MCC
IN INDIA
1976/77

BY THE SAME AUTHOR
Testing Time: MCC in the West Indies 1974
Assault on the Ashes: MCC in Australia and New Zealand 1974/75

CHRISTOPHER MARTIN-JENKINS

MCC IN INDIA
1976/77

MACDONALD AND JANE'S · LONDON

To Rupert and Rosemary; Tony and Jenifer; Bill;
Taff and Norma; and Bryan, with thanks

CONTENTS

ACKNOWLEDGEMENTS

I would like to thank the photographers, Patrick Eagar (2nd and 3rd Tests), Adrian Murrell (2nd and 5th Tests) and G. Bhagwan (4th Test) for their contributions to this book; Patrick Allen for the statistics and tour notes; and not least the BBC for sending me on a memorable cricket tour.

INTRODUCTION

This is indeed India ... the one land that all men desire
to see, and having seen once, by even a glimpse, would
not give that glimpse for the shows of all the rest of the
globe combined.

MARK TWAIN

The politicians, the businessmen and even the cricketers of both
nations may argue, bitterly at times, but there is a peculiar bond
between the British and the Indian people. It is even more of a love-
hate affair than the 'special relationship' often referred to between
Britain and America, but it exists and its origins are as old.

The first seed was the voyage to India in 1600 of a 500-ton
galleon, the *Hector*, commanded by William Hawkins. Acting on
behalf of the newly formed East India Company, he obtained an
imperial authorisation from the last of India's great Moghul rulers,
Jehangir, to open up trading depots around the port of Surat, north
of Bombay. A great adventure began through this modest meeting
between Hawkins, a name synonymous with those brash sea-dogs
of Elizabethan England, and Jehangir, a name instantly evocative
of the fabled wealth of India. From their agreement in Agra
stemmed the process which was to make Britain the imperial
successor of the Moghuls, and there is, for the British at least, a
particular romance about the development of that original commercial role into one of military and civil government.

The Raj, with all its associations of grand living and stiff upper-
lip administration, was the showpiece of the British Empire. Its end,
with Partition in 1947, heralded the break-up of the Empire. As
Churchill remarked, sixteen years before Partition when Gandhi's
agitation for Indian independence was gaining ground: 'The loss of
India would be final and fatal to us. It could not fail to be part of a
process that would reduce us to the scale of a minor power.'

The process is now complete as Britain still struggles to find a new
role beyond a mere quest for economic stability and as India,

becoming increasingly industrialised and making fuller use of
science to produce enough food for a population growing at the rate
of a million a month (an increase every year equal to the entire
population of Australia), struggles to find a political system suited
to its needs. But the vestiges of the law and order imposed by Britain
remain. So do the language and, not least, the recreations of those
British soldiers and civil servants who lived and died on the sub-
continent.

None of the legacies of the Raj have been so universally accepted
within India as cricket. The game seems to override the complex
differences of religion, race, language and custom which make
India a country virtually impossible to generalise about. Mrs
Gandhi has said that no statement about her nation can ever be
wholly true. There must be places, of course, where the gospel of
cricket has not spread, but they were not on the itinerary of Tony
Greig's team. Wherever MCC went they were greeted with warmth,
generosity and fascinated stares. The autographs of the players
were incessantly requested. Often the requests were stubborn and
tactless; sometimes they were refused with equal tactlessness by
irritable players. But it was not easy for them to remain patient,
and impossible for them to please everyone. Even their hotel
rooms were not guaranteed sanctuaries: Geoff Cope once found
a man sitting on his lavatory waiting to meet him, and Derek
Underwood was having a bath when someone came in wanting
a photograph. Outside the room of the idolised Greig a police-
man was permanently posted in Calcutta to keep the admirers
at bay. But even the law could not prevent the telephone ringing
endlessly, and if the caller was not asking Greig and his team
to sample yet more Indian hospitality he was probably asking for a
pass to the match.

Tickets for Zonal games against MCC were valuable enough, but
many an Indian has doubled his annual salary by acquiring and
reselling a pass to a Test match. In England an MCC member
pays £20 a year for the privilege not only of joining an exclusive club
but also of being able to gain free entry to Lord's for all the
important matches of the season – Tests, one-day internationals,
cup finals. But Indians simply do not seem to think twice about
paying £25 just to see one Test match alone: this in a country where
the estimated average wage is £20 a month.

In England, Australia and also the West Indies crowds have
become more sophisticated. They pack grounds only if the series

proves exciting; but in India the gates were closed on would-be spectators on each day of the first three Tests against England, and there was scarcely less interest when the series was decided. An estimated 80,000 people arrived at Eden Gardens, Calcutta, on the final day of the second Test, knowing that they might see no more than a few overs bowled. In fact, the match could have finished in three balls. It is possible, but unlikely, that televised Test matches, which are still a novelty in India, will dampen the near-blind enthusiasm for going to watch. Even for the three-day Zonal games MCC packed stadiums larger than any Test ground in England. In Gauhati, for instance, a remote town in Assam with a relatively small population of some 200,000, a crowd of 30,000 people came every day to see a moderate match of ephemeral significance. What profit was made by India's Cricket Board, and what will be done with that profit, can only be guessed at, but it would surely be in their interests to use as much of the money as possible in the development of their young cricketers.

Without doubt India's crowds are partisan. To a greater or lesser degree, so are most sports crowds around the world. But if they can sometimes be blindly chauvinist – at Calcutta a massive crowd renowned for its furious roar was almost uncannily silent while Indian wickets were falling – there is not the same cynicism as British soccer crowds sometimes display. Run your binoculars round an average Indian cricket crowd and you will see thousands of smiling faces. Bombay, the most westernised and cosmopolitan of Indian cities, was the exception. At times the crowd during the fifth Test was morose and at others hostile.

From time to time crowds in India have fallen from grace. On one famous occasion tickets for a Test were double-sold, and those who had paid hard-earned money only to find their seats occupied by others relieved their fury by burning down a stand. Another riot was sparked by police beating up an erring spectator with *lathis*, and the nearest thing to trouble in the series with England followed Dennis Amiss's century in the first game at Delhi. A spectator came on to the field to congratulate him and when police tried forcibly to evict him from the ground there was such a universal uproar that a wise commanding officer decided to let him be. That, indeed, was people power in action.

For most Indians who learn to play cricket, a ticket to a Test match will be the height of their ambitions. To play first-class cricket means being a member of an organised club, which

presupposes education and a certain wealth and status. Amongst
India's current players only Ghavri and Solkar (dropped after the
second Test) are of lowly birth and the latter's chance arose because
his father happened to be groundsman at the Bombay Gymkhana
Club. Yet wherever one went on the sub-continent one saw cricket
being played – amongst the pigs and cows in the dust of the mud-hut
villages; on the banks of rivers; on beaches; by the side of roads and
on every available grassy space. In the two most densely populated
cities of Calcutta and Bombay one can see upwards of 500 people at
any time of the day involved in matches on the spacious maidans.
Parker's Piece at Cambridge, the wide, grassy common where Sir
Jack Hobbs learned to play, seems small and underused by
comparison. Amongst all this fervour for cricket the odd flower
must surely be 'wasting its sweetness on the desert air'. A fast
bowler perhaps? A good many of these young players run in and
bowl fast, but India's attack, mainly because of the hot climate and
the slow pitches, remains firmly grounded on spin. There is a certain
irony, indeed, in the fact that England's fast bowlers should have
been the major reason for India's disastrous start to the series when
only a few months before Tony Greig's team had been so heavily
outgunned by the West Indian pace bowlers.

Whether the success of the MCC side in India marked the start of
a revival in England's cricketing fortunes or just a pleasant escape
before the nightmares began anew against the Australian fast
bowlers, this was certainly a trip the players could never forget. To
become a household word overnight, like John Lever after the
Delhi Test, or an adored clown, like Derek Randall, who had only
to exaggerate the natural jauntiness of his walk in the field to have
thousands in rapture, or to be like Tony Greig a demi-god, was
extremely testing at times for players who need privacy like
everyone else. But for cricketers used to plying their trade in the
county game before polite spectators who can usually be measured
in hundreds rather than thousands, the unbridled fervour for
cricket in India must have been inspiring.

Moreover, though there were frustrations for players, journalists
and broadcasters alike, and though most of them suffered illnesses
from time to time, those who went had more than just a glimpse of
Mark Twain's 'one land that all men desire to see'.

Chapter One
SELECTORS' CHOICE

An overseas tour is important for the career of any professional cricketer, but for one man in the MCC party which left for India on 23 November the four months ahead were to be climactic. Tony Greig's fortunes had already turned one full circle since his appointment as captain of England for the Lord's Test against Australia in 1975. Now he – like his team – was at a point from which improvement might fairly be expected.

Greig became England's captain because he possessed courage and confidence: qualities badly needed at a time when England's leading batsmen had been battered and demoralised by Dennis Lillee and Jeff Thomson. His attitude unquestionably owed much to his upbringing in South Africa. He was born there, at Queenstown, in 1946, the son of a Scotsman who had joined the RAF and been posted to the Cape Province towards the end of the war as a pilot teacher. Greig senior had married a local South African of English origins. He was a keen cricketer, and his son's early enthusiasm for the game was fostered at Queen's College by a succession of coaches from Sussex County Cricket Club. One of them, Michael Buss, suggested that Tony Greig should return with him in 1966 to try his luck with Sussex, and the following year a 6-foot 7-inch Adonis announced himself to a wider public by scoring 156 in his first Championship match against Lancashire at Hove.

Greig first represented England, which for all his South African accent he quickly adopted as his second home, against the Rest of the World in 1970. He played for another Rest of the World combination against Australia in 1971–72, making a particular impact with his fast-medium seamers, and he enjoyed another successful series under Ray Illingworth in the English summer of 1972. But even in these early days his cricket wavered between the ridiculous and the sublime. The strain of his first taste of captaincy for Sussex in 1973, plus the effects of continuous hard cricket between 1972 and 1973, when he played in eleven Tests at home and eight in India and Pakistan, sapped even his prodigious energies.

He lost weight, and there were those who suggested that he was an overrated all-rounder, jack-of-all-trades perhaps, but certainly master of none, who warranted a place in England's team neither as batsman nor as bowler. Yet under Mike Denness in successive tours of the West Indies and Australia Greig was consistently the outstanding player, the pivot of a struggling side. When England, beaten 4–1 in Australia, lost the first home Test at Edgbaston in 1975, the selectors overlooked indiscretions such as the infamous Kallicharran run-out at Port of Spain, and called on Greig to produce a miracle.

For a time, it seemed indeed that miracles were not beyond him. He came to the wicket in his first Test as captain when his side were in a familiar state of collapse against Lillee, with the score at 49 for four wickets. Supported by the stubborn technique and indomitable spirit of David Steele, the grey-haired artisan who in his first Test became an instant national hero, Greig stopped Lillee and Thomson in their tracks. Like an untried general determined to lead from the front, he scored 96 commanding runs in a little over two and a half hours. When soon after lunch on the second day Australia were tottering at 81 for seven in reply to England's 315, the water had almost been turned into wine.

English supporters who had read and listened with growing despair as Ian Chappell's Australians took the Ashes back by storm the previous winter, now chattered and cheered in delight and disbelief. 'Greigy' had the enemy on the run at last. He hustled them with close fielders, and taunted them by choosing the very moment when they were settling over their bats to run across the field and have an ostentatious word with the bowler. He made the very most of his hour of glory, and if he had known what lay just twelve months ahead, his behaviour would have been even more understandable.

But Greig is no Messiah, and the Australians fought back. They saved the second Test at Lord's despite their perilous position, and after the left-arm spin-bowler Phillippe Edmonds, playing in his first match for England, had induced another collapse in the third Test at Headingley they again recovered. The Australian team arrived at the ground on the final day needing 225 to win with seven wickets left, but a situation pregnant with possibilities never developed because of the infamous 'oil on the pitch' demonstration by the supporters of George Davis. From that morning, which had dawned with England still favourites to win the match and square the series, the fortunes of Greig as England captain went into decline.

In the fourth and last Test of the series, England themselves fought back after being asked to follow on 341 runs behind. A long and determined rearguard action produced another cricketer on whom the new captain might depend for the future, the Kent all-rounder Bob Woolmer, who spent six hours thirty-six minutes scoring a century and who went on to make 149. But for Woolmer, as for Steele, Edmonds and Greig himself, the arid, interminable summer of 1976 was to be a progressively humbling experience. Like marauding Vikings, the West Indians arrived under Clive Lloyd, equipped with weapons the English could not match, and after three months of ruthless rape and pillage, they left their opponents to lick their wounds. The smouldering remains of English cricket once again awaited reconstruction.

The tour of India offered in one sense a welcome respite, especially for batsmen who had faced an unrelenting barrage of fast bowling in three successive series. But everyone knew that not only would the respite be brief, with a Centenary Test against Australia, scheduled as the finale to the tour, being followed by a full-scale struggle for the Ashes again in England in 1977, but also India's cricketers would themselves present a quite different, more subtle, yet equally difficult challenge.

India had not been defeated in a series on their home grounds by an England team since the first official visit under Douglas Jardine in 1933–34. The rigours of the climate, the skill of the Indian spin bowlers and the experience of batsmen like Gavaskar and Viswanath made Bishen Bedi's team clear favourites when the tour began. India, it is true, had suffered a dismal reverse in England in 1974 after several years of success under the taciturn leadership of Ajit Wadekar. But whereas England had just been beaten in three successive Test matches by the West Indies, after draws at Trent Bridge and Lord's, India had emerged with considerable credit from their tour of the Caribbean earlier in the same year. Though they were finally battered into submission by the alarming speed of Michael Holding's fast bowling, their defeat at Sabina Park which gave the West Indies a 2–1 win in the series could not altogether wipe from the memory one of the most famous victories in the history of Test cricket in the previous match at Port of Spain. There India's batsmen, led by Viswanath, Gavaskar, Patel and Mohinder Amarnath, broke one of the longest-standing records in the game by scoring 406 for four in the fourth innings to win the match against all the odds. And now, whereas Greig was leading an unsettled team about whose potential the only certain thing one could say was that it was limited, Bedi had a settled combination of largely experienced players who had warmed up for their main business by trouncing New Zealand in as one-sided a series as India had ever won.

New Zealand were, perhaps, ripe for the picking. They had lost all three tosses on their preceding tour of Pakistan, whose tremendously powerful batting side had taken full toll of a weak attack. New Zealand had hung on bravely to save the third match against Pakistan, but in India nothing went right for them. Umpiring decisions, they felt, went against them too often, and both the captain, Glenn Turner, and the manager, Murray Chapple, were openly critical. Friends were lost off the field and matches lost on it, yet one had sympathy for Turner's side. They were without some of their best players, notably Bevan Congdon, and it is desperately difficult to stop a losing run on a tour when injuries and illnesses multiply and internal differences fester until they become squabbles. Moreover Turner continued to lose the toss.

In the first match at Bombay, Sunil Gavaskar opened the series with a fine innings of 119, but India only achieved a big score because of a recovery lower down the order which was led by the wicket-keeper, Syed Kirmani, who scored 88. When Bishen Bedi made 36 and Bhagwat Chandrasekhar 20 not out, New Zealand must have known their luck was never going to turn. Still, they made India work for victory, John Parker making a century and Turner 65 in their first innings, in which Chandra took four wickets. But after Brijesh Patel, with a rapid 82, had set up the declaration for Bedi, the great left-armer himself completed the job, finishing with remarkable figures of 5 for 27 from 33 overs.

At Kanpur New Zealand did better, holding on for a creditable draw after India had piled up 524 for nine declared. Mohinder Amarnath, Gavaskar, Viswanath, Kirmani and Ashok Mankad all passed fifty; so too, for the first time in Tests, did Bedi. New Zealand responded with 350, Turner scoring an overdue century and Bedi, Chandra and Venkataraghavan sharing the wickets. India again scored quick second-innings runs, Viswanath making a brilliant 103 not out and Anshuman Gaekwad 77 not out, but New Zealand had three wickets left when time ran out for India.

They were frustrated too in the third Test at Madras, though this time only by the weather. A cyclone which struck the east coast a few days before the game caused severe flooding, and a depleted, demoralised and bitter touring side was outplayed by India. Turner again lost the toss, but for a while his opening bowler, Lance Cairns, had the Indians in trouble on a damp pitch. But Viswanath with 87 rescued them, and Bedi and Chandra hustled out New Zealand for 140. India scored a quick 201 before declaring and Bedi finished the job with four second-innings wickets for 22 runs and match figures of 9 for 70.

The bearded Bishen Singh has had many moments of triumph in his career, but few as sweet as this. He led his side on a lap of honour around Chepauk Stadium, received a telegram of congratulations from the President of India, and was soon named captain against England for all five Tests.

Against India's established and confident team, MCC prepared to pit a side which had to be pieced together in difficult circumstances. Their opponents were immensely strong in spin bowling, yet traditionally weak against fast bowling in conditions that were generally unfavourable for bowlers relying on speed or swing. The selection committee consisted of Alec Bedser, Sir Leonard Hutton, Charlie Elliott and Ken Barrington, aided by Doug Insole, the Chairman of the Test and County Cricket Board Cricket Committee, and by Tony Greig, the appointed captain. In choosing their bowlers they had to select seam bowlers good enough to exploit any Indian weakness, and spinners good enough to make the most of turning pitches. The two leading English spinners on the previous visit to India, under Tony Lewis in 1972–73, were Derek Underwood and Pat Pocock. Both had earned their wickets relatively expensively, neither had at any time been a match-winner, and now Pocock, after two Tests bowling at the insatiable bats of Vivian Richards, Gordon Greenidge and others in 1976, was discarded by the tour selectors, who chose two other off-spinners, Geoff Cope and Geoff Miller, ahead of him. Underwood was marginally England's leading wicket-taker against the West Indies, but for all his fine career record some thought him a little fortunate on the evidence of his last visit to India to be preferred to Phil Edmonds. Indeed if Edmonds, whose form returned at the end of the summer as Middlesex made their final surge to become County Champions, had not pulled out of the fifth Test because of a cut finger, he must have come even closer to making his first tour for MCC, probably instead of one of the off-spinners. His ability in the field and with the bat would have been welcome, not to mention his orthodox slow left-arm bowling, which would surely have improved in the land of spin.

But Edmonds was not the only man ruing his misfortune when the party was announced. Two other bowlers, Surrey's Robin Jackman and Derbyshire's Mike Hendrick (who, admittedly, had been given every chance in recent seasons and who had again been affected by injuries in 1976), challenged strongly for the places gained by Mike Selvey and John Lever. The most controversial omissions, however, were those of the two Northamptonshire batsmen, David Steele and Peter Willey.

Selectors have to make difficult decisions, and no one envied their task of sorting out six specialist batsmen for the party of sixteen. They must have been tempted to choose seventeen players and in doing so give themselves one less painful decision, but in the past this had often created problems: it was difficult to keep all the players in match practice. There will always be unlucky players on a tour who do not quite find selection in the Test team and who often become bored as a result; in these days when players can be flown out at short notice to replace the ill or the injured, it is certainly wiser to keep the numbers down. Six batsmen, therefore, it had to be, and although a wide choice of more or less equal candidates was available, including a group of players under the age of 25 – Gooch, Tavaré, Parker, Gatting, Gower, Athey and Botham amongst them – the crucial problem that confronted the selectors was which two to leave out of a shortlist comprising Steele, Willey, Amiss, Brearley, Fletcher, Barlow, Randall and Woolmer.

Dennis Amiss was almost an automatic choice despite a disastrous series against India on the previous tour. In three matches before being dropped, he made only 90 runs at an average of 15, falling three times to the spin of Bedi and three times to Chandrasekhar. Then Amiss was given the benefit of a net against these bowlers in simulated Test match conditions, an act of kindness such as sportsmen do not normally bestow upon rivals. It worked – and an extraordinary turnabout in his fortunes began. In the second half of that 1972–73 tour he started to score runs like a machine, and his form continued to be so good throughout 1973 that he came near to breaking the Test record for runs scored in a calendar year (a record which was to be positively shattered by Viv

Richards in 1976). But Amiss has never been one to do things by halves, and after breaking a thumb facing Jeff Thomson in Australia, he completely lost form and confidence again. The 1976 season began for him with another surge of runs, and he only had to play reasonably well against the West Indian fast bowlers for the MCC at Lord's in June to regain his England place. Instead, the worst happened. He opened with Mike Brearley on a clear, sunny evening against Roberts and Holding, two thoroughbred, intelligent fast bowlers who knew the significance of the moment. Holding's speed that night was terrifying, even when witnessed from the safety of the pavilion, and a fatal indecision in Amiss's mind as he got into the line of a swift, short, kicking delivery resulted in a sickening blow just above the left ear. Farewell Amiss, until the main business of the series had been concluded.

But cricket is, as they say, swings and roundabouts. Having dealt him this untimely cuff around the ears, Fortune next permitted him a glorious batsman's summer to recover his confidence and work out a new method against the fast bowlers, and then gave him a slow, even pitch on which to test it in the final match at the Oval. Taking an enormous step across his crease with his back foot as the bowler delivered, Amiss settled in to make the most of his 'final chance'. The selectors had said that if he were to fail at the Oval there would be no point in picking him for India and then having to leave him out again when the Australian fast bowlers returned. No doubt to their immense relief (since Amiss remained, except for Geoff Boycott who had voluntarily turned his back on Test cricket, the most authoritative batsman in the country), the artificial technique worked like a dream. The terrifying trio of Holding, Roberts and Daniel were crisply flicked off the toes for four after four. By committing himself to back-foot strokes and opening wide his shoulders Amiss was not prevented from driving straight and through the covers with all the familiar strength and timing. He scored a double century and although England as a team were routed by Holding, whose antelope grace and speed earned him fourteen wickets on a fast bowlers' graveyard, one man at least was sure of a passage to India.

After Greig and Amiss, Bob Woolmer was probably the next name to be ticked off. Son of a British business executive who had captained Uttar Pradesh at cricket, Woolmer had been born in Kanpur and had lived there until he was seven. When his English education began, he used to travel East for the holidays from his prep school until his parents returned to England when their son was twelve. No one looked forward to his first tour for MCC with greater keenness, and although the West Indies fast bowlers had tarnished the shining promise of his early Test performances against Australia, Woolmer had never looked out of his class. He began the tour a thoroughly competent all-round cricketer, immeasurably improved as a batsman from the moment Kent had allowed him to bat high in their order, and able to play with a Cowdreyesque poise which promised to captivate spectators in the land of his birth. Unhappily this promise was not to be fulfilled.

Now came the really difficult decisions for the selectors. With one eye on the poor records of MCC sides in India since the distant days of Jardine, they knew that they must take some experienced batsmen. The question was how many. Under the label of experience they had Fletcher, Steele and Brearley; under the label 'up-and-coming' were Willey, Barlow and Randall. The situation was complicated by the need to provide Greig with an experienced vice-captain. To me the choice seemed to lie between Brearley, a man of outstanding intellect and proven worth as a captain but a relatively junior Test cricketer, and Fletcher, who had wisely been rested from the fray after his traumatic experiences against Lillee and Thomson and now, almost overnight it seemed, had become something of a veteran. Fletcher had always been widely respected amongst his fellow professionals both as a batsman and as a shrewd reader of the game. He had never been of more worth to England, either as run-maker or as tactician, than on the 1972–73 tour to India, and although he was reluctant to leave his family behind in Essex there was a sound case for lending his solid experience to Greig's somewhat unpredictable flair. Equally, Brearley, quite apart from his qualities of leadership (and the academic distinction he added to the team as someone who had won a first-class honours degree at Cambridge), had done well enough in his two Tests against the West Indies to merit another chance. Over the last few seasons he had rediscovered the ability to play long, sound innings of the type which had made him a prolific scorer as an undergraduate.

But if there were good cases individually for both Brearley and Fletcher there were also sound reasons for thinking that one or other of them should be left behind. Either could have served as vice-captain and it was Brearley, who had led Middlesex into two knock-out finals in 1975 and to the Championship in 1976, who got the vote. But the choice of both meant that David Steele had to be passed over. 'Stainless' Steele had captured the public imagination in an extraordinary way with his grey hair, his seafaring gait, his native Staffordshire grit, and his unpassable forward defensive. He had averaged 60 against Australia when Fletcher had averaged 19. He had averaged 30 against the West Indies when Brearley had averaged 17. In addition he was a distinctly useful reserve spin bowler and a sound fielder. He had never toured for MCC and he desperately wanted to do so. Yet he was left out on the rather vague theory that he was a less reliable player of spin than he was of pace. How correct this theory was may never be known. The fact is that Steele was unfortunately, even unjustly, treated.

There was a second snag about taking both Fletcher and Brearley: it meant that one of the three batting hopes of England's future to have emerged from the ruins of 1976 would have to be left behind, and moreover that of the two who were lucky, Randall and Barlow, one or other was unlikely to gain extensive Test experience on the tour, since only five batting places needed to be filled above Greig in the Test team and four of these were always likely to be taken, at least at the start of the tour, by Amiss, Brearley, Fletcher and Woolmer.

If a place had been found for Willey, at the expense of one of the more experienced players, the chances were that England would have been able to give *two* new batsmen a full blooding. If the evidence of 1976 had been before Australian rather than English selectors, they would almost certainly have picked Willey as well as Barlow and Randall, and no doubt they would have sent a real youngster as well.

But English and Australian selectors are products of different cricket systems: they do not think alike and they never will. So why Barlow and Randall, rather than Willey? On the face of it, this was another unjust decision. Of the three, Willey was the most experienced cricketer. Aged 27, he had been playing on and off for Northamptonshire since he was 16, and if he had not had remarkable ill-luck with a series of knee injuries he would surely have played for England before 1976. Only in that long, hot summer, however, did he start to bat consistently enough to attract the attention or the selectors. He played in two Tests against the West Indies, batting with skill and courage in a losing cause, revealing a good temperament and a desire to hit the bad ball very hard. In county matches he bowled off-spinners tidily and was improving all the time, having ceased bowling medium pace because of his knee problem, and he was a safe fielder. Peter Willey, in short, was a virile, positive all-round cricketer with immense natural ability. As a particularly useful player in one-day cricket it was a major surprise when he was not named in England's team squad for the one-day internationals against the West Indies at the end of the 1976 season. The story goes that his place was in doubt for India even before the fifth Test at the Oval, as a result of his 'having a slog' in the nets against the England spinners, an attitude the watching selectors considered to be one of inappropriate levity. During the match itself Willey played less fluently than at Headingley, and it is true that he looked frail against the occasional unorthodox spin of Roy Fredericks. Yet to dub him a poor player of spin on these two pieces of evidence seemed harsh. If seventeen players *had* gone to India, Willey would almost certainly have been the seventeenth and, amongst the batsmen, he was first reserve.

Unlike Willey, Graham Barlow and Derek Randall *were* chosen for the one-day internationals (so, strangely enough, was Steele, who needed a rest and had nothing more to prove, gain or lose). The first to make an impact was Graham Barlow. His innings of 80 against West Indies at Scarborough capped a memorable season for this gifted left-hander who, like many a good player before him, had taken time to settle into the testing atmosphere of county cricket. He had made an orderly way to the county staff by dint of consistent success for Ealing Grammar School, Middlesex Schools and English Schools, but that he did not attain a regular place in the county side until he was 26 was due mainly to the fact that he spent three years at Loughborough qualifying as a PE instructor. Once established in the side, however, in 1976, he became a major force. He scored runs regularly and authoritatively, with a dash and vigour that hustled bowlers and stirred spectators. I became convinced that Barlow was a player of Test class when I saw him seal the Championship for Middlesex against Surrey at the Oval. The pitch had received an overnight dousing and batting conditions were quite difficult, especially against spinners of the ability of Intikhab and Pocock. But Barlow used nimble footwork, quick eyes and decisive strokes to counter-attack and in little more than an hour he had made certain that Middlesex would get the bonus points they required. Here was a batsman determined to take the initiative, and capable of doing so. England were in need of players like him. Equally they were in need of fielders of Barlow's bursting athleticism and infectious joie de vivre.

Derek Randall was a similar case: a man brimming over with enthusiasm and natural ability. If anything, he is too much of a jack-in-the-box. The nervous and physical energy he expends in the field is exhausting even to onlookers, but it puts batsmen in mortal fear and Randall partly owed his selection to the brilliance he had shown in the field when touring South Africa for the Derrick Robins team the previous winter. Batsmen there had been as terrified of running when the ball was anywhere near Randall as English batsmen had been in the days of that panther of a cover-point, Colin Bland.

Having started 1976 a candidate for the England side, however, Randall had a setback when, like Amiss, Roope and one or two others, he failed against the extreme pace of Holding and Roberts during the MCC v West Indies match at Lord's in June. Against these two Randall looked like a startled rabbit, and so obvious was his discomfort then that it came as a surprise to many when he used the one-day internationals to show that he could not merely stand up to fast bowling, but dominate it. On a rain-affected, unreliable pitch at Lord's he unleashed a dazzling variety of shots, some orthodox, many improvised, and he played well in another losing cause at Edgbaston. With his rolling walk, nervous twitches and black hair plastered to his forehead, Randall might be taken for the village simpleton or the music-hall fool. But there is plenty of wit in him and a streak of genius too.

Success at cricket, as in any career, is partly a matter of timing. Had Barlow or Randall played for England earlier in the summer and Willey not done so until the less stern one-day internationals, it is likely that Willey would have been chosen for India at the expense of one of the others. Instead he spent the winter as groundsman to Northampton Town Football Club, consoled only a little no doubt by the likelihood of his getting another chance for England against Australia in the near future. He also had tangible consolation in the shape of his Gillette Cup Man-of-the-Match award, placed on his mantelpiece alongside a trophy presented by BBC Television, whose countless cricket viewers had voted him Cricketer of 1976. Incidentally, his predecessor for 1975 had been David Steele, and, to complete a miserable trio of Northamptonshire's Test players, the county captain Mushtaq Mohammed was dismissed as captain of Pakistan for leading a players' revolt against the terms offered to them for the tour of Australia and the West Indies. (He, at least, was soon reinstated.)

Barlow and Randall were the batsmen to whom England looked to point the way to a brighter future; but Test series are won primarily by bowlers, so the role of MCC's relatively untried bowling specialists was going to be even more important. Discounting the experienced Underwood, the remaining six bowlers— Willis, Old, Lever, Selvey, Cope and Miller—had played only 45 Test matches between them when the tour began, and they were faced by some thoroughly competent Indian batsmen whose confidence and reputation had been enhanced by the series against New Zealand, which was concluded shortly after MCC's arrival.

The two off-spinning Geoffs, Miller of Derbyshire and Cope of Yorkshire, had travelled very different paths to the Orient. Cope is one of cricket's irrepressibles. He took over as Yorkshire's off-spinner from Ray Illingworth and for a long time he suffered, inevitably, by comparison. Moreover, there were mutterings around the county circuit of a kink in his action, and in the second half of 1972 he was banned by the Test and County Cricket Board. Cope, with that quiet dedication and determination that often seems to go with bespectacled cricketers, went back to the drawing-board, and with the patient aid of Johnny Wardle he developed a new action which was passed the following season and which received the final seal of approval when he was selected for MCC. The dominant feature of the changed action was the late appearance of the bowling arm from behind Cope's back as he moved into the delivery stride, a method Wardle himself had employed. It took time, but Cope's confidence returned and he improved steadily, thinking hard about his bowling and learning from his mistakes. In 1975 he took 69 first-class wickets, playing a major part in Yorkshire's rise to second place in the Championship. Then, early in 1976, he was selected for the Test trial at Bristol and in the second innings he exploited a dusty wicket to take five for 27. This was an ideal trial for India, and although he wasn't chosen against the West Indies (rumours persisted that the selectors didn't dare risk his being no-balled) that performance at Bristol, plus his overall haul of 93 wickets in the season, was not overlooked when the time came to choose the touring team.

For Geoff Cope it had been a hard road to the top, with frequent setbacks. Geoff Miller on the other hand had travelled smoothly since his days at Chesterfield Grammar School. A talented natural games-player who had also represented Derbyshire at table-tennis,

he won the Sir Frank Worrell Trophy as the outstanding Boy
Cricketer of 1972 and when he made his debut for Derbyshire the
following year he had already toured twice with the England Young
Cricketers – to India in 1970–71 and to the West Indies in 1972.

1976, however, was Miller's real breakthrough year. Despite
such a glittering schoolboy record it was difficult for him to
develop, let alone catch the selectorial eye, in a side struggling as
badly as Derbyshire were. The turning-point for Miller, and
possibly for Derbyshire too (time will tell), was the signing-on of
Eddie Barlow, the charismatic and ebullient all-rounder from Cape
Town. Barlow was made captain of the county soon after the start
of the season when Bob Taylor resigned in order to concentrate on
his wicket-keeping, and one of the first things the South African
captain did was to promote Miller in the batting order. There was
nothing spectacular about Miller's response, but he did play several
mature and worthy innings in the course of scoring 820 first-class
runs at an average of 25. He also began to take wickets with growing
frequency, and Barlow made him work to get them. Under the kind
of tough leadership which would not have been disowned by
Barlow's television namesake, Miller was taught a new discipline.
Once, in a crucial one-day game, Barlow literally commanded
Miller to pitch every ball on a certain spot. Here was a future
England off-spinner learning from an overseas captain the old ethic
of the professional: first learn your craft inside out; then experiment
if you really need to. England's best post-war off-spinner, Jim
Laker, has always said of his successor at Surrey, Pat Pocock, that
he tries to experiment too much. Patience is perhaps the spinner's
most essential virtue, and Miller was sure to learn plenty about it
from Bedi and company.

Though he did not bowl badly against the West Indies, Pocock
did not do enough to convince the selectors, and Miller was chosen
for the fifth Test at the age of 23. He could not have been given a
much sterner baptism: a slow, bounceless Oval pitch (though,
incredibly, it was neither too slow nor too bounceless for Michael
Holding) on which to bowl against the most punishing batting side
in the world. Again, Miller did nothing extraordinary but he
relished the occasion, bowled tidily and, when his turn came against
the fast bowlers, stood up, played straight and got behind the ball,
making light of a nasty bruise on a finger received during his first
Test innings of 36. A cricketer of talent and character had arrived.

Derek Underwood made up MCC's hand of spinners: a unique

bowler, renowned and respected the world over, grinding his way remorselessly to a probable record haul of Test wickets. He had finished the 1976 season a tired and battered cricketer, but two months' rest at home in Kent were enough to rekindle his instinctive zest and competitiveness.

The four seam bowlers in the touring team were not a particularly distinguished bunch when one considers England's traditional strength in this department, but they pulled a good deal more weight than their Indian counterparts. Bob Willis was the one bowler of genuine speed, but the problem which lay ahead of him was clear enough: he must pace himself to last what was bound to be an arduous four months, and so guard against the injuries which, largely because of his size (6 feet, 5 inches) and his awkward action, had plagued him to date. At the same time he was England's main cutting weapon, their one shock bowler, and he would be of little value if he did not make use of his sheer speed to exploit the Indian weakness against his type of bowling.

To a lesser extent Chris Old had the same problem. For all his smooth action and natural athleticism Old had a history of persistent injuries, the most serious of which had involved damage to both his knees. Until late in the 1976 season this had threatened to prevent his going to India. Once declared fit, however, he was one of the few automatic selections. He had done well under Tony Lewis in 1972–73 and apart from his bowling was a punishing player of spin bowling and an accomplished fielder both close to the bat and in the deep.

John Lever of Essex had earned his passage to India after a long apprenticeship. His virtues were his fitness – he had rarely had any injury problems during his nine years as an Essex player – and his ability to swing the new ball, aided by the awkward angle from which any left-arm, over-the-wicket bowler delivers. When the tour began he was not, and had few pretensions to being, another Alan Davidson, nor even – as far as anyone knew – another Gary Gilmour, but he was picked as an honest performer, a good fielder and a cheerful contributor to the off-the-field activities. His selection, incidentally, had been helped by achieving what at one time in the English summer had seemed the impossible feat of dismissing Viv Richards for nought. The Indian tour was his big chance.

Lever had been in the running for higher honours for some seasons. This was not so with Mike Selvey, who had been a useful but run-of-the-mill opening bowler for Cambridge, had failed (like many another) to come up to Surrey's expectations and had laboured with only moderate success for Middlesex since 1972. But right from the start of 1976 he was seen in a different light. Greatly helped by the arrival at Lord's of another fast bowler, Allan Jones, he suddenly started to bowl sides out. Not genuinely fast, he was still sharp enough to make batsmen hurry, strong enough to keep going for long spells and to extract bounce from pitches giving him help. Moreover, he could move the ball in the air, as the West Indians found to their discomfort when an extraordinary succession of injuries to England's fast bowlers persuaded the selectors to choose him for the third Test at Old Trafford. Selvey started with a dramatic spell of three wickets in his first fifteen balls in Test cricket. Although he was soon brought back to earth and indeed left out of the next Test before returning for some punishment in the fifth, he had done enough to suggest that he would be a useful workhorse, and perhaps rather more, on a demanding winter tour.

The final problem facing the tour selectors was the choice of wicket-keepers. In contrast with the other departments they had to fill, there was an embarrassment of riches in this one. Alan Knott was a certain selection. He had not had a particularly good series against the West Indies, despite officially breaking Godfrey Evans's record of Test victims during the course of it, but as one of England's few proven world-class players he remained an automatic choice. Moreover, if his wicket-keeping had been variable his benefit year for Kent had been a successful one with the bat and included the fastest hundred of the summer.

The place of reserve keeper went, as it had on the previous Indian tour, to Roger Tolchard of Leicestershire. As before, he was chosen more because of his ability as a batsman than for his wicket-keeping. As a nimble and decisive player of spin bowling he was going to be especially useful. But his selection meant that the man considered to be England's most consistently able wicket-keeper, Bob Taylor, was left to spend his winter in Stoke-on-Trent and that a chance was missed to blood anyone to succeed Knott when the time comes to replace him. David Bairstow of Yorkshire, Derek Taylor of Somerset, Andy Brassington of Gloucestershire and Geoff Humpage of Warwickshire must all have listened to the announcement of the sixteen names with their fingers crossed.

There were consolations for these men and others who narrowly missed selection. So hectic is the peripatetic life of a cricketer that a gentle winter at home has its attractions – and indeed a tour has its hardships as well as its pleasures. But they must all have felt a twinge of envy as the Ashoka Empress, an Air India jumbo jet, heaved its way off the runway at Heathrow on a frosty November morning at the start of the eleven-hour flight to Bombay. What lay ahead was uncertain, of course, but one's feelings at the time were that this could be the starting-point of a better era for English cricket. The MCC team had clear, if limited potential; it was unlikely to have devastating success, but equally unlikely to be disgraced, and its fortunes were bound to be closely identified with those of its leader, Tony Greig.

Chapter Two
WARMING UP

The tour began on the right note. Four-thirty in the morning is not the best time to arrive anywhere in the world, and there were the usual problems of sorting out the touring party's copious baggage once the Ashoka Empress had touched safely down at Bombay Airport. But there was no doubting the warmth of the welcome awaiting the MCC team as a whole and the captain in particular. Indeed Ken Barrington, the tour manager, who spent part of his 46th birthday on the air flight from London, might have pondered on the transitory nature of fame. He was a national hero in India in the days when he used to score prolifically there for MCC teams, but though Air India remembered to bake him a special cake it was Tony Greig who became the centre of attraction from the moment he set foot on the sub-continent.

Two hours after landing, Greig was leading his players through smiling crowds as eager to touch him as American voters are to shake hands with their President at election time. The coach taking the team to their hotel was accompanied by an old Morris Ambassador whose occupants diced with death as their driver weaved in and out of the traffic to allow himself and his passengers to wave and shout at the players. Occasionally the car would come to a screeching halt, narrowly averting a fatal accident. Then for a time the driver would turn his attentions to the road – just for a change – and miraculously the old car would pop up beside the coach again for another session of waving and laughing. It was seven o'clock and a new day was dawning in a temperature of 85°F when a weary party arrived at the sanctuary of the Taj Mahal Hotel at Apollo Bunder. This cool, spacious, elegant building overlooks part of Bombay harbour and the Gateway to India, a splendid stone archway erected to celebrate the arrival of King George V in 1911. The English architect of the Taj Hotel is said to have thrown himself over the side on the day the building was opened because it had been constructed facing the opposite direction from which he had intended. Yet his creation remains for comfort and character surely one of the most delightful hotels in the world.

Not that there was much time for sleep that day: by noon Greig and Barrington were conducting the opening press conference. In a wood-panelled room beneath an immense chandelier Greig answered most of the questions with effortless charm. He was happy to be back in the land that loved cricket, and he believed the crowds would like the cricket his team would play, not least the fielding of Barlow and Randall. He would make no predictions except that Indians would know his side had been amongst them. Asked about the umpiring decisions which had disturbed New Zealand's players in the preceding weeks, he said he believed Indian umpires to be fair – as good, and as human, as umpires anywhere in the world. Just near the room in which he was speaking was a large bedroom known as the 'Diplomat's Suite'. Greig might well have been offered the room himself.

Soon, however, the talking gave way to action, as the cricketers prepared themselves with three days of net practice at the Wankhede Stadium. This beautiful ground is only half a mile or so from the old Brabourne Stadium, which – but for an internal political wrangle between the cricketing authorities of Bombay – would still be the centre of cricket in the city. Impressive though the new amphitheatre looked it was not ideal for practice because, quite apart from the heat and the unusually heavy humidity, the net wickets were not conducive to confident batting. While practising Graham Barlow received a bruised thumb and Geoff Miller a black eye from balls that popped unexpectedly. But nothing could dampen the enthusiasm of these two or the other young players. The older ones, who had been through it all before, paced themselves gently, though in the sessions of physical training under the equally experienced eye of Bernard Thomas, the team's physiotherapist, no slacking was permitted.

Once again Tony Greig was a special case. To help take the weight off his shoulders Dennis Amiss and Keith Fletcher organised the net practices, but even in his short innings in the nets he was eagerly watched by spectators and faced the problem of keeping them entertained whilst simultaneously concentrating on his own game.

Social functions can easily take their toll of the unwary and there was no shortage of evening receptions to greet the team. Not all the entertainment was on one side, however: at one early function, when the players were individually presented with a tie, Derek

Randall suddenly whispered out of the side of his mouth to Keith Fletcher: 'When I go up to fetch me tie, I'm going to do a cartwheel.' Sure enough, he broke free from the circle of hosts and guests and performed his cartwheel, bringing the house down in the process.

Five days after their arrival the MCC party moved inland from Bombay to Poona, the scene of their opening match. Rather than get up for a 4.30 a.m. flight they preferred to take the Deccan Queen, the Sunday evening express train, which – whilst not as regal as her name suggests – was still a perfectly pleasant form of travel. The 120-mile journey took three hours, and such was the warmth of the reception awaiting MCC at every station along the way that a deft piece of organisation allowed the team to leave the train at the station before Poona and then to travel the last few miles by coach. So the crowd waiting at Poona station itself was disappointed, but no offence was intended and cool drinks and garlands of flowers awaited the players at their hotel.

For many the name Poona (now Indianised to Pune) is synonymous with the Raj, and it was here that the serious business of the MCC tour began on a gloriously sunny day at the Nehru Stadium, a handsome ground ringed by hills and reminiscent of Scotland. The temperature, even at nearly two thousand feet, was in the eighties, but MCC got away to an encouraging start despite losing the toss and also one of their selected team before the match began – Graham Barlow had been in and out of the lavatory during the night, the first of the team to go down with the inevitable tummy upset. His replacement, Geoff Miller, spent a long but rewarding day in the field.

Bob Willis seized the first headlines of the tour. A startling spell with the second new ball brought him four wickets for two runs in seventeen balls and rapidly put an end to a stubborn recovery by the West Zone middle order. Willis had received unexpected encouragement from his very first ball in India, which had the former Test opener Ramnath Parkar backing away anxiously and losing his sun-hat as the ball flashed past his head. The pitch continued to have enough bounce in it to keep a spring in the heels of Willis and Old all day. Old also bowled very well, especially in his opening spell when he swung the ball a good deal. So too did Greig, who appropriately took the first wicket of the tour bowling in his medium-pace style.

MCC, however, were held up by a sound innings from the tall, lean right-hander Dilip Vengsarkar, who had played his first few

Tests for India the previous year against New Zealand and the West Indies at the age of 19. He stood up well to the bouncing ball – certainly a good deal better than Parkar – but the major resistance came in a fifth-wicket stand of 103 between the experienced left-hander Eknath Solkar and a determined little Poona bank clerk, Raju Bhalekar. The latter was twice dropped and things seemed to be going badly astray for MCC, especially as Mike Selvey had limped off with a pulled muscle after bowling only nine overs; but there were consolations, even during this long stand. The most noticeable was the bowling of Geoff Cope who, though he didn't take a wicket, bowled not a single bad ball in a spell of 22 overs, conceding only 40 runs. Miller's first spell was less accurate but it was he who dismissed Solkar and so paved the way for a reasonably dramatic end to the first day.

Once Willis had bowled Bhalekar for 66, the tail succumbed to him in a few overs of straightforward fast bowling. One ball, to the wicket-keeper Shetty, broke a stump in two and Willis generally made a hostile first impression which would not have gone unnoticed by the Indian Test team simultaneously engaged in their last match with New Zealand in Madras. If only Willis and Old could remain fit . . .

MCC's modest success in the field on the first day was followed up by something of a triumph on the second when Mike Brearley announced his presence in India by batting all day for 195 not out. He went on the next morning to 202 before getting himself out, having recorded the highest innings by a member of an official MCC side in India. It was an innings which developed from a studious application to the details of technique in its early stages to a complete domination of all the bowling. Having lost his opening partner Dennis Amiss at 50 Brearley was cautious, especially against some good left-arm round-the-wicket inswing bowling from Parsana, who twice had appeals for l.b.w. against Brearley narrowly turned down before getting the answer he wanted when Amiss aimed to glance a delivery through the short-legs. But the close fielders gradually receded as the new ball lost its shine, Brearley accelerated and Keith Fletcher settled happily in without a trace of his habitual early-innings nerves.

These two went on to a record stand for any MCC wicket in India, adding 292 in 247 minutes before a carefree Fletcher was l.b.w. sweeping at Solkar after an innings of wristy skill. Brearley, after reaching a chanceless hundred in 223 minutes, with 19 fours, scored his next 50 in 47 minutes as he aimed to hit out or get out. It was one of those days, however, and a stream of handsome strokes flowed from his bat through the covers off spinners and medium-pacers alike.

The vice-captain having had his say, the captain proceeded almost to upstage him. In under three and a half hours on the third day Greig scored 162 not out, and such was the spectacle he put on for a 20,000-strong crowd in the later stages of his innings that he would have been declared a god instantly if the citizens of Poona had powers of deification. Greig had seen Brearley sacrifice himself to enable other players to run into form, and then had lost Randall, unfortunately run out for nought. But Roger Tolchard now joined him in another double-century stand and for a long time neither was in any undue hurry since Bob Willis was in bed suffering from a tummy bug and one or two of the other bowlers were feeling unwell. But to placate those members of the crowd who wanted him to declare, Greig suddenly launched a devastating attack, which took him from 94 to 147 in 12 balls. The actual sequence of scoring shots was 6,4,6,1 off Parsana, 4,6,6,6,6 off Joshi (all immense legside heaves), and 4,4 off Parsana. The declaration he later made was a token gesture but the start to the tour had been an altogether happy one.

It was, of course, early days to get too enthused. A better batting wicket than the benign strip at Poona could scarcely be imagined, and the bowling and general atmosphere were a good deal more friendly than England could expect when the Tests began. All the same, to have recorded three centuries and one five-wicket performance (by Willis) only a week after leaving home was a considerable achievement.

From Poona the party moved back to Bombay for a night, and then north to Jaipur, the famous 'Pink City'. The climate here was delightful with the temperature in the seventies during the day but so cool at nights that at least two blankets were needed for warmth. The pity was that there was not enough time to see more than a few of the magnificent buildings which attract an increasing number of tourists each year to the capital of Rajasthan. In former days hunting tigers was the main sport in this desert area. Now the animals are protected, and visitors are taken instead to see the truly fabulous palaces, some still in the private possession of the princely family.

Due to delayed flights the team did not arrive until mid-

afternoon on the day before their match against Central Zone, and
they were too weary to sight-see. With play starting at 10.15 each
morning and the light quickly fading after dark, only those who
were not engaged in the match had the chance to visit the Amber
Palace, set high amongst rugged hills, with its elegant marble
courtyards and exquisite carving in ivory, glass and marble. The
royal palace itself stands behind a long wide street of stone
buildings all covered in the same pink hue, the personal whim of the
great-grandfather of the present Maharajah. In this age of tourism
it has proved an inspired idea, but one feels that if, say, the mayor of
High Wycombe were to decide to paint his town yellow, the effect
would not be quite so pleasing.

Certainly few if any of the great houses of England still preserved
by the National Trust can match the splendour of the royal palace,
though where princes once lived a huge family of monkeys now
patrols the ramparts, giving the lavishness below a rather faded and
melancholy air. Of all the beautiful objects to see, perhaps the most
quaint were a pair of enormous solid silver urns which the
grandfather of the present Maharajah used to fill with water from
the Ganges. Even when he travelled abroad his urns and his holy
water went with him. Two more of the royal palaces are now
flourishing hotels.

The Sawai Man Singh Stadium, where the cricket was played, is
not without a certain splendour itself, though it is situated some
way from the old city. An elegant pink-and-white pavilion, topped
by twin cupolas, stretches the full length of one side of a vast, open
ground. Here a cheerful first-day crowd settled down rather more
peacefully than some other crowds in India to watch MCC compile
another good score. This time Graham Barlow was the main
contributor with a confident, assertive hundred in three and a half
hours. It was an innings marked by firmly punched, decisive strokes
and a general air of cockney chirpiness.

Dennis Amiss, who shared with Barlow a stand of 109, could not
match the enthusiasm and self-belief of his partner, being too
wrapped up in his own intense world of technical theory. At such
times he reminds one of Colin Cowdrey in one of his introspective
moods. Still, he made 60 and was out only because of a brilliant
pick-up and throw by the wicket-keeper Chopra as Amiss dropped
his bat on the ball and ran. Derek Randall also played a long
innings of 48 not out on the first day, at the end of which Brearley,
always an enterprising captain, declared.

John Lever, the find of the series, who had such a spectacular Test debut at Delhi, in action.

Above Patel makes Greig hop about in self-defence.

Below Knott whips off the bails, Greig appeals—but Viswanath is unimpressed.

Above The Calcutta crowd, 80,000-strong even on the last morning of the second Test when the end was a pure formality.
Below Rolling the pitch between innings: umpire Sharma (right) supervises.

Above The crucial moment of the first session of play at Calcutta: Gavaskar is caught by Old at third slip off Willis in the first over.
Below The second wicket to fall was that of Sharma, caught by Greig at second slip off Lever: India were 23 for two.

On a wicket of slow pace and unreliable bounce the Central Zone batsmen responded with extreme caution, Deshpande playing a patient innings of 64 in four and three-quarter hours. Lever, Underwood, Cope and Miller all had useful bowls but Chris Old was less fortunate. His first ball provided a dramatic start to the day: Ansari backed away from it and his off-stump, to borrow an Indian commentator's expression, 'went for a walk in the fresh air'. But a mere eight balls later Old was straight-driven and, trying to turn as he followed through, he slipped as if on ice and fell heavily on the hard ground. For an anxious moment he lay still. Shaken and heavily bruised on his thigh and shoulder, he was unable to bowl again in the match, which naturally reduced MCC's chances of winning.

Hanumant Singh, an experienced and respected cricketer, declared with eight wickets down, 91 runs behind, and whilst Bob Woolmer settled in for a long, steady look at Indian conditions, Alan Knott responded to the invitation to open the innings by playing a carefree, impish innings of 108 in 102 balls. His brilliance outshone anything else in the match. When Central Zone in turn responded to Brearley's challenge – 247 in 190 minutes – they quickly came unstuck, losing four wickets for 26. The fourth, rather sadly, was that of the popular Salim Durrani, the tall left-handed all-rounder who, since MCC's last visit, had made an abortive attempt to become a film star. (Film stars in India are perhaps the only professionals to enjoy a higher popular status than cricketers.) Durrani is prepared to admit that his reported age of 39 might be something of an understatement and he was certainly being unduly optimistic when he tried to take a second run to Derek Randall. Randall's antics in the field, notably his ability to pick the umpire's hat from the back of his head when he wasn't looking, spin it into the air and catch it on his own head, had made him almost as popular as Durrani himself, so the crowd were not sure in this instance whether to laugh or cry. A fifth wicket fell at 51, but the odds were always against the bowlers forcing a win on such a slow pitch and Hanumant Singh stopped the rot in company with the Test candidate Sharma.

A few hours later a weary team was packing its bags again and setting off in a little Avro Anson for a night stop in Delhi. There was a stop en route at Agra and with typical Indian willingness to please the pilot crossed the river to show us the Taj Mahal by moonlight. Alas, on that occasion, one needed an elastic neck and a good imagination to claim to have witnessed one of the wonders of the world.

The overnight stop in Delhi will never be forgotten by poor Geoff Cope or indeed by Tony Greig, who was telephoned early in the morning by Cope's wife with the sad news that his father had died. Cope at the time was very much in the running for a place in the first Test and his father had been reading a report about his son from India on a sofa in his Yorkshire home shortly before he died. Cope returned home at once, Indian Airways delaying a flight to help him to catch the first plane home. He returned to the fold before the first Test in Delhi, but the news inevitably cast a shadow over the whole team, whose morale so far had been very high. By a sad coincidence Pat Pocock, the chief off-spinner on the previous trip to India, also lost his father whilst he was touring there.

Ahmedabad, the next stop, was not destined to raise the spirits very much. Once the greatest city in western India it was in 1615, according to Sir Thomas Roe, 'a goodly city as large as London'. Were Sir Thomas to visit the modern Ahmedabad, an overcrowded manufacturing centre, he might be a little less enthusiastic. Modern buildings and slum dwellings sprawl untidily along the Sabarmati river, across which Gandhi's Ashram constantly attracts pilgrims. The team's hotel was the least modern of those they had stayed in to date, but any inconvenience was compensated for by the extreme friendliness of the Gujeratis, very few of whom spoke good English. The youngsters knew enough, though, to stare through the hedge which separated the hotel from the smelly river and to yell at any MCC cricketer they saw: 'What is your good name?'

The enthusiasm for the game was reflected in a noisy crowd of 35,000 which packed the dusty Patel Stadium for the first day's play of the match against the Board President's XI. The main grandstand is a concrete construction whose roof has an ominous-looking crack about a foot wide in the middle where the two sides do not quite meet. This, however, has stood the test of several years. Round the remainder of the ground, which was in superb condition and compared favourably with most of the county grounds of England, spectators watched from deeply tiered seats under the cover of red and white awnings. They saw MCC score 289 for five declared on the first day, despite a middle-order collapse in the course of which four wickets fell for 22 runs in ten overs.

The major innings of the day was again played by Graham

Barlow. He was promoted to open the batting when Bob Woolmer had to withdraw with a heavy cold and Mike Brearley had to drop down the order because of a stiff neck. From the moment that he strode out with Amiss, Barlow exuded total confidence. He got under way with a straight-driven four off Ghavri and a little later pulled the same bowler for a six to square-leg. Ghavri nevertheless introduced himself to MCC with a lively if wayward opening spell which included plenty of bumpers, and he came back in the middle of the afternoon to take three quick wickets. By this time Barlow had reached his second successive hundred, a chanceless and thoroughly impressive innings. On the whole he played the off-spin of Erapalli Prasanna very well, but the old teddy bear got him in the end, caught low down at slip by Vengsarkar as he played without getting to the pitch of the ball.

If this was a lesson to Barlow that you must never relax against the top Indian spinners there was a timely reminder to Greig and Old that India's seam bowlers were not necessarily to be discounted either. Both played over-confident shots against Ghavri, who had also trapped Randall l.b.w. with a ball which kept low, and it was left to the experienced Tolchard and the youthful Miller to steady the ship. The latter played especially well in his first innings in India since his tour here with the English Schools' side.

Greig declared overnight, and in addition to the 35,000 watching within the ground on the second day some 200 more found a vantage-point on the top of a high block of flats which must have been at least a quarter of a mile from the stadium. Even with the help of binoculars the players can have seemed little larger than ants to them. Twenty-six people had been injured on the first day when a wooden floor inside the stadium collapsed, but the collapsing on the following day was left to the President's XI, who lost three of their first four batsmen for 27 runs as Lever, Old and Selvey swung the ball around on a rather murky morning. However, Parthasarathy Sharma, playing a lucky but admirably stubborn innings, survived four dropped chances to rectify the situation, in company first with Patel and then with Mankad, who were both fresh from their successful series against New Zealand. Sharma made 111, Mankad a chanceless 51 not out and Patel 23, but the other players on trial, Vengsarkar, Chauhan and Yajuvendra Singh, a splendidly Ranji-esque figure in a yellow-and-black striped Bombay Gymkhana cap and cream flannels, were all worms for the early birds.

The Indian selectors rewarded Sharma's patient effort with a place in their squad of fourteen for the first Test, but they dropped Mankad: a decision which cannot have worried MCC unduly because on the evidence of Ahmedabad Sharma had more holes in his defence than Mankad did.

For the MCC bowlers the second day of the match turned out to be a good hard workout and the right sort of preparation for long days they could expect in the field during the Tests. Lever and Selvey both bowled well enough to suggest that it would be a hard choice between them for the position of third seamer – assuming the fitness of Old and Willis. Underwood also had a steady bowl, but Greig and Miller had innocuous and occasionally inaccurate spells of off-spin. Cope seemed to grow in stature, even in his absence.

Prasanna, reinstated in the Indian Test squad, declared the President's XI innings 76 runs behind and MCC were obliged to look for quick runs whilst simultaneously getting as much practice in the middle as possible. The two who resolved the dilemma best were Brearley and Randall, who played fluently for 59 and 47 not out respectively. Amiss, Greig and Old, the others who got a chance to bat, were less successful and Greig made the game's third declaration, a generous one which left the President's XI to score 204 in 157 minutes.

The combination of a slow start and a slow over-rate, however, soon quenched the ambitions of the batting side, and it was MCC who came nearer a win, thanks largely to an excellent second spell by Chris Old, who finished with three for 29, and to some testing bowling by Derek Underwood on a pitch now starting to turn quite substantially. But though there were still ten overs left and not much batting to come when the fifth wicket fell, Mankad resisted with a forthright piece of batting which showed clearly enough what he thought of the selectors who had just dropped him from the national side.

The third match, like the others, had ended in the almost inevitable draw, but it had hardened some opinions about the side England would field in the first Test. Particularly it had shown that, with Cope absent, Greig apparently reluctant to give Miller much bowling (he had nine overs late in the first innings and none in the second) and Greig himself bowling his off-spinners indifferently, England would have to rely on three seam bowlers to form the basis of the attack at Delhi. Willis and Old were the obvious choices if fit, but it was touch-and-go at this stage between Lever and Selvey. As for the batsmen, everyone was now in reasonable form. By scoring his second century Barlow had become a certain selection along with Greig, Amiss, Brearley and Fletcher, but the extra place was wide open. The problem would somehow have to be resolved after the fourth of the warm-up matches, played against the North Zone at Jullunder.

'Warm-up' may not be the appropriate term here. The weather in Jullunder, a town situated close to the Himalayas and not far from the Pakistan border, was extremely cold at nights and even in the bright sun of the day there was an autumnal nip in the air. The journey had been a circuitous one, the party travelling nearly 1,400 miles in all. The team stopped for five hours in Bombay before going on to Delhi for a night. In the morning Graham Barlow, who had been sharing a room in Ahmedabad with Bob Willis, awoke with the chest infection which Willis had only recently managed to shake off, and Barlow was left behind in Delhi with just six days to recover before the first Test.

So with Cope still at home in Yorkshire only fourteen players moved north, travelling by air as far as Amritsar and then on to Jullunder by coach. The last hundred miles of the flight were memorable for a distant but still breathtaking view of the snow-capped peaks of the Himalayas, rising out of a blue haze on the horizon. Yet the agricultural land around Amritsar and Jullunder, a mere hundred miles or so from the foothills, is so flat that if you look only at the trees and fields you might imagine yourself at times to be driving through Suffolk in early summer. But the blanketed peasants, the high proportion of turbanned Sikhs and the abundance of smartly uniformed and strongly built soldiers are all unmistakable features of the Indian Punjab. This is the front door of India, through which invaders of many races have entered in the past. This and the bracing climate has bred a strong military tradition and a relative sense of urgency and efficiency amongst Punjabis.

By this stage of the tour there had been many frustrating moments for the journalists covering the tour, but the difficulties of communication they sometimes faced were impossible to condemn since everyone was so willing to help in every possible way. One young man to whom I had shown impatience when calls to London which he was handling constantly came through late, totally disarmed me by thanking me for my 'superb hospitality' and the 'warm and sweet friendship' we had enjoyed! Certainly the MCC batsmen were treated with friendship and hospitality by the North

Zone bowlers after Tony Greig called correctly when Bishen Bedi
spun the coin with him for the first and least significant time. As
usual the batsmen found a pitch of low bounce and slow pace, and
as usual the seam bowling they faced bore no relation to the type
they had been facing against Australia and the West Indies. This
was so even though North Zone's opening bowlers had both taken
the new ball for India – Madan Lal and Mohinder Amarnath. Once
Greig and Woolmer, who opened for MCC, had played themselves
in against the military medium of these two, the innings faltered
only twice in the day and on both occasions the magic of Bishen
Bedi was in the air.

Despite the formidable MCC score of 389 for six declared, Bedi
escaped the carnage, finishing with three for 38 after a relatively
light workout of 15 overs. When he was bowling it was a different
game: batsmen played and missed when they tried to defend,
mistimed their shots when they tried to attack. For the rest of the
day Bedi seemed content to look on from slip with a philosophical
air, taking mental notes on the form of the opposition he would
soon be meeting. He can only have been impressed by much of the
MCC batting. Woolmer and Greig began with a generally fluent
opening partnership of 110, the start of a delightful day's cricket
before a capacity crowd, many of them in turbans, others
overflowing into the branches of the stately eucalyptus trees which
fringed the ground. Woolmer was out, sweeping against the leg-
spin of Shukla, just before a lunch interval made memorable by the
playing of a regimental band of pipes and drums.

Thus inspired, Bishen Bedi dismissed Tony Greig in the first over
after the interval, and when Keith Fletcher drove outside Shukla's
googly three wickets had fallen for nine runs. But Mike Brearley
with calm, careful batting and Alan Knott with audacious,
inventive strokeplay quickly wrested back the initiative and Knott
went on to score 71 at a run a minute, his innings a small gem of
calculated aggression. Chris Old was the ideal batsman to keep the
attack going and he quickly settled in to play one of the best innings
of his career. On form Old is a graceful as well as powerful hitter of
the ball. In reaching his fourth first-class hundred he hit thirteen
fours and three sixes, one of them a tremendous blow which sent the
ball onto the pavilion roof. Brearley was the fifth MCC batsman to
score more than fifty on the first day, and if he was slower than the
others he also looked the soundest of all. By now he was past 300
runs in three innings and although Bedi had him stumped he must

have recognised the Middlesex captain as one of the most serious threats to India's chances in the forthcoming series.

The festival atmosphere of Sunday's play dissolved into Monday morning blues. Tony Greig, suffering a chill on top of a cold and a boil in one ear, not surprisingly stayed at the hotel in bed, and Mike Brearley was forced to do the same after a night of diarrhoea and vomiting. When, forty minutes after play began, Miller had to leave the field suffering from influenza MCC had only eleven men available to take the field and three of these were substitutes. Cope, of course, was still in Yorkshire and Barlow in Delhi, and though the fighting fit stuck to their guns well in the field there was a sense of unreality about the play. Nevertheless, every day has significance for somebody and John Lever took the opportunity to have three long, steady bowls which further enhanced his reputation. His most important victim was Mohinder Amarnath, the Indian number three against New Zealand, who tried to hook his third ball, miscued, and was caught at mid-on. Lever's opening ten-over spell earned him figures of two for 21 and he finished the day with four for 51 and a Test cap almost in the bag.

Bob Willis eased himself back into some sort of match fitness by bowling fifteen overs; even on a pitch of extreme docility he made the occasional ball lift unpleasantly and picked up a couple of wickets. Mike Selvey worked hard for no visible reward and under the temporary captaincy of Alan Knott, who was at his sparkling best behind the stumps, MCC generally concentrated like good professionals. The North Zone batting was almost uniformly dull, apart from a few good shots by Surinder, the left-handed son of the famous Lala Amarnath and brother of Mohinder, and a few healthy blows later in the day by a slim little wicket-keeper named Ved Raj. He is one of the few players of lowly parentage to get the opportunity to play first-class cricket in India (though one sees games played by children of almost all castes everywhere one goes in the sub-continent), but Raj has a special advantage in that he is the son of the groundsman – itself considered a humble position in India – at Jullunder, and he lives on the edge of the ground at Burlton Park.

The biggest cheers on the second day, however, were for Bishen Singh Bedi himself, whose home town is nearby Amritsar. He brought a smile to every face just by walking out to bat late in the day and when he opened his shoulders and deposited a ball from Lever over the boundary line for what the Indians call a 'sixer' the crowd's ecstasy knew no bounds.

He declared next morning, when MCC could technically have forced a follow-on but preferred to settle for batting practice. Ironically both Fletcher and Woolmer were out to Madan Lal before Bedi came on, and when Randall, having soundly played himself in, was l.b.w. to a googly from Shukla his last chance of seizing a first Test cap had gone. It was a shame, because his electric-hare fielding had made all the difference to MCC in the field: his running, jumping and clowning were an entertainment in themselves.

Bedi bowled only five overs on the last day of the game before leaving the field to 'rest', and against a moderate attack Chris Old took the chance to increase his match aggregate to 163 without being dismissed. Again he stroked the ball handsomely, hitting the left-arm spin of Goel for one lofted onside boundary after another with a casual, almost lazy swing of the bat. Would he be able to play like this in the Tests to come?

Bob Willis, batting high in the order in case he might be needed to come in and make runs or stave off defeat at a vital stage in the Test, had a good long bat in the middle to score 37 and John Lever also played quite presentably whilst making 11.

Alan Knott declared the second innings with no thoughts of being able to bowl North Zone out in only two hours, but Lever, coming on after tea, took two wickets in his first over, completing Mohinder Amarnath's pair in the process. During his brief moments at the crease Mohinder, who also found time to give an unaccepted chance to mid-on, hardly played like a Test number three. Lever finished with three second-innings wickets for eight (7 for 59 in the match) and was by now comfortably the touring side's leading wicket-taker. The match ended with Randall bowling at one end and Fletcher at the other, but though as a contest the game had been meaningless at least it had decided the two doubtful places in the Test team. Woolmer had secured his despite the challenge from Randall and partly because of the illness to Miller and continued misfortune of Tolchard in being considered as a wicket-keeper first and batsman second. At this stage Tolchard had played eight innings in India (including the previous tour), been out only three times (never for less than 35) and averaged over 100.

The preamble to the Tests matches was over. It had been a hectic three weeks, and the strong feeling as the side made their roundabout journey back to Delhi was that instead of four three-day matches, all more or less certain draws before they even began, three four-day games would have been more sensible from every point of view. After the brief settling-in period in Bombay the team had been either travelling or playing every day. There was no time to take stock, to relax, or even to get under the skin of India as a country. The great writer on Indian themes, Ruth Prawer Jhabvala, entitled one of her recent novels *Heat and Dust*. To many of the MCC team, leaving the dusty air of Jullunder behind them and feeling the faintly nauseous excitement that settles in the stomach in the hours before a crucial Test match, those three words might have summed up their attitude to India.

It is strange that a country much of which is so noisy, so seedy, so poor, on its surface indeed so depressing, should have been for so many a place of retreat and solace, where a deeper peace than that reached by the five senses has been frequently sought and sometimes found. No doubt it is the very poverty of the life of so many Indians, and the absence of Western-style material comforts, that has enabled them to discover a deeper meaning to life.

Spiritual thoughts were far from the minds of any of the players as they drove through the spacious, elegant streets of New Delhi and settled with relief into their hotel. The mood of the team was optimistic. Everyone was fit enough to attend a cheerful reception at the British High Commission and next morning all but Derek Randall were able to attend the final net practice before the first Test team was announced. Randall had caught the unrelenting stomach bug overnight, but his chances of an immediate place in the team had gone anyway. The surprise in store for everyone was the appearance at the nets of Geoff Cope and his subsequent selection in England's twelve.

Cope's flight back from London, after attending his father's funeral in Yorkshire, had been delayed and he had only emerged through the customs after more than fourteen hours of wearisome travel at 6.45 in the morning. Yet three hours later, when most cricketers, thinking they had no chance of selection, would have been sleeping, Cope was in the nets and he bowled so well on a turning wicket that the selectors decided he must be included, postponing their final decision until the morning of the match. Otherwise England's team was as expected, with Graham Barlow and John Lever winning their first caps. For them and the other members of the team the moment of truth had come.

Chapter Three

VICTORY AT DELHI

The Farozeshah Kotla cricket stadium lies on the borders of Old and New Delhi. The ground takes its name from Farozeshah's Fortification which still stands nearby – a relic of a pre-Moghul Empire. On 17 December 1976 the sandstone ruins of the old ramparts shook again as 30,000 people made their way to their expensively acquired seats on a cool, sunny morning.

England left Geoff Cope out of their twelve, and India, as expected, made only one change from the side which had won their last Test against New Zealand, Sharma replacing Mankad. Tony Greig, so unlucky with the toss against the West Indies, called correctly this time and when Dennis Amiss straight-drove the first ball of the match from Ghavri for a confident boundary it seemed that the time had come again for the gods to smile on England. In Ghavri's third over Amiss glanced and hooked successive balls for four and six and in the seventh over of the innings, with the score 24, Bishen Bedi peeled off his sweater, handed his spectacles to the umpire, and bowled one testing over. It transpired that he was merely allowing Ghavri and Amarnath to switch ends, and although Ghavri had Brearley in trouble for a while he and Amiss must have been relieved that the serious battle against the spinners had been temporarily postponed.

But relief turned quickly into dismay. Amiss had already taken one or two chances in running short singles to keep the scoreboard ticking over and now Brearley, who had acquired only five rather nervous runs, pushed a ball from Ghavri gently towards mid-off and called for a run. Patel, prowling at extra-cover, moved to the ball like lightning, scooped it up off the ground, threw in underarm and hit the stumps, running Brearley out. The total was 34 for one, and at once Bedi, a quiet master of the art of pressure tactics, brought himself on to bowl against Graham Barlow.

Normally a man playing his first Test might not expect to go straight in at number three in the order, but England hoped to counter the threat of Bedi's left-arm spin by confronting him as early as possible with a left-handed batsman. Bedi met the challenge head on and, at least on this occasion, won. Barlow, having – on Ken Barrington's advice – walked to the middle slowly and calmly so as to get used to the light and the noise, pushed forward to his fourth ball and, unable to smother Bedi's lethal spin, directed the ball straight into Amarnath's hands at short-leg.

England were thankful now that Amiss had got some runs under his belt and also for the calm, unhurried defence of Bob Woolmer. But already the grey, grassless pitch was taking spin, and when Woolmer went back to a ball from Chandrasekhar it whipped in, kept low and trapped him l.b.w. England were in trouble at 51 for three and they looked to the battle-hardened pair of Amiss and Fletcher to pull them through the crisis. Fletcher started confidently enough, moving his feet to Bedi and once on-driving him sweetly for four. But with the unnaturally rapid swingover of a right arm withered by polio Chandra is always liable to surprise a batsman for pace, and when Fletcher was bowled playing back to a fully-pitched ball on his leg-stump his dismissal was an exact copy of the way he had got out to Chandra in the corresponding match at Delhi four years previously.

At 65 for four England's plight was becoming desperate, but Tony Greig marched out, arms swinging, fifteen minutes before lunch, and he and Amiss almost doubled the score with sensible, positive batting. Chandra always mixes some bad balls amongst his unplayable ones and Amiss took advantage of three of them in one over to cut and drive his way to a fine fifty. Without him a good morning for India would have been an excellent one but between lunch and tea Amiss remained a solid, determined obstacle in the way of the spinners as England advanced from 84 for four to 198 for five. Amiss called the tune during his fifth-wicket partnership of 60 with Greig, but the captain played without any semblance of error until a ball from Venkataraghavan kept low and turned enough to have him l.b.w. for 25.

The real transformation of the innings occurred during the stand for the sixth wicket between Amiss and Knott, and this time it was Knott who dominated. Of all the innings he has played for England, some stubborn, some daring and inventive, few can have been more brilliant than this one. His fifty came in 63 minutes with ten fours. At times he was impossible to bowl at, as Venkat found when he was hit three times in an over for impudent fours: first a finely timed dab to third man, then two lofted strokes to leg, struck from several yards down the pitch. But Knott was to dance out of his ground once too often. He did so to a ball from Bedi which pitched wide of the off-stump and turned sharply away. He tried desperately to get back before Kirmani removed the bails but in the umpire's opinion just lost the race. Knott had scored 75 and after his dazzling performance the day ended with Amiss and Old quietly playing out time.

The word quiet is a misnomer, though, when applied to Indian cricket. All day the game had been played in a hubbub of noise which frequently developed to a crescendo as ball hit pad or a shot was struck in the air anywhere near a fielder, and now, as the shadows lengthened, the spectators, knowing that another wicket would mean the exposure of the England tail, bayed for blood. Chandra was the man they felt could do the trick and each time he approached the wicket he was accompanied by a deafening roar of encouragement. Amiss, however, was not to be moved. His innings had been a personal triumph after his failures in India four years before, and showed that he had gained from his bitter experience then. As the day wore on he played with less fluency, content to retreat into his shell and bide his time. In fact, at 92, he ought to have been caught off Bedi by Patel at extra-cover, but he got to three figures in the end, the second time he had done so in successive Tests for England and the eleventh in his Test career. It was a valuable innings not just in the context of the match but also for the fact that, as the first Test centurion of the tour, he earned himself a hundred bottles of champagne presented by the Victoria Sporting Club of London.

The same organisation had promised twelve bottles to any journalist who correctly guessed the scorer of the first hundred in the series. Along with two others I had named Amiss, and the prize was to go to whomever of us had come nearest to estimating the eventual score. Since I had guessed rather pessimistically at a mere 128, and since England needed every run they could get on the second day, I was delighted to concede the champagne to John Woodcock of *The Times* – a man who had once received a regular income from another journalist as a result of a bet he made about the number of runs Amiss would make for England.

After a brief period against Ghavri and Amarnath with the new ball next day, Amiss was soon playing the spinners with great skill as he led England on to 300 and beyond. On the way he lost the help of the last of England's recognised batsmen when Old, after playing with almost excessive circumspection, edged to slip a ball which floated on with Bedi's arm. With England 263 for seven India had a right to think that it would now be just a matter of containing Amiss and working their way as quickly as possible through the tail. But it turned out to be a long process and at lunch England were 297 for seven with Amiss in sight of 150 and Lever, playing with a straight bat and great good sense, 12 not out at the other end.

Lever's red-letter day, indeed, was only just beginning. Needing the occasional slice of luck against Bedi outside the off-stump he stuck to the crease by playing each ball on its merits, and there were enough loose ones for him to pick up runs with increasing regularity, as a tiring Amiss battled solidly on at the other end. In desperation Bedi was forced to abandon spin and reintroduce Ghavri, but such was the relish with which Amiss tucked into him that the experiment was quickly abandoned. And it was spin, plus Amiss's own fatigue after eight and a half hours' unwavering concentration, which finally ended his innings when he struck a ball from Venkat straight to deep mid-on. He had hit a six and twenty-two fours in his 179, shared an eighth-wicket stand of 94 with Lever, and before the end of the day was back in his hotel bed with a temperature and a cold on his chest. As a result he missed the dramatic end to the day.

Once Amiss had gone the game pursued its expected course until tea, when England were all out for 381. Bedi and Chandra took the last two wickets, but not before Lever had completed a memorable fifty in his first Test innings. Bedi's figures – four for 92 from 59 overs – were deservedly the best among the bowlers. The Indian innings got away to such a steady start that England's fears about the pitch being altogether too docile to be of any use to their fast bowlers seemed about to be realised. The tall, bespectacled Gaekwad got behind the line of Willis's fastest short balls, as he had done against Holding earlier in the year at Kingston, Jamaica, where India had been battered to a humiliating defeat by bowling which was apparently not just fast but physically dangerous. Today whilst Gaekwad exercised his attacking strokes off the back foot, Gavaskar, the pint-sized perfectionist, settled in with plenty of time for his shots, and all was proceeding serenely for the opening pair when the new ball went out of shape.

This is a familiar problem in Test cricket today. Balls do not seem to have the lasting qualities they once had and in this series the teams were experimenting with a new type of Indian-made ball which until now had proved quite satisfactory. One of its great qualities, so far as the MCC team was concerned, was its ability to swing considerably whilst the shine remained, but the particular ball with which the Indian innings started had neither swung nor, being unusually soft, had it bounced much either. Fortunately for England it was now exchanged for another one which immediately moved around much more.

Lever, operating from the pavilion end, had already bowled five overs when he struck Gaekwad on the back leg as he aimed to play the ball through mid-wicket. Gaekwad looked as disappointed with umpire Reuben's decision as had one or two of the England players condemned to the pavilion by his fellow-umpire Nagendra the previous day. But Mr Reuben's bony left finger had not finished its work. Lever's next ball ducked into Mohinder Amarnath's boots at the last second and without any hesitation the umpire upheld the bowler's triumphant appeal. Poor Amarnath had now been out three times to Lever in a week without scoring a single run, and his last two dismissals had occurred as the result of identical deliveries, the only practical difference being that the ball at Jullunder had hit the stumps and the ball at Delhi had hit his pads. Thus India were reduced to 43 for two with their two premier batsmen, Gavaskar and Viswanath, at the crease. Two more overs from Lever and they were 49 for four.

The crucial wicket was that of Viswanath, who fell in the same way as Amarnath, l.b.w. to another late inswinger pitched right up to the pads. He walked to the pavilion in a sepulchral silence. Clearly India could not afford another loss before stumps, so they sent in Venkat as the nightwatchman. He was able to leave the first ball outside his off-stump, but Lever's next delivery was the lethal well-pitched inswinger and out went the off-stump. Lever's first active day as a Test cricketer had brought him 53 runs with the bat and four for 16 with the ball. Red-faced and smiling in the dressing-room afterwards he was more willing to talk about the luck he had had than the skill he had shown: 'I have to keep pinching myself to appreciate that it really has happened.'

His bowling on that second evening, and indeed again the following morning, reminded me of another startling first appearance on the international scene, made in England two summers before by the Australian left-arm fast-medium bowler Gary Gilmour. In misty, humid conditions at Headingley in the World Cup semi-final Gilmour had undone England's batting with a similar demonstration of artful swing bowling. (If there was a difference it was that Gilmour had been more easily able to swing the ball away from the right-handed batsman as well as in to him.) Some of Lever's team-mates admitted that they had never seen him produce the inswinger with the regularity he had shown this day. Time would tell whether it was just a once-in-a-lifetime inspirational performance or whether England had suddenly unearthed a bowler of real international quality.

The impression that they had indeed done so gathered strength on the third day. Lever, whose stamina and determination had never been questioned, bowled thirteen overs off the reel on what, fortunately for the England team, was a cool, summery morning with a thin fleece of cloud and a gentle breeze. (Sitting in the shade, however, one English scribe wore six woollen pullovers and was not in any way moved to sympathy by news from home that it was snowing.) Lever was only one hero in a morning's session that saw England tighten their grip on the match still further. Another was Bob Willis, who held two remarkable and totally dissimilar catches.

For a time it had seemed that the Indian wickets would only be acquired by a long, slow process of winkling out stubborn batsmen. Patel and Gavaskar, suitably cautious but still eager to look for runs, took the score to 96. The usual capacity crowd at the Farozeshah Kotla ground applauded every run and when Gavaskar off- and cover-drove Lever for successive fours their roars made the kop at Anfield sound like quietly chattering guests at a vicarage tea party.

But Lever persevered. When Patel had made 33 he received a ball which cut in to him and edged it low down the leg-side. Knott pounced and caught the ball expertly in his left hand and the slide had begun again. Three runs later Gavaskar hooked at a rising ball which skidded off the top edge of the little man's bat and Willis ran twenty yards along the long-leg boundary to catch the ball at full stretch and clasp it triumphantly to his chest as he fell. With two for 28 in the morning stint Lever rested, and Underwood replaced him in the hope of another wicket before lunch. It came when Sharma aimed a firm drive, the ball flying off a thick edge to Willis fielding close in between gully and point. With instant reflexes Willis stuck out a long right arm and fastened onto the ball.

After lunch the innings was killed off ruthlessly. The wicket-keeper Kirmani had played some valuable knocks for India in the series against New Zealand, but Lever produced yet another of his special swinging yorkers to spreadeagle his stumps and Bedi and Chandra came and went almost in the blink of an eye. Bedi was caught in the slips off Old, and Chandra, second ball, lost two of his three stumps to end the innings on a suitably spectacular note.

Had India batted for another half-hour or so Greig might have thought hard about whether or not to enforce the follow-on. But with a lead of 259 he had a considerable insurance against the outside possibility of India's being able to make a big second-innings score and then embarrass England on a turning wicket on the final day. Rightly, Greig took the orthodox attacking decision. But at first the pitch was as good as gold when India began their long rearguard action. With the total 20 Bob Willis took his only wicket of the match with a very fast off-cutter which penetrated Gaekwad's defences and knocked back his middle stump. But this was to be England's only success for a long time. Bedi had wisely decided to drop Mohinder Amarnath down the order to number six, promoting Sharma to number three, a move I had expected India to make in the first innings as well. Sharma had already proved himself a difficult man to dislodge, and as the only batsman so far to have scored a hundred against the MCC bowlers on the tour his opponents had a healthy respect for him. Like Gavaskar Sharma played with coolness and determination against the new ball. He appeared to be fortunate to get the benefit of the doubt when struck on the back pad by a ball from Old, but Lever was naturally tired, and Willis, after striking his one important blow, could not settle into a consistent line and length.

Soon the spinners were in harness: Underwood left-arm medium-slow, Greig right-arm off-break. The ball turned, sometimes negligibly, sometimes quite sharply, but on the whole the bounce was true. Towards the end of the day the pads were frequently struck, and Indian hearts sank as one of the four close fielders on either side of the wicket caught the ball in vain hope of a bat-pad deflection. But what luck there was on the third afternoon went India's way and Gavaskar, clearly relishing the fight, led Sharma into the pavilion at close of play with relieved cheers ringing in his ears. India were 82 for one, still 177 behind, but matches had changed course from such situations in the past and their position was far from hopeless. At a reception given by the Indian Cricket Board that Sunday night in a big Delhi hotel, Bishen Bedi was bold enough to imagine himself spinning England out late on the final day. Certainly, stranger things had happened – and a captain must have faith in his side.

The term 'rest day' can sometimes be a misnomer in a Test match. It is, at least, a day of physical rest and after all the hectic travelling and cricket on the tour to date this was welcome in itself for the players. It was, in fact, the first full 'day off' that they had had since the start of the tour. But physical relaxation is one thing, mental relaxation another. Sometimes, when a team has not won a Test for a long time (and in England's case this was nearly two years) there is almost a fear of winning – or at least a fear that, whatever they do, nothing is going to change their luck. England knew that they still had nine wickets to take on a very slow wicket and after Gavaskar and Sharma's patient defensive stand doubts were creeping in.

Yet despite their apprehensions the team had no intention of wasting their precious free time. Some played golf in the morning on the beautiful course in the heart of New Delhi where almost the only buildings visible from the tree-lined fairways are fifteenth-century sandstone temples. Roger Tolchard, cheerfully accepting his role as reserve, produced the most impressive form when a team of visiting players and journalists got the better of their match with the British High Commission – whose hospitality throughout the stay in Delhi was delightful. Meanwhile, members of the side were content to rest by the hotel swimming-pool, though only the bravest actually took a dip because the cold 'winter' nights made the water almost prohibitively cool. In the afternoon came one of the most memorable of all the many receptions the team were everywhere invited to. The President of India, F. A. Ahmed, who sadly died some weeks later, was a keen cricketer and he lived in one of the most beautiful palaces in the world, a masterpiece of symmetry and splendour in red-and-grey sandstone, commissioned by King George V and set in 380 acres of trees and beautiful gardens. There is even a golf course in the grounds, which the 75-year-old President made full use of and on which his local knowledge proved too much even for so skilled and competitive a player as Ken Barrington. Sir Edwin Lutyens and Lord Hardinge, Viceroy of India, conspired to plan the elegant showpiece of New Delhi with the palace overlooking the majestic 'Rajpath', a long and broad tree-lined avenue to the war memorial arch known as India Gate. The British legacies to India are many, whatever may be thought now about the days of Empire, but – apart from cricket – few have been so readily appreciated as this 'garden city' within a city. It makes a startling contrast to the crammed, narrow streets of the old town. But amidst the teeming bazaars Old Delhi has its own architectural splendours like the massive Jama Masjid Temple, with its onion-shaped domes and tapering minarets, and the famous Red Fort – both legacies from another Empire, that of the sixteenth-century Moghuls.

The time for sightseeing was strictly limited. On Tuesday it was back to business, though not as early as England's team would have wished. When play was due to begin, at ten o'clock, a misty smog hung around Farozeshah Kotla, made up partly of natural moisture in the air and partly of pollution from nearby power stations and factories. As usual one sympathised with umpires who have to decide at such times when the light is fit for cricket, and one wondered again why the International Cricket Conference will not experiment with 'light-meters' to guide the umpires towards a decision. My view on this occasion was that play ought to have begun an hour or so earlier than it did, when the sun had dispersed the worst of the haze. England of course were doubly the sufferers both because valuable time was being lost and also because the ball might have swung considerably in such conditions. Although a frustrated Greig resisted the temptation to 'pressurise' the officials, something he had promised he would not do at the start of the tour, he did go over to the crowd and tried unsuccessfully to get them to call for the cricket to begin. This was one occasion when the England captain and the crowd who adored him were not in accord: they wanted cricket, of course, but with even greater force they wanted India not to lose.

In the end, twenty minutes' play was allowed before lunch, during which time India moved from 82 for one to 93 for one and Sunil Gavaskar reached his fifty. He also scored his 1,000th Test run for the calendar year, an achievement greeted by a mass invasion of the field, and he was buried beneath garlands of roses and carnations. A necklace of rosy apples and one of rupee notes were thrown in as well. As an example of India's extraordinary cricket mania it was notable; but the England players had already lost enough time, and they were not amused.

For the spectators, however, the delay served only to make the afternoon's cricket still more urgent and tense. After two overs from Lever at the start of the day Greig brought himself on to join Underwood, and these two were to bowl unchanged for the remainder of the dim, cool day. Although the occasional ball turned considerably Gavaskar continued to play with great skill, whilst Sharma reminded one of John Edrich in the way that he rode his luck and battled on without a thought for the ball before. But he was much more vulnerable than his partner and appeared to be missed by Knott off Greig in the over before he was out. England's by now desperately needed breakthrough came at last when Sharma, who had put on 90 with Gavaskar in 198 minutes at the crease, pushed out at Underwood and edged the ball via his pad to Fletcher at slip. Sharma walked only when the umpire had raised his finger, but soon afterwards Mr Reuben refused vociferous appeals from Underwood and Knott for catches behind the wicket. On both occasions Gavaskar was stung into action, moving forward to drive Underwood down towards the packed open seats opposite the pavilion. But the firecrackers which greeted the second shot had only just faded when Gavaskar turned Underwood's arm ball off his leg-stump and Woolmer, fielding at square short-leg, stuck out his right hand and caught him. Gavaskar had batted 263 minutes for his 71, hitting seven fours and a six, although he had scored so slowly that the possibility of India getting back into the game with a chance had now gone. The almost total silence which accompanied Gavaskar's walk back to the pavilion indicated the seriousness of his team's plight. Much depended now on Viswanath's ability to take on Gavaskar's sheet-anchor role.

It had been good to see Woolmer getting into the act at last and he almost accepted another very hard chance a few minutes after Gavaskar's demise when Patel whipped a ball from Greig straight into – and out of – Woolmer's comfortable midriff. Greig did not have to wait long for the wicket he so much deserved. Since at least two spinners are invariably needed for Test matches in India England had taken a chance in treating him as their second spinner when he had bowled so little on the tour and so indifferently at that. But Greig has time and again been able to raise his performance when he plays for England and the stakes are high. Today he had dropped on to a length from the start, varied his flight and speed with some subtlety and thoroughly justified the attacking field he was able to set for himself. His first reward came from one of his less distinguished balls, pitched just short of a length. Viswanath slashed, snicked and was caught by Knott. Now the slide was really on.

At tea India were 156 for four, still 103 behind. The new ball had been due for some time, but with the pitch increasingly responsive to spin and the relentless Underwood gradually strengthening his stranglehold Greig had rightly delayed taking it. In only the second over after tea Patel drove Underwood hard back down the pitch and the bowler took the catch at the second attempt. Kirmani reached ten before pulling Greig to mid-wicket, and though Mohinder Amarnath played some brave attacking shots he spooned a rare full-toss from Underwood straight to Randall, fielding substitute at mid-on.

With the slow bowlers in operation Amarnath and Ghavri had made an unsuccessful appeal against the light, and now with clouds gathering ominously Greig dared not take the new ball as he would like to have done in an effort to finish the match in four days. Ghavri took the chance to hit 23 relatively speedy runs before the umpires intervened on their own initiative. Only three hours and twenty-five minutes' play had been possible but in that time England had taken six more wickets and now only a meteorological freak could deny them their first Test victory since February 1975, their first also under Tony Greig, and only their fifth ever in India.

After the strain and tension of the fourth day the end came swiftly on the fifth. Some 10,000 spectators watched the final few overs in bright early morning sunshine, proving either that hope does indeed spring eternal or that devotion to cricket in India knows no equal anywhere in the world. No one in the English camp seriously thought that victory was anything other than a formality now, but they were thankful nonetheless that there was no long-drawn-out tail-end resistance. Underwood finished the over that had been curtailed because of poor visibility the previous evening, and then it was back to Willis and Lever with the new ball. Willis bowled fast but a little short. I doubt anyway if he was much concerned at which end the wickets fell, so long as they kept falling. Certainly it was appropriate that they should have been taken by Lever, who had been the leading matchwinner.

Venkateraghavan was the first to go, in Lever's second over, fending off a short, rising ball on his leg-stump into the gloves of Knott. Ghavri remained, but the serious business was now over and it was only a question of how long Bedi and Chandrasekhar could entertain the crowd. Bedi middled his first delivery from Lever but could not score from it, then took a sightless heave at the next and lost his middle stump. While the left-handed Ghavri, who revealed a good eye but a certain apprehension against the quickest balls, picked up further runs to lessen the margin of victory Chandra actually played a full maiden over from Lever. He had almost survived a second one too when Lever produced the swinging yorker that was required and England had won by an innings and 25 runs. Bedi and Chandra, free scorers in the previous series against New Zealand, had both collected a pair.

The extent of England's victory may possibly have been a little flattering to Greig's team. It had really been determined by the suddenness of India's collapse on the second evening of the game. But it had been an altogether more convincing win than the one in Delhi four years previously when Greig himself and Tony Lewis had kept their nerve in England's second innings to guide them to a six-wicket win. Greig and the other survivors from that game – Fletcher, Amiss, Underwood and Knott – were all the wiser now for the mistakes that had been made later in that series. They knew that a long struggle lay ahead. Only two winters before, Clive Lloyd's West Indians had won the first two Test matches, only to lose the next two – and their subsequent wrapping-up of the series at Bombay owed most to Lloyd's winning the toss and getting the all-important big first-innings score. So celebration had to be tempered by qualification – the toss in this game at Delhi had been an important advantage to England too.

Victory in a Test is always sweet. It is sweeter still when it has come after such a long period of disappointment and defeat and when, as in Delhi, it had been strained and sweated for. India had been beaten by a performance of sustained excellence. At lunch on the first day England were in serious trouble, but Amiss's staunchness, his absolute bloody-minded determination not to become strokeless and creasebound as he sometimes had before, had enabled his side to weather the storm. Then Knott's sheer genius had wrested back the initiative – which the winning of the toss had originally given to England. From that moment the game belonged to J. K. Lever: surprising the pundits, the Indian batsmen, his own team-mates and even himself. His was one of the most famous debuts in Test history; not since Alec Bedser had a bowler taken ten wickets in his first Test for England and the fifty which preceded his performance with the ball gave the story a touch of Boy's Own fantasy. Now Lever became a star overnight. Second only to Greig's, everyone wanted his autograph. When I played golf on the rest day I was asked four or five times if I was Lever, and one man simply refused to accept my denial. Cricket being the humbling game it is, it was unlikely that he would ever again have quite the same success, but his performance was already on its way into the record books, and there would be more to come.

Graham Barlow's first Test, in contrast, had been a disappointment. But he could console himself with the knowledge that as many great batsmen had made noughts on their first appearance as had made hundreds. Time was on his side, along with his own flair and exuberance.

One interesting technical point arose from this opening victory by England. The Indian ball, which was being used for the first time in the series and which, much to the England team's delight, had swung so noticeably in the opening games of the tour, had played a very significant role at Delhi. Ken Barrington had shrewdly agreed to play with it instead of with the English ball which had been used in the past, and this naturally pleased the Indian authorities. However, the England players said that the particular make of Indian ball used at Delhi was not produced again for the subsequent Tests. Certainly Lever and the other seamers never swung the ball so prodigiously again, but they had the upper hand now, and they were in no mood to relinquish their hold.

So Greig and his team, after a visit to the incomparable Taj Mahal, left for Christmas in Calcutta. Their tremendous start had been more than a seasonal present to themselves. It had, perhaps, done something to boost the morale of a whole nation at a time when it was struggling to combat an apparently interminable economic crisis. Perhaps as a result of this mood of national despondency the performances of British teams abroad seem to take on a disproportionate importance. The medals predicted for British athletes in the Montreal Olympic games had not come in the expected profusion. The English soccer team had been beaten by Italy in the World Cup match in November, and they, Scotland, Wales and Northern Ireland were all apparently unlikely to qualify even for the last sixteen. The newspapers wept and gnashed their collective teeth. Petrol was up, booze was up, and inflation was getting worse, so it was not surprising, amidst all this misery, that England's cricket victory in distant Delhi should have pierced a thin shaft of light through the surrounding gloom.

Chapter Four
INDIA MISS THEIR CHANCE

Because they had started so auspiciously there, and because New Delhi is the most British of Indian cities, MCC were naturally sorry to leave it behind. Calcutta awaited them, the second largest city in the Commonwealth, where shocking slums alternate with tall modern buildings; rickshaws, buffaloes, goats, and ceaselessly hooting cars and buses share the teeming streets with rumbling trams, and almost every pavement can serve a man as his bedroom, his dining-room, his bathroom, even his latrine. During the relatively cool nights of winter the air above these streets is thick with choking smoke from thousands of wood and cow-dung fires lit to warm the kerbside sleepers and the inhabitants of the 'bustees'. Apart from the spacious Maidan (a wide park offset by the splendid Victoria Memorial) it is undeniably a squalid city, as well as a colourful and fascinating one, yet the Bengalis treated the MCC team with charming warmth and friendliness, and the players were delighted with the quality of the hotel where they stayed.

Christmas was enjoyable if untraditional: golf on Christmas Eve, swimming by the pool and a visit to the polo on Calcutta racecourse on Christmas Day. Through private generosity almost everyone had a bite of turkey. The desire to please was universal, and only Keith Fletcher was unable to make the most of the hospitality. On Christmas Eve he had stumbled against a stone step and flaked a piece of bone from his left ankle. He was at once pronounced extremely doubtful for the second Test and stayed behind in Calcutta with Alan Knott and Dennis Amiss, who were given a rest whilst the remainder of the team left for their match against East Zone at Gauhati.

Their flight into India's far eastern region was frustratingly delayed for four hours by fog, but when they reached their destination they found Gauhati to be a charming shanty town, rambling amidst copious palm trees along the southern shore of the fabled Brahmaputra river and surrounded by the mist-shrouded, heavily vegetated hills of Assam. There was a pleasantly relaxed and welcoming atmosphere here, not least at the team's simple and unpretentious hotel overlooking the broad grey waters of the Brahmaputra. At one point the river is six miles wide and at monsoon time it can cause terrible destruction, estimated to average £15 million a year. But although the wettest place on earth is only 100 miles away, those few amongst the countless thousands of Britons who spent the best years of their lives in India surely chose well when they settled for the life of a tea planter in Assam.

Tony Greig and Bob Willis would probably agree with that sentiment. When they arrived at the hotel they found the beds too small for comfort. The locals were not used to men of 6 foot 7 inches and 6 foot 5 inches staying with them, but the problem did not bother them. By the second night both were sleeping in beds seven feet long by five feet wide which had been constructed for them during the day. That is service of a kind which you would find nowhere else but in India. Although there is now a population of some 400,000 in Gauhati and a thriving oil refinery there, it truly remains an unspoilt place, which in many ways has remained unchanged for centuries. I was taken to a 600-year-old temple, high on a local hill, where a goat is taken from the mountain every day, purified in holy water, then brutally guillotined and sacrificed to a Hindu god.

Gauhati's amenities include its stadium, the Nehru, which holds 35,000 spectators, more than any English Test ground. But the pitch on which East Zone played MCC was a poor one for cricket, very slow even by Indian standards, and turning sharply for spin bowlers from the start. At least it opened the prospect of a positive result to the match as MCC were put in to bat and spent the first day patiently laying the foundations of what they hoped would be their first win against a Zonal side. In making 213 for six, however, the MCC batsmen gave little help to the selectors who would have to choose England's second Test side later in the week. Randall, Tolchard and Miller all played equally well and these were the three rivals for Fletcher's place if his ankle injury ruled him out.

Randall got the first chance to gain promotion when he opened the batting with Barlow. For over an hour these two faced seam bowling on a pitch of uneven bounce and with the ball swinging about, but they scored 65 together and it was only the spinners who posed really perplexing problems. Dilip Doshi was well-known to the English players. He has bowled his left-arm spin with consider-able success in India for several years and apart from playing for

Nottinghamshire had made a recent impact on English cricket when he helped the minor county Hertfordshire to knock Essex out of the Gillette Cup in 1976. He bowled with too flat a trajectory and too wide a line to be a real menace on this occasion and he had less success than an interesting 26-year-old right-hand off-spinner, Alok Bhattacharjee, who looked for all the world like a leg-spinner until a last-minute twist of the wrist gave the ball a tremendous tweak and spun it in the opposite direction. He dismissed Brearley third ball after Doshi had got Barlow l.b.w. and he had Woolmer in the same way, caught at forward short-leg after Woolmer had spent a most uncomfortable hour at the crease for eight runs.

All this while Randall was playing as he had throughout the tour, patiently, soundly, unspectacularly. He had become the outstanding character of the team, as ready to mount a stage and take over from the local band as he was to scamper about the field, ape-like arms hanging down from clothes-hanger shoulders to keep everyone amused. His team-mates wanted him to succeed and they were delighted when he produced this timely fifty, his first of the tour. In truth, though, he played no better than either Tolchard or Miller, who came together, just as they had done at Ahmedabad, with their team in trouble. Again they played with resource and coolness. Miller, cap-peak pushed up at an angle like a jockey's, à la Tom Graveney, gave an impression of total unflappability. It was his second innings of the tour but he played like a man in ripe July form. Tolchard, though, was the senior partner, showing once again what an outstanding player of spin bowling he can be. He moves his feet nimbly to disrupt the bowler's length and plays the ball so late that he is able to dictate his own terms, and this he proceeded to do although the conditions were against him. Bhattacharjee was less of a worry when he was played as an orthodox off-spinner, and Tolchard and Miller had put on 93 when late in the day Tolchard was given out l.b.w., much to his surprise, as he shaped to leg-glance a ball from the persistent but otherwise ordinary seam bowler, Burman.

Greig declared overnight and MCC's apparently sluggish performance on the first day was placed in better perspective by East Zone's summary dismissal for 147. Despite the extreme slowness of the pitch, treated, I was told by a local first-class cricketer, with a potion of water and buffalo dung in order to take the fire out of it, Willis was fast and hostile enough to put the wind up the early batsmen. In six overs, three of them maidens, he took three for 14 in his opening spell. His first victim was caught behind by Tolchard off a bouncer, and his next two were clean bowled, the second one so cleanly that the middle stump was split down the centre.

The experienced Ramesh Saxena, however, brought with him an atmosphere of calm, and a slim, youthful bespectacled right-hander, Raju Mukherjee, settled down after a streaky start to play the only innings of substance. He might have been caught in the slips several times early on, especially off Old, but he rode his luck well and played some fine drives, both through the covers and off his toes. The stand of 51 between these two marked the only period when it looked as though East Zone might not be bowled out cheaply, and with Cope turning the ball sharply as soon as he came on the only surprise was that Willis managed to take five for 29. He finished the job he had begun so well with his second spell after lunch. Cope had to settle for three for 39 and the knowledge that he would be sure to have a good bowl again in the fourth innings. The other two off-spinners, Miller and Greig, did not even get on.

The batsmen had their usual problem when they went in again, that of scoring as fast as they could in the interests of forcing a win whilst at the same time taking the chance to practise against good spin bowling on a pitch as difficult as any they were likely to encounter on the tour. As it turned out both Randall and Brearley were out for single-figure scores before the spinners came on, but Barlow, in making 43 not out by the close of the second day, and 61 in all, did have a good duel with Doshi, who by reputation is India's best left-arm spinner after Bedi. Barlow did not by any means have everything his own way but from his reaction he clearly thought he was unlucky to be given out caught behind off bat and boot. This was only the first of a number of dubious decisions given by two umpires on the Test panel as MCC suffered a collapse which otherwise was of no significance, although it gave another immense crowd a morning of excitement.

Woolmer made 22 and Old 33 before they were given out stumped, in Old's case with the back foot apparently very firmly planted behind the crease. But Greig, Miller and – at last – Tolchard all went cheaply and fairly to Doshi and Bhattacharjee, who finished with three wickets apiece.

Greig declared at lunchtime, giving himself three and a half hours to bowl East Zone out and thus record the first win against a Zone side in India since M. J. K. Smith's tour thirteen years before. But in the field his captaincy was faulty for the first time on the tour and a great chance was missed. Greig, who did not want to bowl himself because he wished to prevent unnecessary wear and tear to his spinning finger, gave Miller only three overs all afternoon on a bare spinner's pitch. Cope, on the other hand, bowled 23 overs off the reel and took four for 55. It was impossible to understand Greig's reluctance to bowl Miller who had, after all, been England's off-spinner in the last Test of the English summer and who had taken 77 wickets in the season. One would like to have heard the comments of Derbyshire's captain Eddie Barlow if he had watched the final day at Gauhati.

There was everything to be said, of course, for an initial attempt to break through with the new ball. Old, indeed, did so when he bowled Banerjee in his second over, but MCC were then held up by a long stand of 82 for the second wicket between Saxena, who played outstandingly well – better than anyone else in the match – and a local boy, Bharali, who was to go on to bat for three and a half hours for his 45 not out. Willis could not summon the same venom as he had in the first innings but Selvey picked up two useful wickets as Greig persisted with endless seam bowling from one end.

Cope bowled eleven overs before he took a wicket. He was getting less turn than his Indian counterpart Bhattacharjee had done, and although he was apparently unlucky not to have Bharali given out caught off bat and pad it was not one of his best days. He was steady rather than venomous as one might have expected him to be on this pitch, but he missed the support which would have come from a spinner hustling through the overs at the other end with a ring of close fielders. When Greig finally turned to Miller, nine overs of the mandatory final twenty had already gone. But he quickly lost faith and called up Willis, which in fading light was an unwise move. Sure enough, the umpires called play to a halt with two overs of the last twenty still to go and MCC three wickets short of victory. It would not have been a win of any great significance, but the momentum gained from the Test victory at Delhi was lessened as a result. For that reason it had been perhaps the most disappointing day of the tour to date. The crucial game at Calcutta was looming ahead, however, and there were more important things to worry about.

MCC returned to find the 8,000,000 inhabitants of the city gripped by cricket fever. Nowhere in the world, not even in Yorkshire or Barbados, is the passion for the game stronger than it is in Calcutta. For a ticket for the five days at Calcutta people paid

£35 and thought themselves lucky. On the black market 800 rupees – over £50 – was the going rate. Yet the annual average income of a Bengali is probably no more than £20 *in toto*.

Two press conferences were held by the Bengal Cricket Association in an effort to satisfy the curiosity of people wanting to know why 26,000 of the 64,300 tickets available should be distributed amongst the officials of various clubs and cricket organisations. 'Officials' seemed mysteriously to multiply at Test match time. In any case it was widely felt that 64,300 was a laughable underestimate of the actual capacity of the magnificent Eden Gardens Stadium with its famous and beautifully maintained green outfield, bordered by a bowl of massive tiered concrete stands and a brand new club house, completed for the Test in less than six months. From the top one could peep over the great black scoreboard on the other side of the ground to see a line of palm trees and the masts of ships passing down the Hooghly River, and behind the club house the wide open spaces of Calcutta's big park, the Maidan, reminded one that the city wasn't all dirt and overcrowding.

After a police escort to the ground to protect them from the sea of smiling faces that followed their every movement the MCC players had their final practice on New Year's Eve, whilst the Indians went through their paces with equally good cheer in parallel nets on the other side of the ground. Between them stood the 22 yards of white-coloured earth and turf which held the key to the game. England's players bowled, batted and fielded with an air of confidence and genuine enthusiasm, though one important figure was missing: Derek Underwood was in bed with a temperature caused by an inflamed throat.

Underwood was of course an integral part of the team and the doubts about his being fit caused the selectors to choose two quite different elevens. Their first choice contained two changes, one enforced, the other voluntary. Fletcher's ankle was nowhere near fit enough for the rigours of a five-day game and he was duly replaced by Derek Randall. In addition the selectors reluctantly asked the out-of-form Woolmer to stand down and in his place named Roger Tolchard, who at the age of 30 was about to get the great opportunity of his cricket career. It was sad to see a player of Woolmer's ability left out, but there was no doubt that Tolchard had deserved his chance. He had an anxious 24-hour wait to hear whether Underwood had recovered, before having his place confirmed. Had 'Deadly' been unfit, Tolchard would have dropped out as well, and Cope and Woolmer would have come in: Cope to play Underwood's attacking role, Woolmer his defensive one. It was a tribute indeed to this unique bowler that it should need two men to cover him. Happily he woke up on New Year's Day 1977 restored to health by antibiotics.

The first roar of the morning came when Bedi signified that India had won the toss by waving his white sun-hat in jubilation to the crowd of 80,000. On a pitch likely to take increasing spin, it had to be a good toss to win. India sprang a mild surprise by announcing three changes from their defeated side at Delhi – Solkar, Prasanna and Madan Lal coming in for Mohinder Amarnath, Venkataraghavan and Ghavri. Madan Lal probably owed his elevation to a fine bowling performance on the Eden Gardens ground against the West Indies two years before, but one felt sorry for Ghavri who had bowled as well as any of India's few seamers in the previous matches against the English team. Solkar's return was due to his reputation as a gritty all-rounder but above all to his brilliant ability at short-leg, whilst Prasanna swapped places with Venkat as he had been doing on and off for years. There was no doubt that England feared Prasanna much more.

The first session was clearly likely to be crucial. India needed a solid foundation; England, with the prospect of batting last on a wearing pitch, simply had to make early inroads, and they got off to a perfect start when off Willis's fourth ball of the morning Gavaskar sparred outside the off-stump without controlling the high bounce of the ball and Old at third slip took a fine low catch. England's fielders hugged each other jubilantly. The hubbub in the vast arena died to an eerie whisper. Lever bowled from the new club-house end and twice beat Gaekwad outside the off-stump in his first over. With the last of the morning dew still dampening the bleached, crudely shaven pitch, every ball of the first few overs had to be closely watched for the extra bounce that had undone Gavaskar. Sharma coolly and studiously blocked one maiden over from Willis, but in the next he edged a ball inches in front of Brearley at first slip. A Simpson or a Chappell might possibly have fastened on to it, but it was not a true chance. This was a side of exceptional fielding strength, especially in the outfield where, with Randall, Barlow and Tolchard all outstandingly quick, it was arguably as strong a combination as England had ever fielded. Nor are Old, Greig and Brearley the worst close fielders to have stood at slip for England, and Greig is certainly amongst the most reliable of recent times. He proved the point when Lever followed up Willis's early blow with a second wicket in the twelfth over. He had been unlucky to have an understandably confident appeal turned down when Gaekwad padded up to his inswinger and unlucky again next ball when only the thinnest of edges on to Gaekwad's boot kept the ball out a second time. Gaekwad retaliated by hitting a firm straight push-drive for the first four of the morning in Lever's fifth over but in his next the latter got a ball to leave Sharma's defensive bat and Greig gobbled up the straightforward chance at second slip. India were 23 for two but by now Willis's furiously fast and admirably straight opening burst was at an end. Although Old replaced him after one exploratory over from Underwood he was not at his most dangerous. Viswanath settled in solidly and Gaekwad kept him gradually more confident company until lunch, which India took at 53 for two after 25 overs.

It had not been an impressive start by the home team and the vast crowd had continued to watch in uncharacteristic calm, but many a poor start by a batting side in India has been followed by a recovery in the heat of the afternoon. Not so this time. Half an hour after lunch, when the third-wicket pair had put on 42 and were just starting to show signs of breaking the grip which Lever and Old were continuing to hold by steady swing bowling, the indefatigable Lever struck again. Gaekwad had scored 32 when the trusty well-pitched late inswinger ducked back quickly and beat the long and slightly crooked downswing of Gaekwad's bat. The ball brushed his boot and carried on to remove a bail.

Now India badly needed a stand of substance between Viswanath and Patel before the soft underbelly was exposed. Viswanath, scrupulously careful over his defensive strokes and playing the occasional attacking shot with wristy skill, was just beginning to give the crowd something to shout about at last when he pushed forward to Underwood and edged the ball to Tolchard at forward short-leg. He had been grafting for more than two and a half hours and with his going the innings was in serious decline. Greig brought back Willis with instinctive good timing and Solkar, returning to Test cricket after a long absence, was quite out of rhythm with his extra pace. In the last over before tea he did not get fully on top of a rising delivery on his off-stump and edged the ball chest-high to Greig at third slip. England's captain was really enjoying himself now and giving the crowd what little they had to smile about. A few balls earlier Solkar had been unsettled as one of the few bouncers

Willis bowled all day brushed past his biceps. Greig went up to rub the offended spot, then took the bat and showed Solkar how to hook the ball towards long-leg. Mild amusement turned to delighted laughter when Greig then rearranged the position of his long-leg fielder just in case Solkar should take his advice seriously. Alas for India he could not do so, and they went into tea with only 99 for five on the board having lost three wickets for a mere 46 runs in the two hours of the afternoon.

Their plight grew worse soon afterwards when Patel trod on his wicket playing back to Willis. But a spirited if lucky partnership between Madan Lal and Kirmani at least brought India within a few runs of 150 by the close. Kirmani needed less luck than Madan Lal, never a happy player of quick bowling, but at least the latter tried to take the attack to the enemy and for a time his policy paid off. Eventually, however, he flashed once too often outside the off-stump and Knott did the necessary to give Old his first wicket. Not long afterwards Kirmani and Prasanna appealed against the fading light and the umpires brought an end to their – and the crowd's –misery. In 69 overs India has scored 146 for seven. England had bowled and fielded outstandingly well and gone a long way towards offsetting the disadvantage of losing the toss. But they knew the ball was certain to turn on the bare pitch and that the match, even the entire series, would probably depend on the way they batted in their first innings whilst its surface was still reasonably intact. It was no time for complacency, but 1977 had begun as well for them as it had for the Australians they would be meeting later in the year. (Australia's second Test match against Pakistan in Melbourne had begun a few hours earlier and their 322 for four underlined the strength of the challenge that lay ahead.)

It was the business in hand that concerned Greig and his team as they took the field on the Sunday before a packed stadium. Prasanna, after two unsuccessful flicks outside his off-stump, scored a run off the last ball of the opening over from Old, but he then played on to the seventh ball of the morning to give Willis his fourth wicket. Bedi appeared in his pink patka, got off the mark for the first time in the series with a risky single to Randall, whose throw was inches wide of the mark, and then hit Old towards mid-wicket where, after an anxious circle or two, Lever held on safely to the swirling ball.

Now it was a question of how long Kirmani could protect Chandra. Greig spread the field wide to invite him to take singles, but though Chandra was willing to take them the little wicket-keeper, a calm-looking figure with his sleeves rolled down to his wrists and his black moustache curling down either side of his mouth like a Mexican bandit's, was not. He managed to delay the inevitable for a while and to take his score to 25 not out before Willis, given two balls at Chandra, knocked out the latter's leg-stump. The innings had lasted exactly 75 overs, and the new ball remained in the umpire's pocket.

Now for the crunch: the decisive phase not only of this game, but perhaps of the whole series. The vast army of spectators shifted uneasily on their hard concrete seats. From the top of the pavilion they appeared as a circular sea of red, white and yellow dots, their sun-hats mingling into one huge kaleidoscope under the bright sun. Amiss calmly played a maiden over from Madan Lal before Barlow induced the first excited roar as he played and missed at Solkar's deceptively gentle outswing. Barlow's first runs in Test cricket came from a controlled thick edge past gully for four.

Amiss had a narrow escape in Madan Lal's second over when he turned a ball inches in front of Solkar at backward short-leg. The fielder damaged a finger on his right hand as he tried to scoop up the ball, but Madan Lal's disappointment was short-lived because, off the last ball of his third over, Barlow drove, got an inside edge and Kirmani dived to his right to hold a brilliant catch. The absent Farokh Engineer could not have bettered it.

For India this wicket before the spinners had come on was a tremendous bonus; for England the loss of Barlow so early was a heavy hammer-blow. The experiment of sending him in first had been costly and, with two new caps at numbers four and five, much depended now on Amiss and Brearley. All their experience and professionalism were under the microscope and Madan Lal, his tail up, was bowling his outswingers extremely well. Brearley, however, hooked him for a solid four and in the tenth over of the innings Bedi, his patka now changed to a blue one, came on in place of Solkar. Brearley played forward to the first two balls and at once the Indian captain brought up a point and a forward short-leg to join the two slips already posted on either side of the wicket. To the last ball of the over Brearley pushed forward again and the whole mighty stadium erupted as the ball carried off bat and pad to Solkar at short-leg. England were 14 for two as Brearley walked discon-solately back without waiting for the umpire's decision, and Randall replaced him, that jaunty, apparently carefree walk

Willis in action during India's first innings at Calcutta. *Left* Gaekwad ducks a bouncer. *Right* Chandrasekhar's off-stump is knocked out of the ground.

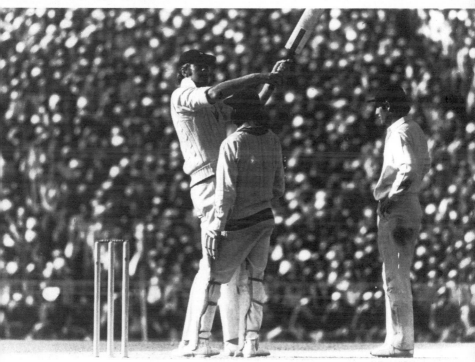

Left Wicket-keeper Kirmani leaps in an attempt to catch Tolchard off Chandrasekhar. *Above* Greig square-cuts Bedi for four and *below* demonstrates the hook to Solkar, who has just been unsettled by a bouncer.

Further incidents at Calcutta. *Above* Brearley is caught by Solkar off Bedi for 5.
Below Viswanath is caught by Tolchard off Underwood for 35 in India's first
innings.

belying the almost unbearable nervousness that must have been bubbling within him. But if tension can paralyse some people it can fire the adrenalin in others. Randall played his first four balls from Bedi with only one hint of difficulty, then late-cut and swept the last two balls of the over for perfectly timed boundaries. Chandra he played with equal confidence and good timing, and England went in to lunch thankful for small mercies and a score of 37 for two. Amiss, eight not out, had merely survived, but he square-cut the first ball after lunch from Bedi for four to give the few English spectators hope that the afternoon would be less hard on the nerves than the first hour of the innings had been. But when Randall had scored 18 he drove a full-toss from Madan Lal through the hands of the diving Bedi at mid-on and Amiss, when 22, was confidently appealed against as Kirmani caught a ball from Madan Lal down the legside which had brushed Amiss's side on its way through.

The initial flow of runs from Randall's bat was soon slowed to a slight trickle by Bedi's teasing accuracy. The fifty partnership came in a little over an hour, but the introduction of Prasanna after an hour of the afternoon session signalled the start of a period of slow torment for England's batsmen. His turn was at once more vicious than that of either Bedi or Chandra and his control was as tight as his flight was subtle. Amiss was becalmed on a score of 31 for some fifty minutes and in the course of this anxious period he was missed behind the wicket off Bedi. But after a stand of 67 in 107 minutes Randall's auspicious first Test innings was ended when he was given out l.b.w. as he played back to a ball of full length on his leg-stump. It may possibly have been Prasanna's floater, but he was turning the ball so much that he must have considered himself lucky to get the decision. A wicket was, however, no more than he deserved, and he followed up by ending Amiss's long and anxious vigil by means of a legside catch by Kirmani in the second over after tea.

Amiss had batted three hours and twenty minutes for 35. When he was out Tolchard's first Test innings had already lasted 45 minutes for a mere five runs. The two statistics tell something of the skill of the spinners and the extent of the turn as early as the second afternoon. Tolchard had come to the wicket intending to break the rhythm of the bowlers by moving his feet and trying to force holes in the ring of close fielders hemming him in like prison walls. But his initial plan had to be abandoned. The bowling was such that survival became the sole intention. Runs had to be scrimped and scraped. 'After a while,' Tolchard said afterwards, 'I really enjoyed

the exercise of just occupying the crease. In county cricket we never
have time to play an innings like that.'

The sight of Greig marching to the wicket in Amiss's place gave
renewed hope, however. His first scoring shot, an off-driven four
off Chandrasekhar, took him past 3000 runs in Tests and a swung
six to mid-wicket off Prasanna took England into three figures at
last. But their target, a lead of at least 100, was a long way off.
Prasanna, up to this point, had bowled twelve overs and taken two
for nine. That single six apart, he continued to demand respect and
ended the day with figures of two for 22 from 19 overs. But Greig
and Tolchard stayed to the close, by which time England's deficit,
with six wickets in hand, was only 19. Their target had at least
become a possibility. Tolchard had served them as well as Randall
in his first Test, his innings becoming increasingly freer and more
authoritative as the day wore on.

The crucial first session of the third day began under another
cloudless sky with a stiff breeze fretting at the blue-and-yellow flags
which marked the boundary between the players and the 80,000
spectators packed together like rush-hour commuters. Bedi from
the club-house end, Prasanna from the Hooghly River end, opened
the bowling and the battle of wits began all over again. Bedi
crowded the bat with five close men – slip, gully and point on the
offside plus a leg-slip and the inevitable Solkar hovering fearlessly
at short-leg. Prasanna employed two men up close on the legside,
with only three fielders in all on the off. Tolchard, sleeves buttoned
down at the wrists, neat and clinical in every movement, looked for
runs from the first ball: a quick dart down the pitch enabled him to
drive Prasanna for three runs between cover and extra to make him
the highest scorer in the match so far. Thirty-eight on this wicket, and
in this testing environment, was worth at least twice that amount in
friendlier circumstances.

Greig had woken early in the morning shaking feverishly from
the effects of yet another 'flu-bug. But Bernard Thomas's pills and
his own guts enabled him to make light of a temperature of 101 and
he settled down to play an innings that was completely out of
character. He began by tickling Prasanna past leg-slip for two more
runs to take England to 150. After four overs Prasanna was relieved
by Chandrasekhar. As the slender, bearded figure approached the
stumps and the polio-withered arm came whirling over the crowd
roared him on in a rising chant, and one or two of the more
unscrupulous amongst them tried to flash mirrors to distract the

batsmen. Greig successfully implored them to desist and then when Bedi pitched short he took a long step back and firmly square-cut him to the boundary to take England into the lead. To the next ball, however, Greig played forward and Solkar at short-leg muffed a catch he would normally have taken with ease. Greig was then only 33 not out, and India had lost a chance that was not to recur all day.

In the 89th over of the innings and the sixteenth of the morning Bedi called up Madan Lal and the new ball. A perfect late outswinger almost immediately beat Tolchard, but after an hour's play England were twelve runs on and inching their way towards a position of command.

Greig was even relaxed enough to start clowning. Just as Madan Lal started to run in a thunderclap boomed from the midst of the crowd and Greig, quick as a flash, fell flat on his back. Tolchard, by now equally at ease, went rushing down the pitch in mock concern. Bedi, however, decided the joking must stop and came back on after Solkar had been allowed only two overs with the new ball. There was another moment of comedy, this time quite unintended, when Tolchard danced down the pitch to Madan Lal, only to find himself confronted by a bouncer when three yards out of his crease. He ducked and scurried back into his ground like a rabbit making for its burrow. In the next over a typical controlled but unorthodox push past cover brought Tolchard his first Test fifty. He had batted 220 minutes and hit only two fours but his innings had been one of almost incalculable value, a triumphant vindication of his selection both for the tour and for the match. No wonder he punched the air with delight as he scampered down the pitch. The gesture reminded one of Gary Player holing an important putt, and after the long, anxious grafting, the hours of concentration, his feelings must indeed have been similar to a golfer crowning his final round with a birdie putt to win a big prize for the first time.

Greig reached his fifty just an over later and England lunched cheerfully, 38 runs ahead. The anxious period was now over for them and they could move on to the next stage of their broad strategy. The lead had been gained by patience and determination; there had been times the previous day when it had looked doubtful whether they would be able to establish any worthwhile lead at all. But if anything the Indian spinners were now turning the ball more slowly and the ironic possibility was developing that instead of having to bat last on a crumbling pitch as they had feared England might instead see India bat out for a draw on a pitch becoming

slower and slower. From an objective viewpoint it seemed that
England needed now to move on to the attack, and with a well-set
Greig at the crease and Knott and Old to follow they were
apparently well equipped to do so. But the two sides were reading
the match quite differently now. Greig, strongly influenced by the
experienced guiding hand of Ken Barrington, who had described
this as a 'grafting' pitch from the start, believed that England must
continue simply to occupy the crease. India, believing the pitch was
crumbling less quickly than England thought it was, were of the
opinion that the longer England batted, the greater India's chances
of saving the game.

In any case the best-laid plans will 'gang awry'. An intelligent piece
of bowling by Bedi and an unintelligent piece of batting (for once)
by Knott changed the complexion of the game again. Tolchard had
scored 67 and had batted for just under five and a half hours when
Bedi decided to change his angle of approach by bowling over the
wicket. The ploy worked. Tolchard, initially looking for the chance
to sweep, adjusted his stroke and pushed forward to a ball of full
length. Instead of leaving the bat as he had expected the ball came
on with Bedi's arm and found its way between bat and pad to the
wicket. This time the crowd's roar was one less of triumph than of
relief. They recognised in Tolchard's five-and-a-half-hour innings,
however, a great piece of disciplined batting and a canny application of all the experience he had acquired in thirteen years as a
professional cricketer. They rewarded him with a long, rolling
round of applause.

Knott came in clearly intent on injecting pace into the scoring. He
began by sweeping Bedi, but in the Indian captain's next over he
tried to square-drive a ball which turned away from him and was
caught off the edge by Gavaskar in the gully. One of the essential
differences between the two sides was emphasised now, however,
because Old, at number eight, compared favourably with Solkar,
the batsman going in two places higher on the opposite side. Not
that Old has often done justice in Tests to his abilities. But now,
when he was greatly needed to play a responsible innings, he did so.
Indeed, though he played and missed from time to time, it was Old
who almost single-handed kept England's score ticking over. One
effortless swing-through of the exceptionally heavy bat he favours
lifted a ball from Bedi over the long-on boundary and an
occasionally handsome drive or pull relieved the monotony of
strokeless defence that was increasingly the pattern of the day.

Greig, tired but determinedly defying his natural attacking instincts to the end, scored only nine runs between tea and the close. 'My old man would have been proud of me today,' he said afterwards in a voice wheezing with cold. 'He always reckoned I was an impatient b...!'

England had scored 147 runs in the day when the long shadows of the towering stands finally met each other in the middle of the pitch. There were times when the batsmen had been so intent on defence that the occasional long-hops and full-tosses were not despatched as they would normally have been. This happens when a mood of ultra-caution grips batsmen. But to their immense credit England had lost only two wickets all day on a pitch which, Greig firmly asserted, was quite unfit for Test cricket. Satisfied but still far from well, England's captain lay recuperating in his hotel bed on the rest day, preparing to hoist India with their own petard.

He needed only one over from Chandra, the first of the fourth day's play, to go from 94 to 101. His eighth Test century, and third against India, came with his seventh four after six hours and 42 minutes at the crease. He reached it with an off-drive about which there was a certain irony, since he had said that the pitch made it almost impossible to drive with safety. Its vagaries, anyway, were swiftly underlined. First Greig was l.b.w. to a ball from Prasanna which kept low and then, after demonstrating again that he is far from a rabbit at the crease, Lever was caught in the gully by a ball from Bedi which turned and lifted savagely.

Old retaliated by unleashing a superbly-struck on-driven six off Prasanna, but after Underwood had also been caught in the gully off Bedi Old's attempt to repeat the stroke gave Madan Lal the chance to make a spectacular running catch on the long-on boundary. Prasanna, with four for 93, had more than justified his recall at Venkat's expense, and Bedi, with five for 110 from 64 overs, must have rested his weary feet with a mixture of relief and anxiety. The way the ball had turned this morning was ominous for his side.

India's attempt to score the 166 that would make England bat again began 35 minutes before lunch on the fourth day. Gavaskar's first runs off Willis were all through the slips and it was plain at once that he did not intend to let the bowlers tie him down. Though both the openers kept the slips on their toes Greig posted only three of them. Seventeen runs came off the first four overs, heady stuff compared with what had gone before. Perhaps India knew that they must make hay whilst the sun shone because the advent of

Underwood would surely put a stop to such liberties.

He came on for the sixth over of the innings and Greig, from the Hooghly River end, followed him into the attack at once. Gavaskar drove his first ball over the top of mid-on for four to reach 15, wildly tried to repeat the shot next ball and was dropped by Amiss at mid-off – the gentlest of chances and an agonising miss for the poor fielder: Gavaskar of all people! But these things happen even to the best fielders and it was not to prove a costly miss because from 31 for nought India's wickets suddenly fell with a rush. Gaekwad, who had looked rather sounder than his partner, went to a straightforward bat-pad catch, which dollied to Tolchard at short-leg. Two runs and one over later Gavaskar played back to Underwood, the ball virtually shot along the ground, and down went the bails. When, at 36, Viswanath hit Greig to Lever at mid-wicket it became a question only of how long India could stave off their first defeat by England at Eden Gardens. The huge crowd accepted it all with relatively little fuss. A minor scuffle or two broke out, but a defeat so thorough, even humiliating, as this was going to be seemed hardly worth a full-scale riot.

But there was to be plenty of excitement for them before the day was out and England must have been disappointed after such a start to the afternoon that they were not able to finish the match in four days. My feeling at the time was that there was no reason why Greig and Underwood should not have bowled in harness until they had finished the innings by themselves. But after Underwood had taken one for one in ten overs from the pavilion end he was switched to the other where, try as he did for the rest of the day, 'Deadly' could not take the wickets he was expected to. Greig himself, who by this time had already taken two, did not bowl another over all day.

The reason may partly have been accidental, because in bringing back Willis, probably as a temporary expedient, Greig got rid of Sharma, and he kept Willis and Old going from the pavilion end for the rest of the day. Sharma, in fact, drove two fours off Willis before hanging his bat out to dry and edging a straightforward catch to Knott. The next dismissal was that of Solkar for three – again, caught Knott, bowled Willis – but this time Solkar got an inside edge to a rapid short ball which fairly flew down the legside. Changing direction Knott flung himself to his right to hold the ball in the fingertips of his right hand at full stretch: an amazing catch.

Patel, very neat and giving himself more chance than most by playing the ball so late, still needed luck to survive. He twice got the benefit of worthy l.b.w. shouts by Underwood but clearly this just wasn't going to be Underwood's day, an impression confirmed when Patel was dropped off a hard chance to Brearley at slip when he had scored 14. Underwood went down on all fours for a moment in his frustration. From that moment Patel never looked back.

After tea at 86 for five he and Madan Lal, who played Willis with more resolution than he had often shown in the past against fast bowling, took India to 97 for five when Old, who had come on in place of Willis, had Madan Lal smartly caught by Brearley at first slip – a swift compensation for the earlier miss. Two balls later Kirmani was bowled by a lethal well-pitched inswinger from Old. India were 97 for seven with an hour still left of the sunlit afternoon and bookmakers would have offered long odds against any play the following day. But the old game does not get any more predictable. With little to lose and a Test place to protect, Patel suddenly began to play with great brilliance. On a pitch which no one had been able to treat incautiously for long he stepped back to pull Underwood against the spin, made room to drive Old and then hit Underwood straight for two audacious fours. The crowd, so sleepy a giant that when Knott had taken his dazzling catch earlier on they had needed conducting and cajoling by Greig to move them even to mild applause, now awoke. Every run from Patel was cheered and the delight was redoubled when Prasanna, catching the sudden mood of confidence, played some spirited shots of his own. At the start Patel deftly stole singles at the end of each over, but when play closed with India 145 for seven Prasanna was batting without much difficulty himself. It may only have been a stay of execution for India, but 80,000 people left Eden Gardens still believing in miracles. Patel's 48 not out had, anyway, taken some of the sting out of his side's defeat, given his colleagues heart for the battles ahead, and extended a most unusual game into its final day.

Where else in the world would 80,000 people come to a cricket ground at 9.45 in the morning to watch the dying moments of a Test match? Come they did, with all the desperate urgency of business-men rushing to catch the last fast train home. Outside Eden Gardens on the hot, sunny morning of 6 January the air was thick with dust swirled up by thousands of hurrying feet; the street sellers offered their betel leaves as if a whole day's refreshment were required, the car horns blared and trumpeted, the police horses stared out of bloodshot eyes at the human wave around them. The gods smiled down on such faith and enthusiasm. They were not so indulgent as to reverse the laws of natural justice. But they did allow the vast crowd at least an hour and a half of entertainment in which they saw their heroes avoid the humiliation of a second successive innings defeat, and this was no small triumph for them.

Willis and Underwood began the attack for England and off the last ball of the second over of the morning Prasanna was out for 13, caught by Brearley at slip, with only one more run added. But Patel continued to play in the neat, unhurried manner of the evening before, and Bedi nobly kept the game going at the other end. Patel's fiftieth run gave the captain five balls of an over from Underwood, which he successfully kept out before getting off the mark against Willis. The crowd's excitement went one key higher when Bedi drove Willis to the cover boundary and then, next ball, dropped the ball in front of his spectacles and somehow Patel completed a perilous single as Willis followed through to break the wicket.

The replacement of Willis by Old after ten overs was a sign that the formalities were not being completed as summarily as England would have wished. Bedi greeted the new bowler by thumping him over the top of Barlow at mid-on for four to reach double figures, and his snick off Underwood between the slips which saved the innings defeat raised the crowd to their feet. A few people invaded the field, and orange peel was thrown on to the ground. You would almost have thought that India had won: hearing the force of that roar one realised just why it had been so hard for visiting sides to succeed over the years.

But Patel's notable innings ended when he shaped to pull a straight ball from Old and, after a moment's cogitation, the bowler's imploring appeal was answered in the affirmative by umpire Sharma. Back walked Patel to such a standing ovation as on other grounds might be reserved for a double century. Bedi and Chandra prolonged the entertainment a while and ten runs were added before Underwood bowled Bedi round his legs for a wicket he richly deserved, and England were left with just sixteen runs to win.

Barlow's luck changed when in the first over from Madan Lal he drove outside his off-stump, impatient to get the job done, and was dropped by Viswanath at first slip. But he and Amiss saw England to their target without further mishap and forty minutes before lunch on the final day England had beaten India for the first time ever at Eden Gardens.

Now the crowd, silent for much of a match that England had

dominated, forgot their disappointment and gave Greig and his team a generous reception. Indeed they would not leave until Greig, arms aloft like someone who had just been elected President of the United States, led his team round the ground on a lap of honour. Bedi, his blue patka pushed back high on his furrowed brow, watched from his dressing-room window, remembering that only a short while ago he had been leading a similar victory lap, and smilingly accepted defeat. After he had won the toss it should have been plain sailing for him. His batsmen had let him down and two of them, Sharma and Solkar, were now made scapegoats, with Vengsarkar and Mankad recalled to the squad for Madras. Bedi said, however, that it was the failures of Gavaskar and Viswanath which really disappointed him. England, he asserted, were not so much better than his side as the first two results suggested. 'If they are forced to pick a wicket-keeper as a batsman, they must be struggling.' He also blamed Solkar for dropping 'four or five catches he would normally have taken'. But words, he knew, could not undo what had happened. The decisive match of the series had been won and lost.

India had fallen into the grave they had made for England. The day before the match, the MCC team were amazed to see ground-staff rubbing away at the pitch with scrubbing-brushes. In other words, the pitch had been shamelessly prepared for the home spinners but because they were bowled out so cheaply the advantage of batting first was lost. As at Delhi England had played cricket of uniformly high standard. Randall, Barlow, Lever and Tolchard, all of whom had gained their first caps on the tour, had transformed them into a slick, smart fielding side – even some of the great Australian teams of the past might have suffered by comparison. The opportunity opened up by the bowling and fielding on the first day was later capitalised on by the batsmen, with Greig playing a true captain's innings. Unlike the context of his previous Test hundred, a solo effort at Headingley the previous summer, his cause this time was a winning one, and rather than being a lone performance it was very much part of a team effort.

In victory Greig could afford to be frank about the controversial pitch. 'I don't feel sorry,' he said, 'for the Indian team, because they're the opposition, or for the ground authorities, who prepared this pitch to help the home side. But I do feel very sorry indeed for the spectators and I feel I owe them an apology for playing the way I did. They looked to me to entertain them but on that wicket there was no way anyone could be entertained.'

The practice of preparing pitches to help the home team is not a new one, though this was perhaps the most blatant example in recent times. Those who went to Australia with MCC under both Ray Illingworth and Mike Denness said that the grass was left on the pitches much more in 1974–75 to suit Lillee and Thomson than it had been four years earlier when John Snow was the major fast bowler on either side. On the other hand the 1975 Australians in England believed that no more than lip-service was being paid to the ideal of hard, fast wickets. (I do not include the 'fusarium scandal' at Headingley in 1972 since it was, without doubt, an accident of nature.)

The ideal of a pitch with enough pace to help fast bowlers but also to allow batsmen to play strokes freely, as well as giving the spinners bounce and suitable speed of turn plus a greater chance in the later stages of a match, remains the one which all countries should strive for. Certainly if India had more wickets of that kind they would not be so backward in the production of fast bowlers, or in the art of playing against them.

Chapter Five
VICTORY AND VASELINE

After the noise and appalling pollution of Calcutta, Nagpur, a pleasantly arboreal town with a population of a mere million or so, set in the very centre of India and famous for delicious oranges like huge tangerines, was something of a haven. The team stayed at a circuit house, one of the resting places dotted around India originally constructed for itinerant civil servants and now used by government ministers. As usual everything was done to please a team whose spirits were so high that they would quite happily have slept in a clearing in the jungle. As it was they were well fed beneath a colourful tent of red, blue and yellow stripes and housed in simple, relatively spartan bungalows dotted about a compound full of lawns, flowers and trees. Uniformed police protected the players from the fascinated stares of on-lookers and the relentless autograph-hunters, and at night only the barking of wandering dogs disturbed a calm that was almost rural. The ground and resting house, indeed, were detached from the centre of Nagpur, which looked as hectic as any large Indian town; on the outskirts there were very few cars and in the sleepy heat of the day, with goats and wandering cows idly grazing beneath magnificent trees, and the occasional kite wheeling in the even blue sky, one had a sense of the timelessness of India.

In the ten days separating the Calcutta Test from the next one at Madras three of England's leading players, Greig, Willis and Underwood, missed Nagpur and for three blissful days rested on the beautiful beaches of Goa on the Arabian Sea, a holiday centre of the future, without doubt. Graham Barlow, after two failures, was made twelfth man for the game against the Combined Universities and India Under-22 side, but he cheerfully accepted the implication that he was going to be dropped from the Test side and no one else complained about playing on a small, tree-bordered ground which, though it staged a Test against New Zealand in 1969, holds only 15,000 people.

Needless to say, it was full when on a perfect summer's day Mike

Brearley won the toss. An early nineteenth-century English stone church, with a mock Norman tower, peeped over the tops of the trees, and if the outfield had not been so bumpy or the pitch such a slow turner, built of hard-baked red mud, Amiss and Woolmer might have imagined themselves at Worcester as they put on 110 for the first wicket. Amiss, crisply driving anything overpitched from a couple of lively opening bowlers, met the ball solidly whilst Woolmer, occasionally hitting the ball with the sweet timing of the natural batsman he is, played and missed far more than he should have done. Instead of meeting the ball with the full face of the bat he seemed obsessed with delicate deflections. When the spinners came on – Dharmaraj Jadeja, a slow left-armer with a distinct jerk in his action, and bouncy little Aswina Minna with his enthusiastic leg-spin – he was hit on the front pad more than he would have wished. But even on this first day the ball was turning considerably, and batting was not easy. This was no sort of pitch on which to try out the young hopefuls of Indian cricket. For the visitors, however, it was a useful foretaste of the likely conditions at Madras. Amiss and Woolmer were out in successive overs to the spinners, neither looking too disappointed (indeed Woolmer gave himself out caught behind) because with Madras in mind it was important for Brearley and Fletcher to have some practice.

Fletcher, playing his first innings for weeks and still in-capacitated and worried by his injured ankle, could not get going and had batted for more than two hours when he was l.b.w. to Jadeja's seam-bowling brother Rajendra for 24. The umpire who sent him on his way, named Swarup Krishnan, must be the heaviest first-class umpire in the world, with a figure like a heavyweight wrestler. With his white coat on, there was hardly any need for a sight-screen. One run later, Knott snicked a legside catch to the wicket-keeper, but Brearley, now back in rich-looking form, took some sort of command in the final session and with Tolchard contributing a tidy 19 not out he took MCC to 237 for four by the close of the day, at which point he declared.

A little before noon the following day, on a hot Sunday afternoon in Nagpur, an insignificant match seemed to be going gently to sleep. The Combined Team were 73 for one and the only entertainment for the usual capacity crowd was a brilliant display of outfield gymnastics by Derek Randall, who added somersaults and leap-frogs to his customary cartwheels, and from time to time had the spectators in stitches by pinching the umpire's hat and

walking off with it, preening himself. But at this point Dilip
Vengsarkar, who had opened out after a slow start with some fine
straight driving against the two off-spinners, Cope and Miller, was
bowled by the latter as he made room to force on the off-side, and an
inexperienced team suddenly folded against two bowlers having a
long overdue chance to show that English spinners can make use of
slow turning pitches too.

Though Cope, with six for 41, had notably the better figures,
confirming his status in the minds of the players, there was not so
much to choose between them. On this distinctly helpful pitch both
turned the ball quite enough to do the job of bowling their
opponents out cheaply, though Vengsarkar and the left-handed
Mohan Raj prevented a rout. Cope's variations were fewer, but
rather more subtle; certainly his action was more grooved than
Miller's and his control tighter. But 'Dusty', as he is inevitably
called, must have considered this one of his best days of the tour.
Not only did Brearley allow him to bowl unchanged for 23 overs but
he also got him in to bat at the end of the day at number four in the
order.

Miller, two not out overnight, scored only one more run in the
morning as, with the pitch now resembling a beach in appearance,
Minna and Dhamaraj Jadeja whistled through the batting with
the ball doing all sorts of strange things. This, of course, only made
MCC's win more certain. The best piece of batting was produced
not by one of the recognised experts but by John Lever, who in the
course of making 17 in a couple of overs hit Jadeja for a six to long-
off and also for two remarkably well played reverse sweeps to third-
man, changing his grip whilst the ball was in the air from right- to
left-hand à la Mushtaq. It takes real natural talent to do that.

Cope, on the other hand, is one of those typical English county
cricketers who has used limited ability to make himself into a
serviceable batsman, and playing only his second innings of the
tour he hung around long enough to prove he was nobody's
pushover. Tolchard yet again demonstrated his skill against
spinners; one noticed especially the way the ball always meets his
bat below the line of his knee when he plays forward, thus virtually
eliminating the chance of a bat-pad catch.

A stand of 33 between these two for the ninth wicket allowed
Brearley the luxury of a declaration, and although Vengsarkar
began the Combined Team's innings with a stream of elegant
strokes during five overs of seam from Lever and Selvey it was

evident to all but the boldest local optimists that once Cope and Miller were on there could only be one result to the game. After Cope had made the initial breakthrough and followed up by having Vengsarkar caught at square-leg, it was Miller who this time ran through the middle order. A couple of run-outs only exacerbated the problems facing an inexperienced batting side on a wicket which Cope and Miller would gladly have carried around with them everywhere. Selvey was involved in one of the run-outs, his second of the match, and it was good to see him getting into the act because at this stage of the tour, though he never stopped trying, nothing much was running his way. He must have reflected ruefully on that seamer's paradise where he had made his Test debut.

Nagpur, where the longer the match went on the more one was amazed at its status as a Test venue, was the exact opposite of that Old Trafford pitch, and it was Cope with three for 20 and Miller with four for 54 who took the honours this time as MCC wrapped up the match soon after tea on another blazing afternoon. An amusing last-wicket stand between Minna and Yog Raj had delayed them for 50 minutes.

This victory in a three-day game, which had eluded MCC ever since M. J. K. Smith's tour thirteen years earlier, was another fillip to morale. But the selectors of England's team for the Madras Test still had plenty to think about. Their problem was that three into two won't go. Success in the first two Test matches had been largely due to the efforts of the faster bowlers, Willis, Lever and Old. But Madras was certain to be a turning wicket. If five specialist bowlers were chosen – the three seamers plus Underwood and either Cope or Miller, with Greig going in at number five and Barlow dropping out – England's batting would be more exposed than ever to the Indian spinners.

If the selectors could have persuaded themselves that Miller was their man to bowl off-spin the solution would have been simple. If, as a genuine all-rounder, he had replaced Barlow the batting would not necessarily have been weakened whilst the bowling would have been strengthened considerably, especially since Greig's spinning finger was liable to become sore during a long spell. This was one of the reasons for his bowling so little in the second innings at Calcutta. But Greig himself, who, though he took advice from Barrington and Brearley, was very much the supremo of the party, believed Cope to be the better spinner. It therefore boiled down, in the captain's mind, to a choice between Cope and Lever.

As to who came in for Barlow, a decision depended on how well Fletcher's ankle injury responded to further rest and treatment after his try-out in Nagpur. At that stage he was clearly not fully fit for a five-day Test, but Woolmer had looked more like a Test batsman again in his latest innings and he stood out as the obvious alternative.

These were the topics under discussion as the MCC party settled in to their hotel at Madras and sampled for the first time the extra heat and humidity and the very different environment of southern India. The skins here are a darker brown, the paint on the trishaws a brighter yellow, the foliage of the bougainvilia on the low white houses more magnificent than elsewhere, and the people more relaxed. On their first evening the players were entertained to evening cocktails in the High Commissioner's garden, then to dinner in the elegant surroundings of the Madras Club, where an old white indigo planter's house looks out across lawns, flowers and majestic trees to a lazy river fringed by palm trees on either side.

Amidst all this tropical sumptuousness it would have been easy for the team to have over-relaxed. Greig announced just one change in his team, Woolmer for Barlow, with Fletcher ruled still unfit and the unfortunate Cope left to wonder, after taking 19 wickets in four matches, if his chance would ever come. When asked to sign a team list of autographs he mistakenly put his name under India. When the error was pointed out he smiled and said: 'I just want a Test. I'm not fussy who I play for.' The captain apologised to those not selected and then set about renewing the killer instinct of those who had been, fearful that two victories might lull them into a false sense of security. At the team dinner the night before the match he spoke with the fire and determination with which he plays.

Next morning Greig carried out his first duty successfully. He won the toss and, taking a leaf out of Bedi's book, waved cheerfully to the 52,000 packed together under Chepauk's concrete circle. The majority of the crowd must have been hopeful that India's luck was about to turn. Of nine Tests played at the stadium in the past only two had been drawn, and in the last few seasons India had beaten Tony Lewis's England side, Clive Lloyd's West Indians and Glenn Turner's New Zealanders. There was talk of the home side playing all their four spinners but from the way the pitch bruised the knuckles when its surface was rapped it was clear that it would have more pace than the normal Indian wicket. (The ground authorities, one senior official admitted to me, had been approached to prepare the wicket for the spinners, but had refused to comply.) India's selectors chose instead to strengthen the batting, replacing Gaekwad with Vengsarkar, Sharma with Mankad and Solkar with Mohinder Amarnath, who was restored to the place he had held in the series against New Zealand as number three batsman and opening bowler.

It was his opening partner Madan Lal, however, who justified the continued inclusion of two seam bowlers when play began on a hot morning with a gentle breeze to temper the warmth and a few clouds on the fringes of the sky. Bowling from the pavilion end Madan Lal got his first ball to Amiss to bounce off the one spot of green on the pitch, which was on a length, and Amiss turned it into, and out of, Amarnath's hands at backward short-leg.

Woolmer, delighted to find a pitch with some pace in it at last, was at once able to caress and deflect in the manner he enjoys and he played exceptionally well from the start – too well, as it transpired. Having had his escape, however, Amiss could not capitalise on it and at 14 he was out l.b.w. as he got tucked up in trying to keep out an off-cutter from Madan Lal.

Woolmer treated Amarnath like a club bowler, off-driving him sweetly for three, placing him through mid-wicket for four, glancing him delicately fine. But though the comparison with Colin Cowdrey was inevitable, the scorer of 107 hundreds would not have reached 22 with such consummate ease only to play a lazy flick, as Woolmer did, at an outswinger from Madan Lal and so direct the ball straight at Gavaskar's midriff at second slip. This loose-wristed throw-away must have made the MCC manager Ken Barrington grind his teeth in anguish inside that proudly jutting jaw. He would have been as likely to play such a shot, on such a wicket in such good form, as fly to the moon.

But India were to receive an even more generous present. Randall, coming in fourth at 29 for two, steered a single off Madan Lal, then played Amarnath fast and all along the ground to Mankad on the third-man boundary. It was an obvious ambled single but an extremely risky two. Yet stirred by some momentary madness Randall went haring up the pitch, turned, called for a second, hesitated, slipped, saw that Brearley, after hesitating himself, had answered his call irrevocably – and as Mankad's throw came sailing over the top of the bails into Kirmani's gloves Randall was run out by three or four yards. England, whose thorough professionalism had earned them their two-nil lead in the series,

Chandrasekhar *(above)* and Bedi *(below)* bowling in the third Test at Madras, with England's vice-captain and captain at the non-striker's end. Chandra's follow-through might almost belong to a fast bowler.

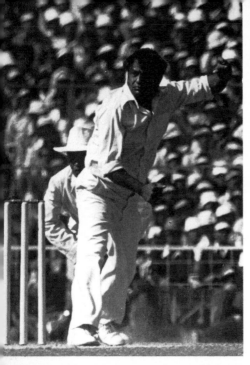

Above left Prasanna, who by the end of the series had proved himself to be the best off-spinner in the world. *Above right* Gavaskar cover-drives. *Below* Mankad's throw beats Randall by three or four yards as the batsman goes for a second run to third-man. Brearley is the other batsman, M. Amarnath the bowler.

Patel is bowled by Underwood for 32 in the first innings of the third Test *(above)*
and Viswanath is caught by Brearley off Underwood for 6 in the second.
Underwood was kept fresh for the Tests and has rarely bowled better.

The 'Vaseline affair' at Madras: Lever and the Vaseline-impregnated gauze strip which caused all the furore.

had given away two of their ten wickets in an uncharacteristically
unprofessional way.

Southern India on this opening day of the match was celebrating
the harvest festival of Pongal as a national holiday, and home
supporters could hardly believe their luck at this stage of the game.
Having won the toss England were 31 for three. But the suspicion
began to harden that it might not have been such a good toss to win
after all. The occasional ball was bouncing in a way which made one
wonder what Willis would have been like, and the difficulties were
not confined to the end with the green patch, because when
Tolchard played forward to Amarnath soon after he came in he was
rapped on the right hand and had to retire hurt with a severe
bruising. Happily, however, an X-ray showed that there was no
fracture.

So, at 11.30 a.m., an hour and a half after he had waved to the
crowd in pleasure at calling 'tails' correctly, Greig was walking out
at number six, no doubt blinking with disbelief at the sorry-looking
score standing out in yellow on the giant black scoreboard which
straggled across three concrete pillars on the far side of the ground.
The only consolation for him was that Mike Brearley had settled in
soundly and sensibly, like a man who knew a big Test innings was
overdue.

After eight overs Madan Lal rested, having taken two for 18, and
for once Chandrasekhar, rather than Bedi, was first change. His
first ball was a bouncer which whistled over Brearley's head and
was stopped by Kirmani only at the expense of a bruised finger.
Bedi came on for Amarnath at the other end but the captain and
vice-captain took England to a shaky-looking score of 53 for three
at lunch.

Less than an hour afterwards, however, Greig and Brearley had
doubled that score. With Bedi off the field for a while with a minor
ailment Chandra and Prasanna began the attack and Greig at once
moved onto the attack against them. He was helped by some long-
hops from Chandra, who was striving desperately but vainly to
recapture his magical form of the early 1970s when his stock googly,
occasional leg-break, 'fizzer' and surprising quicker ball made him
such a difficult bowler to contend with. Straight after lunch Greig
received two long-hops in an over from him and clubbed them
powerfully to mid-on and mid-wicket. At the other end Brearley
waited patiently for the bad ball and, when it came along,
persuaded it smoothly to the boundary off the full face of the bat.

The aggressive, extrovert, excitable captain and his cool, studious deputy made a nice contrast.

Brearley had passed his previous best Test score (40) with a back-foot force for four off Madan Lal when in the same over he was vehemently appealed against for a legside catch by Kirmani. Umpire Reuben, the tall, calm figure who had sent Amiss on his way earlier with characteristic certainty and decisiveness, stood motionless now as Brearley indicated the ball had brushed his side, not his glove as Madan Lal, making his dismay crystal clear, believed.

Madan Lal was being used by Bedi now mainly as a tactical weapon to keep the batsmen quiet and the over-rate down. He was doing the job outstandingly well. But England, their crisis over, were in no hurry. Greig reached his fifty soon after tea with a straight-driven four which scorched through Chandra's fingers on its way to the boundary. The crowd, quicker to appreciate good cricket by either side than those at Delhi or Calcutta, applauded him warmly. So they did Brearley when he reached his first Test fifty at the age of 34 in his fifth game for England. But in the next over Bedi took his 200th Test wicket and the one his side badly needed. Greig drew back to cut a ball which was probably not quite short enough for the shot to be played with safety and sliced a high, sharp chance to Viswanath at slip. Greig and Brearley had put on 109 and effectively stopped the rot, but with Greig's going the chances of a sizeable first-innings score were reduced at a stroke.

Knott came in with no big score to his name since the Delhi Test and with typical cheek began to sweep Bedi against the spin, a policy fraught with risk but also infuriating to the bowler. But he had to forget any thoughts of cashing in on a tiring attack because with twenty minutes of the day to go Brearley's fine innings was ended in a most unfortunate way. Aiming a hard and perfectly legitimate sweep at Prasanna, he hit the ball firmly against the back of Amarnath's head at close short-leg. It rebounded up the pitch for a grateful Prasanna to take a gentle catch off his own bowling. The fielder was bruised – in fact it was the second time he had been hit that afternoon – but Brian Close would not have smiled more happily on realising the unintentional outcome of his bravado.

So England ended the day back on their heels again. India had taken two important wickets in the session between tea and the close and an interesting and balanced first day ended with England 171 for five, Knott 21 not out and Lever, who had batted twenty minutes as night-watchman, still to score. One felt sorry for

Brearley, who had played flawlessly for most of the day and was apparently set for a century when his innings came to such an unususal end. But one also felt glad for India and their captain Bishen Bedi, whose 200th wicket gave clear evidence for the widely held belief that he is the greatest exponent of orthodox left-arm spin of his generation. At last his side was in a match with at least an even chance. Apart from Chandra they had bowled well; their ground fielding had been good and, but for the inexpensive miss off the first ball of the day, they had taken their chances. An interesting match was developing.

India had bowled only 79 overs on the opening day, a rate of just 14.33 an hour, and they took the new ball at once on the second day, which England began apprehensively since Tolchard's injured hand was now badly swollen whilst Amiss had become the latest victim of the remorseless flu-germ. His innings over, Amiss would not be missed if he spent the day in bed, but the injury to Tolchard was obviously a worry and much was clearly going to depend on Knott and Old.

First, however, India had to be rid of J. K. Lever, the fair-haired lad from Ilford, who had begun the tour as a little-known name to Indian crowds but who now seemed a permanent thorn in the flesh. The first 'near-thing' of the morning was the result of a mistake not by Lever but by Knott, who tried to hook a short ball from Amarnath which was well wide of his off-stump and top-edged the ball into no-man's-land between slips and third-man. In Madan Lal's next over, however, the ball went out of shape and when the bowler overpitched his first two deliveries with the new one Knott glanced and on-drove him for successive and nicely timed boundaries. Another driven four, this time past extra-cover, persuaded Bedi to return to the attack after ten overs with the new ball, and at 201 he got the wicket he wanted most.

Knott had continued to sweep at Bedi, even from outside his off-stump, and he was attempting another when the ball dollied up behind the wicket on the leg-side, where Viswanath ran from slip to take a simple catch. Knott stood his ground, apparently suggesting that the ball had come off his boot, but he was given out after a confident appeal.

Old spent some twenty minutes playing himself in and looked quite at ease, but Bedi by now was dropping the ball on the very blade of grass he wanted, taking his time before stepping up and wheeling over that double-jointed left arm as if it were based on ball-bearings. He dismissed Old in a straightforward way with the assistance of a smart catch round the corner by Amarnath, at which point Tolchard, his injured hand swollen and bandaged, resumed his innings.

Tolchard was able only to keep the ball out of his stumps whilst the tailenders made what they could in their differing styles. Lunch came with Lever still there, England having added only 49 more runs in 27 overs as India's over-rate continued to be sluggish. But in the afternoon session there was a good deal more urgency shown by both sides. Lever's innings had lasted a further two hours and twenty minutes on the second day when he drew back to hit Bedi through the covers off the back foot and was caught behind. It was a valuable knock in its own way, but Underwood scored as many runs in some two hours less as, with the aid of two legside fours off Bedi, he made the most of the pace in the pitch.

Underwood was bowled off his pads by Prasanna, and with Tolchard still able to do no more than scamper down the pitch and block the ball Willis aimed some heavy blows before a misunderstanding with his partner resulted in a second run-out and the end of the innings. A total of 262 in 512 minutes was no more than a moderate performance by England after winning the toss, but after a start of 31 for three and with their number five batsman immobilised it represented a good enough recovery.

The score soon looked a good deal better too, as India in turn lost three quick wickets. It was clear that they were going to have to bat well against the fast bowlers because the pitch was faster than they were used to. Old and Willis shared the new ball and Amarnath, who had opened in place of Vengsarkar because the latter had a back strain, was bowled by the last ball of Old's first over, hopelessly late on an off-drive.

Both Willis and Old were distinctly hostile in the opening overs, but the balls that bounced highest were those that pitched outside the line of the stumps and Gavaskar and Viswanath restrained themselves from sparring. Viswanath, indeed, played one cracking square-cut when Lever replaced Willis and looked as though he really meant business this time when he flicked fatally at a rising ball from Lever outside his off-stump and was taken gleefully by Knott. When in the same over, continued after tea, Mankad was yorked by Lever for a duck, India were reduced to 17 for three. But they had cause to be very grateful now for the resolution of Sunil Gavaskar. It was he who, with stubborn and scrupulously correct defence, took the sting out of Willis, whose second spell was as fast as his first and a good deal straighter. There was one half-chance, a very fast slice past Lever at fourth slip, but otherwise no further alarms as Patel gradually gained confidence at the other end. Then, as at Calcutta, he suddenly began to play his attacking strokes, driving and hooking Lever with a panache that reminded one of Doug Walters. Patel, indeed, has something of Walters in him – both the good and the bad. He can flirt horribly outside his off-stump, and he is always liable to get himself out, but at times he is capable of brilliant cricket, both in the field and with the bat.

India began the third day on a score of 58 for three, knowing that to have any real hope of victory they must bat all day. Underwood began the bowling from the northern end and Willis from the pavilion end, bowling towards the green patch outside the line of the off-stump from which the ball sometimes bounced high towards Knott's head – shades of Sydney where simultaneously Australia were sinking to their first home defeat at the hands of Mushtaq's talented Pakistan side. World supremacy in cricket never lasts for very long. Was Australia's star starting to decline as England's rose? It seemed possible, but if England were to go to Australia in March for the Centenary Test with genuine confidence they must first finish the job they had begun so well in India.

Gavaskar and Patel were the immediate obstacles in their path, and they began the day promisingly. But Patel had played Underwood uncertainly each time they had met on the tour and after making 32 of a partnership of 52 he was bowled playing outside a fast, well-pitched delivery on his leg-stump. So at 69 for four Vengsarkar, one of the great hopes for India's future, joined Gavaskar, one of the great stalwarts of their past and present. Vengsarkar, tall, good-looking and in calm control of his nerves, coolly played out the remainder of Underwood's over and then got off the mark with a leaning drive off Willis through the open spaces on the off-side.

The young batsman needed all his skill, and a slice of luck, to keep out a superb over from Underwood in which he received almost every variation in that great bowler's repertoire – the quicker ball, the arm ball, the one bowled from wide of the crease, the flighted delivery inviting a drive and a caught-and-bowled, and finally an orthodox spinner away from the bat which bit more than any ball Underwood had yet bowled and which spun off the edge to give Old at gully a low chance which he could not quite take.

Old had been ill for some days with stomach trouble. He had been sick in the middle of the previous night, which was no doubt partly why Greig asked Lever to take over from Willis in the next over. And to Old's relief, but to the disappointment of many, Vengsarkar, for all his talent, displayed the club player's weakness for wanting to play his shots before he was set. Knowing that he had already played one uppish hook off Willis, knowing too that Greig had posted a square-leg and a fine-leg to snare him, he nevertheless pulled at his first short ball from Lever and was caught at square-leg.

Madan Lal was beaten by three of the first five balls he received from Lever, then dropped at short-leg by Woolmer off Underwood. If the catch had been taken India would have been 87 for six, but Madan Lal, after a stern talking-to from Gavaskar, stayed to see the little master off-drive, glance and on-drive Lever to take India past 100. The sight of Willis coming back after Underwood had taken one for 11 in 13 overs apparently decided Madan Lal that his luck could not hold. He connected for two fours but then swatted a short ball towards mid-off. Underwood set off, caught the ball at full stretch in his right hand and toppled over, holding on to the ball with his arm fully extended.

This dismissal might have occurred at any time. But Gavaskar had played with such resolution and restraint, with such noble defence of a slowly sinking cause, one thought he might carry his bat. Instead he was seventh out when Old, in his first over, produced an ideal outswinger which Gavaskar edged for Brearley to take a smart, straightforward catch at first slip. When a game is slipping away from a side catches often go straight to hand.

Thus did Kirmani and Prasanna join forces shortly before lunch, and the score at that point, 126 for seven, is worth noting because of the extraordinary incident which followed. During the interval John Lever went to the physiotherapist Bernard Thomas to ask him for something for his sore foot, which had been troubling him during the morning session. Thomas rummaged amongst his bag of tricks but could find nothing suitable except a tin of Vaseline-impregnated gauze, which had been given to him in Calcutta by the big firm of chemists Smith and Nephew, along with various other medical aids. Thomas is a most sympathetic man who freely gives his advice and help not just to the cricketers on a tour but to anyone who asks for it – which often includes journalists and broadcasters who are as prone to stomach or chest ailments as the players. He is the kind of man who will get up at three in the morning to stop an attack of enteritis with the appropriate pill, and his skill and exceptional abilities in his field have enabled him to set up and help to run a thriving clinic in Birmingham. It is not normally the job of physiotherapists to save lives; but when two years previously the New Zealand Test bowler Ewan Chatfield had been hit on the temple by a deflected ball from John Lever's namesake Peter, Thomas saved his life by the prompt administration of mouth-to-mouth resuscitation.

Not surprisingly he is a very popular and highly respected man. The job he does on a tour gives him small recompense for the considerable work involved and on occasions like this one he must wonder why he does it, because a large mountain was about to be made out of a very innocent molehill. He had noticed during the morning that Willis and Lever were both having trouble with sweat running down into their eyes from their ample supplies of hair. As he placed the gauze on to Lever's sore foot Thomas remembered that marathon runners sometimes grease their eyebrows to divert the sweat down the sides of their faces. The more obvious remedy would have been a sweat-band round the forehead like those used by long-haired tennis players. But sweat-bands were not in his box of tricks; the gauze was, and since this was the first time on the tour that the heat had been intense enough to worry the bowlers an immediate expedient was necessary. So he experimented by placing two bits of gauze over the eyebrows of both players.

'It probably won't work, but there is no harm in trying,' said Thomas as he sent the players on their way. And he was right: Willis discarded his at once; Lever did so after a few overs, by which time Prasanna had been out, caught and bowled by Underwood, having shared a spirited partnership with Kirmani which held England up for 45 minutes after the interval. Bedi had just arrived at the crease when Lever decided that his gauzes were doing him more harm than good. He has a habit of applying perspiration from his forehead as he walks back, to keep the shine on the ball, and it was partly because grease and sweat were getting onto his fingers and making it difficult for him to grip the ball that he took the strips and threw them down by the stumps. Despite counter-allegations those who were watching on television confirmed that Lever clearly discarded the gauzes, rather than that one dropped off as the Secretary of the Indian Cricket Board said in a statement to the press at the end of the day. At any rate umpire Judah Reuben picked up one of the

gauzes and with encouragement from Bedi took it to show Greig to
complain politely that he thought they should not be used. Reuben
apparently said at the time that he understood the need for various
kinds of protection against the sun – he used them himself – but he
felt that this might result in grease getting on to the ball, thus
enabling the shine to last longer than it otherwise would.

Reuben reported the matter during the tea interval, by which
time India's innings had been 'polished off' by Lever, though not
before Kirmani had scored 27 creditable runs and generally played
with some panache. It is possible that the matter would have ended
there had not several journalists gone down to the dressing-rooms
to find out what the talking in the middle had been about.

If India had been leading two-nil, rather than losing two-nil,
Bedi's answer would no doubt have been something very diplomatic about the possibility of using Vaselined gauze for the wrong
purpose. But Bedi was a man under intense pressure at that
moment. After two defeats he had received letters of abuse from the
more ignorant members of a vast, passionate cricketing public
whose heroes can so easily become villains overnight. Worse, India
had just succumbed again to England's bowlers and a deficit of 98
was almost bound to be fatal with the pitch getting worse all the
time. Like a wounded animal trapped in a corner, Bedi struck out.
And the statement which really fanned the flames was the one which
suggested that England's bowlers had illegally greased the ball at
Delhi. Nor was this a heat-of-the-moment accusation, because he
afterwards allowed himself to go on record as saying he thought it
was 'disgusting that England should stoop so low' (a quotation
used by Reuters) and that he had suspected something was wrong
when the ball with which Lever bowled India out at Delhi (the
replacement for the first new ball which, in fact, had swung
dramatically from the start and without any assistance from
Lever's perspiration or from anything else) had continued to
'wobble' after about forty overs. What is more Bedi added that he
had told the umpires to watch out for signs of grease on the ball.
When one heard that, one thought of two things: Tony Greig's
start-of-tour statement that his side would not be putting pressure
on the umpires; and various accusations in the past about bowlers
using artificial aids – intentionally or not. From Keith Miller's hair-
grease through to the lip-salve which Bob Massie was subsequently
accused of using during his sensational performance of swing
bowling at Lord's in 1972, when he took sixteen England wickets,

these aids had been known about by those playing the game and, I suppose, reluctantly accepted as one of the 'unacceptable faces' of cricket. Law number 46, note four, subsection three, prohibits the use of oils, waxes, resins etc., but the plain fact is that lip-salve and sun-cream are frequently used by cricketers genuinely seeking to protect skin from getting cracked or burnt by hot sun, and bowlers of all nationalities have from time to time taken advantage of them to add a little extra shine to the ball.

Now, by the innocent action of a well-meaning physiotherapist, one bowler was about to be unfairly victimised for this general malpractice. What happened was that the tour committee of the Indian Board, in some cases perhaps, like Bedi, not unhappy to encourage a diversion from the unpalatable truth about the cricket – which was that India were being beaten as they had never before been beaten on their own grounds by England – began an elaborate farce. They sent the pieces of gauze and the ball to the Tamil Nadu Forensic Science and Chemical Laboratory for analysis. Meanwhile, England's manager, Ken Barrington, anxiously explained the truth about the gauzes to anyone who wanted to listen, pointing out that the ball had not swung for Lever after lunch, and that anyway if England had wanted to grease the ball they would have employed rather more subtle methods. Lever had to spend the remainder of that day, the rest day which followed and the whole of the fourth day wondering what on earth the Board would produce.

When he arrived at the ground on the fourth day he found a huge flag on which the words were printed: 'Cheater Lever go home; Tony Greig down down'. Later that evening, when the match had swung still further towards the expected outcome of another England victory, his anxious wait was ended by a long and inconclusive statement by the tour committee, consisting of five senior Board members: R. P. Mehra, S. K. Wankhede, Fatesingh Rao Gaekwad, M. A. Chidambaram and P. M. Rungta. After announcing that the chemical analysis had revealed that there was Vaseline on the gauze (surprise, surprise) and a small trace of it on the ball (which presumably came from the fingers of Willis or Lever after sweat and grease had got unavoidably and unintentionally mixed together), the committee said they were unable to come to a conclusion about whether the actions of the bowlers were deliberate or not and therefore decided to refer all the information to the MCC.

As to Bedi's statement about the Delhi match, he now made it known, through Barrington, that he had never said anything offical about this – although he had clearly been quoted on the subject in the Indian and English papers that day. Barrington and Greig said they were glad India's captain accepted their word. Off the record they chafed and cursed along with all the MCC players that what they considered to be a colossal red herring should have taken the glamour out of what they were about to achieve on the field.

Poor Barrington was struggling badly in deep diplomatic waters. So far he had been an ideal manager for the players, advising, encouraging and amusing them like the cheerful, gutsy sergeant-major he is. Problems on the field he understood and could deal with. Off the field he had done as good a job as anyone in keeping players and press happy and, equally important, in keeping all the invitations which the team received, along with the interminable requests for autographs, to an acceptable minimum without offending anyone. But this was a totally different matter – one in which commonsense and logic did not necessarily help, because when passions are aroused, as the crowd's partially hostile reaction to Lever showed they were in this case, logic does not always triumph. The matter was left for the time being with two contradictory statements being issued – one by the Board sub-committee saying they were unable to decide if the bowler's actions were deliberate, the other by Barrington thanking the Board, and Bedi, for accepting that they were not.

Lest there be any doubt it was very clear to me, and to most who were able to view the matter reasonably objectively, that Lever was entirely innocent and that suggestions about England shining the ball by illegal methods at Delhi ignored the fact that the early destruction of India's first innings was achieved by Lever with a virtually new ball which swung freakishly from the outset.

One could also say, however, that it was naïve of the two England bowlers to have taken the gauzes on to the field and that it would have saved a lot of time and speculation if Barrington had immediately taken the tin of gauzes to the Indian Board and explained the circumstances.

So much for one of the stranger storms in a tea-cup which from time to time disturb the sporting scene. Some of the glory was thereby taken out of the crushing victory which England completed on the last two days of the game. The evening session of the third day had lasted an hour and fifty minutes during which time only twenty overs were bowled and the ball was changed three times because each previous one had gone out of shape. With sight-screens being switched and bowlers slowing the game as much as they could England were able to make only 44 despite the fact that Dennis Amiss played very well. Woolmer, with a team position to consolidate, was cautious until shortly before the close he swept at a straight ball from Prasanna and was given out l.b.w. on the front foot.

The fourth morning was as action-packed as any in the series. England looked for runs with great urgency and were delighted to find that the pitch had lost none of its pace, whilst it had clearly begun to break up after another day's grilling from the hot sun on the rest day. Lever, who had come in as night-watchman, soon departed the scene, caught at short-leg off Chandrasekhar, who was embarking on his first successful spell of the series. It was good to see him whipping the ball in from the off with all his old deadliness, but the pace of both the pitch and the outfield meant that anything off line could be cut or glanced and anything overpitched driven. Both Amiss and Brearley produced succulent cover-drives and the score had moved to 83 when Amiss was caught at short-leg just as Lever had been.

Randall came in with the crowd now getting right behind Chandra and when he aimed to cut a ball which achieved sudden lift Kirmani took an excellent catch. This neat little wicket-keeper had his work cut out to 'keep to Chandra, who twice bowled genuine bouncers which cleared not just the batsman's head but Kirmani's as well.

India's progress was once more halted by Greig's arrival at the wicket. He liked the sort of situation he was in now, when controlled aggression was called for, and he played an innings in perfect tune with the situation, forcing Chandra off the back foot for four to announce his arrival, then sweeping both Bedi and Prasanna for fours before moving three paces down the pitch to drive Bedi straight for six. As in the first innings Brearley played equally well before he pulled over a straight ball from Chandra and was bowled. Knott made a hasty 11, then drove Prasanna against the spin into the covers, and when, just after lunch, Old also hit a catch off Prasanna England's lead, 239 with only three wickets left, was not enough for complete peace of mind. But the way the wicket was allowing the ball to lift and turn was ominous indeed for India.

Greig was not the same player after lunch; indeed he struggled and miscued so much against Prasanna and Chandra that he must have been deeply thankful both for the presence of Underwood in his side and for the fact that he had won that important toss on the first day. He perished eventually to a dubious l.b.w. decision by umpire Shivashankariah when he walked two long paces down the pitch, found that Prasanna had bowled a short one, swept and was hit on the pad. Underwood was brilliantly stumped by Kirmani and the rest of the innings was taken up with Tolchard's noble efforts to score what he could with one hand until, half-an-hour before tea, Greig declared, setting India 284 to win.

In the twenty minutes before the tea interval Vengsarkar was hit on the left wrist by the first ball he faced from Willis, and it was only with remarkable courage that he stood up to everything that came his way before retiring hurt at tea with what turned out to be a cracked bone. If there was any consolation from the defeat to which India now careered it was this twenty minutes of youthful defiance by Vengsarkar. His day will surely come.

Gavaskar's partner after tea was Mohinder Amarnath, who played his best innings against Greig's side though his score of 12 might not suggest so. The fact was that as soon as Underwood came on there was simply no escape for India. The pitch was too difficult and Underwood altogether too hot to handle. He began by having Gavaskar caught at short-leg with the delusory score of 40 on the board; then he had Amarnath in the same way, and when Prasanna came in to try to play out the remainder of the over and thus leave some hope for the home side the next morning Underwood had him caught at slip first ball. Prasanna just smiled.

The denouement on the final day was so swift as to be almost cruel. Certainly the one and a half hours play was so one-sided that it was exciting only to the England players. For them a tremendous triumph was about to be completed.

Underwood and Willis began the bowling and the serious business of the day was settled by them in the fourth and fifth overs. In the fourth Patel wafted outside the off-stump and was smartly caught by Old at third slip; in the fifth Viswanath got a ball which turned sharply and quickly and was brilliantly caught, low and left-handed, by Brearley at first slip.

Oddly enough, it was Underwood's last wicket. Two catches were missed off him, and once again his figures, good though they were, did him less than justice. Viswanath's wicket made India 54 for five, or effectively six with Vengsarkar out of action. The slide accelerated, with Kirmani giving Brearley another catch in the first-slip position which Fletcher normally occupied (Brearley's fourth in the match) and Madan Lal stepping shamelessly away to snick a high, fast catch to Knott.

Two wickets remained to be taken at the end of the first hour, when Lever was called up by Greig to take over from Willis. To the delight of both, he further rubbed in the message that he didn't need artificial aids to take wickets. Mankad played across the angle of his delivery and gave Old yet another slip catch, and then Lever sent Chandra's off-stump cartwheeling through the air to end a game which, for very different reasons from those at Delhi, may always be linked with his name.

Chapter Six
BANGALORE: SPINNERS PREVAIL

England's three-nil lead in the series had made a nonsense of the record books. Their third successive victory had been completed with almost ridiculous ease. No wonder Greig was chaired from the field by jubilant team-mates. The players vied for the privilege of seizing a souvenir stump as they set off on a victory lap around Chepauk, keeping well away from the outer perimeter to avoid the orange peel which was hurled in their direction, not with any hostile intent but more as an expression of disgust at what the spectators saw as India's catastrophic capitulation.

Their second-innings total of 83 at Madras was the lowest by India on home soil. Over the years Indian batsmen have tended to specialise in all-time lows, but they excelled themselves on this occasion. It was the thirteenth time they had been bowled out for under 100 and their sixth-lowest score in what, neatly enough for statisticians of the lagubrious, was their 150th Test match. Their lowest score of all was scraped together at Lord's in 1974 when Chris Old and Geoff Arnold bowled them out for 42. England did not care in their moment of triumph now to remind themselves that their humiliation of India then had been followed by their own disasters at the hands of Thomson and Lillee. For the moment it was Indian cricket that was in mourning. When things are going against a side it needs all the luck it can get, but the loss of the toss at Madras had not helped much. Not that England's first-innings score of 262 need necessarily have been a winning one, nor, on the other hand, that India would have found batting on the first day any easier than they did later in the game. The plain and painful truth was that their batting was not good enough. Delhi had suggested this, Calcutta confirmed it and Madras proved it beyond all doubt.

Back at home in Woking Alec Bedser must have been feeling both delighted that at last the tide was turning for England and also sorry for his opposite number C. D. Gopinath and the other Indian selectors. As Bedser has so often said himself, you can only pick from the players you have got. For the Bangalore Test, India's harassed quintet – Gopinath, Mamasahb Ghorpade, Raj Singh, Vijay Mehra and Pankaj Roy – left out the injured Vengsarkar and dropped Mankad and Madan Lal, bringing into the squad the reserve wicket-keeper-batsman Bharat Reddy, the left-handed middle-order batsman Surinder Amarnath, brother of Mohinder and son of Lala, and a newcomer, Yajuvendra Singh. The latter had been mentioned by Indian journalists as a possibility but against MCC in his two matches earlier in the tour he had scored 16, 2 and 6 not out and had looked not much more than an elevated club cricketer.

For different reasons both Mankad and Madan Lal were unlucky to be made scapegoats. Mankad had batted as well as anyone in India's second innings except for Gavaskar, and it is certain that Madan Lal had never bowled better against England. He was dropped because he had failed to live up to his billing as an all-rounder. In any other Test side the truth was that Madan Lal would have been going in at number nine or ten – against fast bowling he is a no-hoper. But India's great problem was that their tail always seemed to begin at seven against any strong bowling attack. In feeling sorry for Madan Lal one also wondered why the selectors had apparently not considered the seam bowler who to me had looked considerably the best of those who had played against MCC – the big right-hander from Rajasthan, Kailash Ghattani. Nor, as he was about to show at Hyderabad, was Abid Ali yet over the hill. But the selectors did the right thing in sticking by players like Viswanath who had proved themselves in the past and who had to come good sooner or later.

England, for their part, looked forward to the Centenary Test at the end of the tour as the next focal point of their ambitions. The bowling and fielding had made great strides forward; the team spirit, which had been good from the start, had been nourished by success, and the first and major part of their job was done. But Greig is a pragmatist. He knew that this same side might fare very differently against Australia, the West Indies and even Pakistan, who had just beaten Australia by eight wickets at Sydney to level their three-match series, and who were now moving on to the Caribbean to flex their muscles there. What England still lacked, as they had since the passing of the May, Cowdrey, Dexter, Barrington, Graveney generation, were three batsmen in the middle order of genuine class. Apart from Brearley and Tolchard, neither likely to be long-term answers to this perennial problem, and Amiss who along with the absent Boycott had been England's best batsman for some years, no one in the first five of the order had got fifty in the first three Tests. For years Greig and Knott had been coming in at six and seven to do what they could to shore up the innings.

The batting form of Fletcher, Randall, Barlow, Woolmer and Miller was going to be the most important feature of the remainder of the tour. All of them knew that a younger generation was eagerly awaiting its chance – Athey, Tavaré, Gower, Gatting, Slocombe and others. Meanwhile two men shivering at home in Northampton, David Steele and Peter Willey, had as much cause to feel themselves wronged at this stage of the tour as they had at the start.

From the sticky heat and tropical splendour of Madras the party moved on by air to the capital of Andhra Pradesh, Hyderabad, on the day that Jimmy Carter was enrolling as 39th President of the United States. The mood on the modern Indian-made version of the old Avro Anson plane was one of relaxed contentment. Nothing could take away from Greig and his men their achievements over the previous two months, and everyone was counting their blessings. The champagne which a generous British firm had provided at £30 a bottle had ensured an excellent party the night before. Now that the team was fully acclimatised, the illnesses were becoming fewer. One or two of the wives had joined the tour and others were to follow. For those who could not afford the journey there was consolation in the knowledge that the long tour had now passed the halfway mark.

Hyderabad is the fifth largest city in India, and for the enterprising there was plenty to see, including the teeming old market area, Charminar, where a huge carved stone monument with majestic arched gateways topped by minarets, looking north, south-east and west, commands an area of open shops and bazaars. Beggars, women in purdah, cattle and goats mingle here amongst a mass of bicycles, and the air is thick with the smell of spices, refuse and drains; the ground is spotted with red stains where the betel juice has been expertly ejected from practised mouths. The knowledgeable and affluent buyers of Hyderabad make for the pearl stalls, which sell natural and cultured pearls of all sizes and colours imported from Japan. The fat gold rings, oiled hair and loud electronic wristwatches worn by these dealers suggest that times are not too hard.

Outside Hyderabad, where the arid ground is strewn with huge

Gavaskar's extraordinary shot off Lever in only the second over of India's first
innings at Bangalore (fourth Test) – he was caught at mid-off by Underwood for 4.

Brearley snicks a ball from Chandra to Viswanath at slip and is given out caught.
The batsman clearly thought the ball had bounced first (first innings at Bangalore).

boulders like a lunar landscape, the old medieval fortress of Golconda looks down from a rugged granite hill across a high plateau to the twin cities of Hyderabad and Secunderabad. It would take many days to appreciate this extraordinary place with the Moghul royal tombs at the foot. The walls of the fort cover a five-mile circumference and in sheer size it dwarfs anything similar in Britain. From the moment you step in through one of eight heavy gates, studded with iron spikes to stop an elephant charge, to the time you arrive panting at the top you find yourself wondering if any warrior in his right mind would ever have contemplated storming it. In fact the Moghul Emperor Aurangzeb conquered the surrounding kingdom of Golconda in 1687 but the fort itself held out for a further eight months and fell not by force but by a trick.

Only one afternoon was available to the sightseers before the cricket began again, because, for the sake of those like Barlow, Fletcher, Cope, Miller and Selvey who had played so little cricket in recent weeks, Greig insisted on a full net session the morning after the team's arrival. Before a Saturday crowd probably a little in excess of the official capacity of 40,000 John Lever must have opened the bowling against South Zone with a feeling of relief, because the strange affair of the gauzes had now finally been dealt with by a statement from Lord's which completely exonerated any MCC player of 'sharp practice' whilst recognising that the wearing of gauzes might have constituted an 'inadvertent breach of the rules'.

South Zone made 228 for seven on the first day when Indian batting showed itself in a better light on another pitch with enough pace in it for shots to be played freely. The most notable piece of batting was Abid Ali's innings of 63. It was good to see this tough, barrel-chested, gutsy, military-looking figure hitting the ball with all his old panache. Abid Ali has never lacked confidence in himself and although at 35 he was old by the standard of Indian cricketers he looked superbly fit and generally cut a rather more impressive figure than all-rounders who had been preferred to him in the series against England.

Viswanath, from whom an innings of substance was positively demanded, recovered at least some of his confidence after getting off the mark with a superb force off the back foot past cover off Lever. But he still played and missed much too frequently for a world-class batsman and he eventually gave Cope some reward for a long and patient stint of off-spin when he played an airy whip-drive back to the bowler. Patel, after playing well for 30, also perished to an undistinguished shot, pulling a short ball from Miller to mid-wicket. Since this was Miller's first over (delivered shortly before tea) he might have expected to settle in to a long bowl. But he was out of luck, because soon after the interval he received a full-blooded sweep above his left ankle fielding at backward short-leg, and he limped off in great pain. This happened during the best stand of the day between Abid Ali and a tall young right-hander, Narasimha Rao, who showed a sound technique, hit the ball hard and refused to be kidded into losing his concentration when Greig played cat-and-mouse with him to the amusement of the crowd. He also bowled leg-breaks and googlies from a high action and looked a genuine prospect, especially when he followed this up by batting even better in the second innings.

Sunday was clearly going to be significant for those batsmen – Woolmer, Fletcher, Randall, Barlow and Miller – who in theory were all in the running for places at Bangalore. The first two, Woolmer and Fletcher, missed their chance. Woolmer shaped to force a rising ball and was well caught, low in the gully off Abid Ali, the 'Hyderabad Express' himself (whose arm was even lower but his persistence as great as ever), and then Fletcher, playing only his third innings in five weeks, played six balls for one run before getting a delivery which might have dismissed someone in peak form. The bowler was Jayaprakash and the ball lifted and left Fletcher to brush his glove and carry to wicket-keeper Reddy.

This brought Derek Randall to join Dennis Amiss, who was already solidly settled in for a long session of match practice. Randall, after his unfortunate run-out and another low score at Madras, was also in need of a substantial innings and he timed the ball perfectly from the start. It was evidence of how well he played that he got to his fifty half an hour faster than Amiss. But Amiss began to take command after lunch, punching the spinners through the covers and clipping them off his legs as he proceeded to his hundred. It was a typical Amiss innings: sure defence against the good balls, equally sure punishment of the bad ones. Like an old TV film, one felt one had seen it all before. Randall's hundred, on the other hand, was anything but inevitable. In his previous innings on the tour he had tended to dry up after a sound start and sometimes got himself out through a lapse of concentration. This time he again went through a sticky patch in the middle of the afternoon. The crowd became restive but Randall did not, and eventually the strokes began to flow again – well-timed placements through mid-wicket off the full face of the bat and powerful flowing drives past extra-cover. He finished the day 110 not out and a crowd estimated at 45,000, reckoned by local pundits to be the largest ever to have watched a day's cricket at Hyderabad, went home reasonably satisfied, for all the scant success of the local bowlers. Amiss had opened out after reaching his 53rd first-class hundred and when he was stumped for 138 he and Randall had put on 221, the most dominant piece of batting since the first match at Poona. But unlike the 1976 West Indians against the English counties this was not such a brilliant batting side that it could throw the bat with gay abandon every time the Test match pressure was off. Practice had to come first, entertainment second. In any case the Test side was never a settled eleven and almost every day of the minor matches was important for somebody's chances of Test selection. Randall's innings – which he extended to 142 on the last day – clearly confirmed his place, but poor Graham Barlow followed Fletcher into mourning when he pushed forward to Venkataraghavan and fell to another bat-and-pad catch. His habit of playing the ball with his bat ahead of his pads proved his downfall again.

Greig reasoned on the last day of the South Zone match that the only chance of winning the game was to extend MCC's overnight lead of 63 as quickly as possible and try to bowl the opposition out. Greig , Knott and Miller, whose ill-luck continued when he was adjudged l.b.w. on the front foot against Abid Ali, were all out cheaply and it was the last-wicket pair of Selvey and Cope, who until this point of the tour had hardly raised a bat in anger, who took the score past 400 by dint of an unbeaten stand of 49. Lever and Selvey took a wicket each in the first two overs of the innings – both to catches by Greig at second slip – but the pitch was still good and Narasimha Rao batted with the confidence and soundness he had shown in the first innings to put the match out of MCC's reach. Rao and Jayaprakash, another promising all-round cricketer, put on 104 for the third wicket, batting out the last two hours and fifty minutes of a hot afternoon. The pitch, which looked good enough for Test cricket, was the only winner, and it had enabled Indian cricket to show itself in a much better light. Geoff Cope, about to step back quietly from the limelight again, with no chance of selection for the fourth Test, bowled eighteen overs for 32 runs and was unlucky not to take a wicket.

Three of England's Test team, Brearley, Old and Tolchard, had stayed behind in Madras to rest, and when they met up with the others in Bangalore there was good news of Tolchard's injured hand. He would be fit to take his place again, so with Randall's innings insuring his place the discussions about the Test team were confined to whether or not Keith Fletcher, now not just physically fit again but also very eager to play, which at Madras he had not been, should come back at the expense of Woolmer. It was not an easy decision for the selectors. Greig had immediately said after the series had been wrapped up in Madras that he would not make any concessions to the future and would play the best possible team in the last two Tests in order to try to win the series five-nil. Fletcher at his best gets into the current England side but after 49 Tests for England he was as enigmatic a cricketer as ever. He had been out of both form and luck since his sparkling hundred in the opening match at Poona, and had fielded unreliably at first slip, where Brearley had been outstanding at Madras. Woolmer had been only slightly less disappointing. The memory of his 149 against Australia at the Oval back in 1975 was starting to fade. The iron and application he had needed then was absent from his batting in India. But he had been playing better of late and there was a good case now for including him and giving him another examination with the coming matches against Australia in mind.

It was Fletcher who was eventually chosen, and the match about to begin at Bangalore was an important one for him. How he played here might determine his selection for the Centenary Test and subsequently for the series in England against the old enemy. His Test average at this stage of his career was better than forty, which showed him to be a very much more successful Test cricketer than many gave him credit for. Yet somehow his failures were more memorable than his triumphs. The summer ahead looked like determining the final making or breaking of his reputation.

Bangalore is supposed to be the most British of Indian cities. I had always thought of it as the birthplace of Colin Cowdrey, and rather like the man himself it turned out be to quiet and charming. Set at 3,000 feet with a delightful climate, it is a relatively affluent city which now has thriving electronic, cotton, wool, carpet, silk, leather, soap and cigarette industries. But the impression it still gives is that of a garden city. Everywhere there are beautiful trees and shrubs which seem somehow to cushion the noise, to soften the glare and to mask the squalor. The atmosphere of many of the streets is akin to that of an English market town. This feeling of peace, almost of sleepiness, induced by Bangalore is nowhere more evident than in the old British club where the aura of colonialism still hangs around the elegant columns of the main clubhouse. As a young subaltern Winston Churchill was once a member and according to the club books he still owes them thirteen rupees. Several people have tried to pay the debt, but no one has been allowed to do so. After all, Churchill is more famous than the club! The few British and the other foreigners living in Bangalore are all members here, but the membership now as in other clubs of its type is almost entirely Indian. Thirty years on from Partition the small upper echelon of Indian society still clings determinedly to such traditions.

It was less because British visitors might feel at home here than because several of the best cricketers in India hailed from the city that Bangalore was accorded the privilege of staging only its second Test match. The first had been two years before when Clive Lloyd's West Indians had won a rain-affected match. The attempts by the Karnataka Cricket Association and the state government to turn their stadium into a modern one along the lines of India's other main cricket centres had begun before that first Test and were still going on, night and day, when MCC arrived two days before the match. Gradually a bamboo stadium was being transformed into one of concrete but only in India could so much have been left until the eleventh hour and only in India would so much be achieved by sheer hard work at the last moment. My own BBC commentary point, for instance, was an unfinished mixture of wet concrete and thin plywood hanging perilously in space two days before the match began, but by the time the first ball was bowled on Friday it was a spick-and-span commentary-booth, with a commanding view of the green outfield and the circle of stands, which had eerie-looking white effigies sticking out from their roofs like scarecrows to frighten away the evil spirits.

The spirits were on Bedi's side, anyway, when the coin landed right for him and he chose to bat first. There is a heavy dew in Bangalore in January, and with play beginning as early as 10 a.m. batting can be a hazardous business for the first half-hour or so. Yet the only wicket India lost in the opening overs and, as it turned out, the only wicket they lost all morning was the result of extraordinary indiscretion on the part of Sunil Gavaskar. Desperate is the only suitable word for Gavaskar's method during his brief innings. He was clearly intent on attack from the first ball, but after one dazzling cover-drive he drove wildly at a ball from Lever that simply was not pitched far enough up to him and the ball spun off the outside edge to Underwood at mid-off.

This opening wicket fell in only the second over of the innings and with India's senior batsman sacrificing himself in such a way one could not help wondering what the rest would do. In fact the second-wicket pair added a further 93 on a brown-coloured easy-paced pitch. Both partners, Gaekwad and Surinder Amarnath, had been absent at Madras, and Surinder, the left-handed elder brother of Mohinder, was playing his first Test innings in India. After a certain amount of luck early on – he survived a confident l.b.w. appeal the first ball he received from Willis and also played one or two hooks of which he was not in control – he settled in to play extremely well. Gaekwad, back for the injured Vengsarkar, was altogether sounder in the early part of his innings, apart from the time that he padded up to Lever and looked palpably l.b.w. He capitalised on this and as usual hit the ball fluently off his legs and stood up straight to get behind the fast bowling.

The nature of the pitch, a typical Indian slow turner, was soon evident. Underwood came on after only four overs from Willis and by the end of the day he and Greig had done more bowling than anyone else. Well as they performed, the England captain must have regretted that Cope or Miller was not in the side to give an extra prong to his spin attack. Ironically this was the first game for which Cope had not even been seriously considered. By lunch Gaekwad and Surinder, who was driving through the covers and cutting with the air of a man who was thoroughly enjoying the exercise, had steered India to 82 for one, and for only the second time in the series India's total reached three figures with only one wicket down, before the patience and accuracy of Underwood and Greig at last paid off. At 102 Gaekwad turned Greig to leg where Tolchard, far and away England's best available short-leg, dived to catch the ball in his left hand.

Surinder, after a long chat with his distinguished father Lala during lunch, had played particularly well afterwards, and he had hit Greig for four fours when he tried to cut a ball which curved into him and dragged it on to his stumps. Two of the local Karnataka heroes, Viswanath and Patel, were together now but dreams of a long partnership between them collapsed when at 134, after an hour's patient struggle during which he could manage only seven scoring strokes, Viswanath was caught by Brearley via bat and boot off Underwood, for whom, once again, a wicket was overdue. Not for the first time in the series Viswanath was unhappy to be given out. This brought to the wicket Yajuvendra Singh, the debonair, moustachioed, 24-year-old from a princely family in Maharashtra, who had been picked by the selectors in place of Mankad in answer to the national demand for new blood. In his innings against MCC earlier on the tour he had looked out of his class, but he batted sensibly until he tried to square-cut Willis and was neatly caught low and to his right by Knott.

So India's position at tea had declined rapidly from 102 for one to 153 for five, and Greig and Underwood had again shown that they are not to be underestimated as a pair of unorthodox but frequently effective spinners. It was Willis who took the last wicket of the day, however, thanks to a superb catch in the covers by Randall, who dived forward to hold a rasping square-cut by Patel. It was a rather unfortunate way for Patel to get out after playing another sensible and disciplined innings.

That India should have reached the respectability of 253 after thus losing the last of their front-line batsmen was almost entirely due to a stand of 66 for the seventh wicket between Kirmani, who scored his first fifty of the series, and Ghavri, another of those restored to favour by the selectors. They guided India to 205 for six by the close of a first day during which England, with the now traditional help of a hold-up due to a ball going out of shape, had bowled only 70 overs.

The new ball was five overs old next day when Willis broke through at last and in a spell of eighteen balls polished off the tail. Kirmani played on to his wicket, Ghavri was caught behind (having survived a confident appeal for a similar dismissal off Lever which Ghavri later admitted should have been upheld) and Prasanna and Bedi were respectively caught by second slip and at the wicket. Willis's extra pace earned him figures of six for 53 on a pitch which, as India's spinners were about to confirm, was made for slow bowlers. Bedi bowled the third over of the England innings, and although Amiss and Brearley scored eleven cautious but safe runs before lunch they ran into deep trouble in the afternoon heat.

There was a fifteen-minute delay after the interval whilst a cloth was found to cover up a large piece of corrugated iron which was glinting in the sun to one side of the sightscreen at the end opposite the main stand. Then, in the second over after lunch, Brearley snicked a ball from Chandra towards Viswanath, who caught the ball, as it appeared from the boundary, after it had bounced. All the close fielders appealed, umpire Nagendra's finger slowly rose and a furious Brearley departed, leaving Viswanath as he passed in no doubt about his opinion of him.

A sticky little stand followed between Fletcher and Amiss which took England to 34 when, an hour after lunch, Prasanna came on and in his first over had Fletcher smartly caught at short-leg by Yajuvendra Singh for 10. Randall made a rather more authoritative 10 before falling in what, according to the scorecard, was an exactly similar fashion – caught Yajuvendra bowled Prasanna. In this case, though, the catch was a more difficult one, held low and left-handed, and there was also a considerable element of doubt about whether Randall had hit the ball. As he walked past the press-box after a long look of amazement at umpire Ghouse's finger, which had shot skywards the instant the ball was caught, Randall said loudly: 'I didn't even play a shot – you can write that.' From the boundary it was impossible to see for sure whether or not he had touched the ball. All one could say was that Yajuvendra made an almighty song-and-dance every time he caught anything, be it off bat or pad. He was clearly a very useful fielder, and equally clearly an opportunist.

When Tolchard was bowled by Chandrasekhar's googly on the stroke of tea England had declined to 65 for four, and two balls later the situation grew worse still when Greig, after hitting his first ball from Chandra past mid-wicket for two, was caught off bat and boot by the rapacious Yajuvendra.

All this time Amiss was playing with the skill and character of the world-class batsman he is. The more the wickets fell, the more venomously he played his attacking shots and the more solid his defence seemed to become. With Knott he now tilted the balance back towards an even keel in a tense and fascinating stand of 70.

Knott began by pushing Chandra in the air past short-leg and in the same over a miscued drive by Amiss spun off the outside edge close to Patel at cover. There was a hint of desperation about the stroke, but Amiss had clearly decided that he must attack whenever possible. In Chandra's next over he cut Chandra, again in the air, past slip for four to third-man and he was hitting the ball so hard that the close fielders had little hope even of seeing some of his shots. It seemed as if he had been angered by the questionable decisions which had undermined his team's position, but he only released that fury when the right ball came along.

Gradually Chandra's own snake-like venom was repulsed. Knott swung him carefully over the inner ring on the onside, and then Amiss drove him smoothly all along the ground past the groping fingers of Bedi at mid-off. When Amiss repeated the stroke, this time off Prasanna, with the ball again evading Bedi, the peculiarly fickle nature of a section of the crowd was demonstrated as scattered booing broke out. If the objectors were not satisfied with Bedi's team today they never would be, for the Indians had bowled brilliantly and snapped up almost every chance.

Prasanna, turning the ball more than anyone else, and Chandra, beating the bat with his leg-break almost as much as with his googly and achieving more bounce than the others, had the best figures at the end of the day but it was Bedi, coming on again half an hour before the close, who struck the final important blow by getting a ball to turn sharply past Knott's slightly crooked defence and bowling him. Amiss, luck on his side at times but his skill and character once more passing every test, walked in on the Saturday evening 76 not out with England still in deep trouble at 138 for six.

However, Amiss did not last long on Sunday as Chandra and Prasanna renewed their attack with even greater zest. For the first time in the match the stadium was full and every ball that beat the bat, struck the edge or hit the pad was greeted with a bellicose roar. This was the roar for wickets which we had expected at Calcutta but rarely heard there. Now there was something to roar about, especially when Amiss pushed forward in Chandra's second over; the ball fizzed back at him and carried off the edge of his bat and his pad into the sure hands of Yajuvendra Singh. The piratical little figure was much less lithe in his movements than Solkar, India's greatest short-leg of recent seasons, but his catching on this evidence was at least as reliable.

Old and his new partner Lever inched their way from 146 to 154 and Old seemed gradually to be getting the measure of the two spinners, who were now hurrying through their overs and hustling the batsmen like wasps buzzing round a ripe plum. But Prasanna suddenly let slip a straight full-toss, Old opened his shoulders, the ball struck the pads and again umpire Ghouse's finger flew heavenwards to confirm Prasanna's appeal. Now it was finally certain that India would have a substantial first-innings lead and, with the advantage of batting first, they had their sights firmly set on victory for the first time in seven Tests – home and away – against England.

The position had been achieved on Sunday 30 January, the anniversary of the assassination of the father of the new India, Mahatma Gandhi. Just as Prasanna was moving in to bowl to Lever, at exactly 11 a.m., a siren began howling above the crowd's hubbub, the players stood erect in their positions on the field and 50,000 people in the stadium rose in sudden silence to remember the tragic end to an extraordinary and noble life. (It did not seem to matter that a silence scheduled for two minutes in fact lasted only about 45 seconds. Indeed it showed a typically Indian sense of timing!)

Bishen Bedi decided that this was the psychological moment to bring himself on in Chandra's place, but Lever and Underwood would not easily be awed and by sensible batting they added 21 valuable runs for the ninth wicket before the lethal combination of Chandrasekhar and Yajuvendra Singh struck again. Underwood's dismissal, after 12 hard-earned and well-deserved runs, was straightforward: a sharp, high-bouncing googly, turned into Yajuvendra's chest. His fifth catch meant that he had equalled a world record in his first Test – that of five catches in a Test innings, established by Vic Richardson in the 1935–36 match between South Africa and Australia at Durban. Richardson was also a specialist close fielder, notably to the bowling of Bill O'Reilly.

Lever and Willis survived until lunch when England, at 182 for nine, had added 44 runs in two hours for the loss of three more wickets: a grim but absorbing struggle. These two extended the innings to 195, batting for another twenty minutes after lunch with rather more freedom than anyone had shown in the morning, until Willis took a long step down the pitch to pad up to Chandra and was adjudged l.b.w.

It had been just like old times for India on a pitch which suited them perfectly: neither too fast nor too bouncy for the England fast bowlers, yet with considerable turn for the home spinners and just enough pace to make that turn dangerous. Chandra, with six wickets, had the best figures, and as this followed his five at Madras it was clear that the old magic had returned. Prasanna, however, had bowled even more admirably, his flight, control, changes of pace, sharp spin and subtle use of the crease making this an exemplary performance by a master spinner.

It is sad but necessary to have to write that the value of these performances, and also of a typically immaculate one by Bedi, was tarnished by poor umpiring, but this was indubitably the case.

Umpire Ghouse, who had caused New Zealand to protest earlier in the season when he had stood as a replacement in the Madras Test because a cyclone prevented the officially appointed umpire from standing, had not taken part in any of the MCC's three-day matches, although the tour regulations agreed between MCC and the Indian Board had stated that wherever possible all the appointed Test umpires would stand in the Zonal games so that MCC might see them and object if they wished. Barrington and Greig took a gamble when they agreed to his standing at Bangalore.

India's lead of 58 on the first innings was clearly going to be priceless with England having to bat last on a wearing pitch, and this time Gavaskar played exactly the innings his side needed as the lead was quickly built upon. The innings began quietly – there was no point in hurrying – and after eight overs with the new ball Underwood was introduced. If it was the moment of truth Gavaskar appeared not to know it, because off his first two overs he moved down the pitch to strike confident offside fours. It was Old, in the course of an excellent spell of straight fast bowling, who achieved England's only success before tea, knocking out Gaekwad's off-stump as he played back.

Greig, becoming gradually more confident and inventive about his bowling changes, now brought himself on in place of Underwood to bowl at the left-handed Amarnath, but for a time before and after tea, whilst Gavaskar was playing exceptionally well, nothing would go right for England. Amarnath sliced a four off Greig past Brearley's upstretched left hand, then miscued a lofted drive short of Randall, who slipped as he came in from cover. Then, in successive overs after tea, the luckless Underwood had Gavaskar missed by Knott behind the wicket – the ball going through his gloves for four although the wicket-keeper had done well to get across in time – and Amarnath missed off an even harder chance to Tolchard, diving at short-leg. But after Gavaskar, with nine fours, had reached a fine fifty out of a total of eighty in two hours he was caught at slip off the outside edge as he pushed forward to Underwood.

Again, Greig showed his growing tactical appreciation when he brought back Willis with immediate effect. Amarnath mishooked a short, fast ball to Tolchard at square-leg, and India were 82 for three.

With Viswanath being held back because of a bruised hand, Yajuvendra Singh, India's new hero, followed Patel in the order. If his record-equalling five catches had exaggerated his abilities as a fielder, it certainly also seemed that his innings against the touring side earlier in the season had exaggerated his failings as a batsman because he now played for time with a disciplined and organised defence against both Willis and Underwood, only for Patel to perish just before the close to yet another bat-pad chance this time carrying to Knott who took a gentle catch behind the wicket on the leg side. India's lead at the end of the day was 163, with six wickets left. Underwood had already taken two for 27 and might well have had two more – close fielders find him difficult to field to because his changes in pace cause the ball to come off the bat at varying speeds – and he had now passed Alec Bedser's former record haul of 236 Test wickets. Only Gibbs, Trueman, Statham, Benaud and McKenzie now stood between him and an all-time record, and he was certain to add to his tally when the game resumed on 1 February. Underwood was congratulated next day by Barrington, who asked: 'Has Alec sent you a telegram yet?' When Underwood said no Barrington added: 'Stingy so-and-so. I'll send you one when you pass my number of runs.'

Test match rest days earlier on the tour had been anxious affairs. The MCC team had in each case spent them with a victory beckoning, and each time they had been a little more confident that the potential victory would become a reality. But there was no mental relaxation until the series was in the bag. Now that it was, England ironically found themselves facing probable defeat. They could afford to be philosophical. There were only cheerful faces round the pool, where the growing band of English supporters was as much in evidence as the players, and on the parched little golf course where the greens are brown. For the more adventurous or extravagant there were trips either into the high, dry, desolate Nandi hills, or south to Mysore, with its palaces and commanding focal point of Chamundi hill, topped by its spectacular Hindu temple.

The relaxed attitude of the England team was demonstrated when Greig called a press conference apparently to discuss the umpiring and some scurrilous articles which were still appearing in Indian publications about the Vaseline affair. Greig sat down in the room of a certain Fleet Street sage, who had bought beer all round in anticipation of some juicy 'quotes'. As the first question was about to be asked Bob Willis came in and said: 'There's someone here to see you, Tony.' At which point a 50-year-old Russian woman in a mini-skirt, with lank red hair and a huge python coiled round her neck, walked in and deposited the reptile on the belly of a reclining and unsuspecting pressman. The looks of naked terror all round had to be seen to be believed, but professional scribes and broadcasters must produce their comments, even on a rest day, and more serious matters were then discussed. Officially there was no comment as to the umpiring, about which Barrington was to report to the Indian Board at the end of the tour, but unofficially six cases were enumerated where England's team felt decisions had been unjustly given against them. In their more suspicious moments the MCC players felt like victims of a conspiracy with the umpires playing the role of hit men. There was even talk of senior Bombay officials anxiously overseeing the game, desperate for an Indian victory lest their splendid new stadium, expensively constructed whilst other more badly-needed buildings in Bombay were held back, might only be half-full for the final Test. Political reputations seemed to be at stake as well as cricketing ones.

But nothing could mask the truth that India's spinners had bowled superbly on a pitch ideally suited to them and the batsmen had performed with much greater resolution this time. They needed to do so for only a little longer now to make the match safe.

The fourth day, naturally, began before a full house, and began well for India. Underwood and in particular Willis bowled beautifully, but luck and commonsense cricket were on India's side as the first hour produced 35 runs for the loss of only the nightwatchman, Prasanna. Helped by two late stabs off Underwood to the fine-leg boundary he made a very useful 12 before cutting Willis to Old in the gully.

Willis had already been unlucky not to win an l.b.w. appeal to umpire Ghouse when Yajuvendra played back to a straight half-volley, and off the second ball he received Viswanath snicked a very fast delivery in front of Greig at second slip. Willis puts a tremendous amount of energy into every ball, and he can bowl only for short spells. Viswanath and Yajuvendra held on and the former emulated Gavaskar by twice moving down the pitch to drive Underwood for fours. At the other end Yajuvendra got a bonus four from a wild throw by Fletcher from third-man, an incident which betrayed the tension amongst the England fielders. Only later would one appreciate the immense significance of these early overs as Viswanath settled in and the possibility of a swift end to the Indian innings receded.

The roles of Viswanath and Greig at this stage were crucial. If 'Vishy' batted well or Greig bowled badly the match would soon go beyond England's recall. The England captain certainly did not bowl badly – indeed he nearly got the man he wanted when Viswanath, then 14, played the ball sharply through the hands of Tolchard at short-leg – but the little man continued to play some skilful shots until after a stand of 30 and a resolute innings Yajuvendra tried to drive Underwood and was safely taken by Fletcher at mid-on. Underwood had been at fault in not inviting him to drive before this.

Kirmani, whose first-innings fifty was looking all the more valuable now, opened his account with a bold pull for four off Greig. He followed this by smashing Underwood over mid-on. It was the buccaneer's approach and in this situation the right one. His rapid 21 enabled India to add another 35 for the seventh wicket at better than a run a minute, but he was caught by Randall at extra-cover soon after lunch.

India's innings had already gone on longer than England had hoped but there was to be no speedy mopping-up of the tail this time. Ghavri played a mute but effective defensive role whilst Viswanath continued to collect runs with wristy square-cuts and drives. The new ball was taken after 76 overs but Ghavri survived several overs from Willis and Lever before cutting the latter a long way through the air to Amiss on the deep third-man boundary.

Bedi, who had enjoyed very little batting glory in the series, now had the crowd on their toes with excitement as he opened his shoulders and hit three fours before his innings was cut short by a brilliant pick-up and throw by Lever, who noticed Bedi ambling down the pitch whistling a happy tune and threw down the stumps from deep extra-cover. Even now Chandra managed to prolong the entertainment by means of some eccentric defensive strokes, but one wondered why Bedi did not declare. His lead now was beyond 300 and he could hardly have been worried by any thought of another England victory. If, on the other hand, England batted outstandingly he might need the time which was frittered away in the last ten minutes before the tea interval.

At tea, anyway, he declared and no doubt thoroughly enjoyed the luxury of being able to do so at last. He set England 318 to win, but everyone knew that, despite the fact that India had extended their second innings much longer than expected, they would have to bat miraculously well to do so. Yet no one was prepared for the extraordinary events which took place after tea.

For England, with batting only a little less brittle than India's, the influence of Amiss was almost as important as that of Gavaskar or Viswanath. It was no coincidence that in India's highest score of the series both these two had scored fifties. By the same token it was no coincidence that the shock of seeing Amiss out for nought in the first over of their second innings was the signal for the most remarkable of all the remarkable collapses suffered by England since the break-up of Ray Illingworth's side.

Amiss was hardly to blame. He got across outside the off-stump to play half-cock to a ball from Ghavri which suddenly stood right up, took the top inside edge of the bat and carried to backward short-leg. Waiting there was our old friend Yajuvendra Singh, who dived forward to take one of the best of the catches which was to make his Test debut a permanent feature in *Wisden*. There was a special delirium about the dancing and leaping of the Indian fielders as they ran to envelop the beaming hero. Amiss out for nought in the first over was almost too good to be true.

Yet this was only the *hors-d'ouevres* before India's feast. Brearley and Fletcher successfully negotiated three overs from Ghavri and two from Gavaskar, who bowled a few testing deliveries at medium pace including one genuine bouncer – not bad for a man of 5 feet 4 inches. He looked like a slower and less serious version of Bill Edrich and might perhaps have made a useful bowler if he had ever wanted to apply himself diligently. Bedi relieved him with a condescending pat and then Chandra took over from Ghavri and in his first over got a ball to spin back sharply to Fletcher, who turned it into the ever-eager hands of Yajuvendra. Thus Greg Chappell's world record of seven catches in a Test was equalled and the way he was going it looked as if Yajuvendra would not only break it before the game ended but overhaul all the wicket-keepers' record tallies as well.

England were now 7 for two. Very soon they became 7 for three and 8 for four. In the tenth over of the innings Bedi pitched a ball short; it popped and turned and as Brearley tried to pull against the spin the ball took the top edge of his bat and carried over the heads of slip and gully, where Gaekwad turned quickly and ran back a few yards to make the catch. Tolchard swept the first ball he received for one and Randall pushed forward to the next, the ball turned again, took the edge and spun up over Gaekwad, who repeated the process. England 8 for four. Like the two-headed monster at the mop fair, it was fantastic but true.

As it turned out the combination of Greig and Tolchard successfully negotiated the remaining three-quarters of an hour of India's day of triumph. But they might very well not have done. Tolchard was dropped off Bedi by Yajuvendra Singh when he had made only one, and three times (twice to umpire Ghouse) bowlers and fielders claimed bat-pad catches which were not allowed. So India could feel that the imbalance of decisions which England claimed had been redressed. In any case, what did they care? At 34 for four England had no realistic chance of survival.

The only question when the final day began under the stainless blue sky which may be taken for granted for most of the year in Bangalore, was how long England would keep India waiting for their sweet revenge. Their lowest Test score against India had been 101, and there seemed every chance that it would not be reached this time when off the last ball of the first over of the day from Chandra Tolchard played back, the ball turned sharply and although it looked like missing the leg-stump umpire Nagendra raised his finger.

Half the England side was out for 35. For the umpteenth time those battle-hardened veterans, Tony Greig and Alan Knott, found themselves together in the middle with a hopeless cause on their hands. No matter what the situation, Greig has one irrefragable rule when he is batting. He will not be dominated. Even in defence at Calcutta he was always playing the game his way. In England the previous summer his attempts to counter-attack the West Indian fast bowlers had on the whole been a failure. But this morning, whilst the effects of the roller were still evident, Greig was able to hit back at Chandra with immediate effect.

It did not last long but for a while he enjoyed himself, pulling a long-hop majestically for a four which some of the crowd indignantly thought was a six and then in the same over stretching his front foot far down the wicket to drive handsomely through the covers. But the wine went to his head. Such liberties could not be taken with Bedi, possessor of a mastery of flight peerless amongst modern bowlers. He dismissed the headstrong, aggressive batsman in the classical manner, tossing the ball up on Greig's leg-stump. Down the pitch came England's captain, intent on hitting the ball high into the crowd, but he missed, and Kirmani, quick as a cobra, did the rest. Before the over was out Bedi ought to have taken his fourth wicket as Old swept and was dropped off the top edge of his bat by Gavaskar running back and looking into the sun.

At the other end Knott was being a little more judicious about choosing the ball to hit, but like so many of his colleagues he seemed obsessed with the sweep against both Bedi and Prasanna. If the series had still been at stake, England's tactics would have been hard to defend. Instead of grim defence they now settled for going down with all guns blazing. It made for splendid entertainment and a less inglorious defeat.

Knott certainly had more to offer than just the sweep. With a quicker movement of his feet he was able to dance down the pitch and with a greater chance of success play the shot which Greig had tried off Bedi. Twice he moved several yards from his crease to get to the pitch, once lofting Bedi straight for four, the second time picking his spot on the mid-wicket boundary with precision. As he warmed to his task the strokes became more varied and inventive: square-cuts, delicate dabs, firm drives. One knew the eventual outcome so one was able to sit back and enjoy this virtuoso solo against subtle spin bowling on a pitch by now affording tremendous turn at times. The immense advantage of winning the toss was paying its dividends. Old played one or two brave shots and resisted any further temptation to sweep, but when he shaped to hit Chandra away on the legside he was struck on the back foot and the appeal was once more answered in the affirmative.

Whilst Knott continued to sparkle to the delight of a crowd who had no wish for an abrupt end to the entertainment, Lever acquired eleven runs with the help of one or two judiciously played inside-edges before guiding a very sharp turner into the gully where Ghavri dived to hold a brilliant left-handed catch. England and the match were still just about alive at lunch-time, with Knott, who had reached his fifty in 85 minutes with six fours, 69 not out.

He had time to add just twelve more in twenty minutes after lunch during the course of which India's victory was appropriately sealed by Bishen Bedi. Underwood perished as so many have perished to his own bowling, mowing against the spin to give a catch at deep square-leg, and then after Knott had survived a confident appeal for a legside catch by Kirmani off Prasanna, which looked like yet another incorrect decision, this time in England's favour, Willis moved yards down the pitch like a father getting himself out on purpose in the annual school match against the sons. Kirmani delicately removed a bail as Willis kept on walking and it was all over.

Nobody begrudged the Indians this moment of triumph. It was both a well-deserved and a timely boost to national cricket morale with the final Test in Bombay due in another nine days. One was delighted for Bedi, whose six for 71 had settled matters on the last day and helped to prove his contention that there was less between the two sides than the first three results had suggested. One was delighted for all the Indian players, not least Viswanath whose second innings 79 not out had taken the pressure off himself and his colleagues. One was delighted too for those anxious Bombay officials and in particular Mr Wankhede; and above all one was delighted for the countless millions throughout the teeming sub-continent who had been following every ball bowled in the series and who had been spending their hard-earned rupees to watch whenever they possibly could.

Like all Indian victories of recent seasons success had been based partially on significant contributions from their only batsmen of world class, Gavaskar and Viswanath, and mainly on their three great spinners. The fact that Yajuvendra Singh, in his first Test, had held seven catches at short-leg was also of the utmost significance, because spinners lose half their effectiveness if close catches are not snapped up. How many fewer wickets, for instance, would Laker have taken without Lock at short-leg – or for that matter Lock without Surridge? And how many more wickets might Underwood have picked up over the years if he had been able to carry around Lock, Roope and Solkar to field for him? He would probably already have overtaken Lance Gibbs.

Not the least satisfying feature of India's 140-run win, indeed, was simply that spinners and fielders had achieved it. After watching so much cricket where fast bowlers held sway one revelled in this totally different brand of game, where guile is more important than brute force. I had seen Greg Chappell set his record of seven catches in a Test in Perth two years before (when he was even more deserving than Singh of a permanent place in *Wisden*) and there was simply no resemblance between that match and this one. Perth had resembled a public jousting, Bangalore a public chess-match, full of wit and subtle touches. Both were dramatic in their way, but this game at Bangalore had been the quintessential Indian Test, a rarity in a cricket world increasingly ruled by the fast bowlers.

Only one feature of the match spoiled this enjoyment. One would like to think that umpires Nagendra and Ghouse went home from

Bangalore with a clear conscience. No one in sport has a harder job than Test umpires. Like referees at FA Cup semi-finals or line-judges at a Wimbledon final they have to make momentous decisions on split-second evidence. An umpire can terminate an innings with one lift of his index finger. His decision must be made in an instant, often against a flurry of pads and an excitement of arms raised in appeal and a deafening roar from the crowd. No one envies an umpire his decision; everyone is prepared to blame him if he makes the wrong one.

Undoubtedly the umpires did make a number of wrong decisions at Bangalore. When that happens players are less likely to help them and more likely to appeal for catches and l.b.w.'s they do not really believe in. The whole game suffers. But the vital distinction between poor umpiring and biased umpiring remains: one is understandable, the other unforgivable. All the objective viewer can really say is that England got far more bad decisions than India at Bangalore.

The fact nevertheless remains that India deserved to win and that it was a thoroughly good thing that they did.

Chapter Seven
THE FINAL SHOWDOWN

England's defeat at Bangalore had been the most painless they had suffered for a long time. But they had a problem now. They needed to return to winning form at Bombay – or at least to avoid defeat here – if the new confidence they had found after winning the series so decisively was not to be undermined. They also had to make the most of the Bombay Test to help them discover the best combination for the Centenary game with Australia.

The loss of the Bangalore Test was the result of another failure by the front-line batting. Of the English batsmen only Amiss, going in first, and Knott, seventh, had scored fifties in the match, and these two plus Greig (number six) had been easily England's highest scorers in the series. Fletcher was not alone in failing twice at Bangalore but in playing he had deprived someone – Barlow? Woolmer? Miller? – of the chance to establish a longer-term claim to a place. With every passing Test the feeling grew stronger that only when England could solve this apparently interminable middle-order batting problem would they be able to win regularly against other countries. Basically there was a lack of the right talent, yet Greig made the telling point after Bangalore that there was also the question of inexperience. Amiss and Knott, after all, had both failed to a greater or lesser extent on the last tour of India. Next time round, perhaps, Randall or Barlow would be scoring the major centuries that win Test matches.

This was all very well, but England now had only one match between the fourth and fifth Tests to sort out a better combination for a match they desperately wanted to win, if only to prove to themselves and everyone else that their first three victories had been no flukes and also that the unbearably smug remarks in some Indian papers about the 'great, ecstatic and memorable' win by their 'superb' team might be placed in proper perspective (just as that very win had itself put the one-sided start to the series in a more realistic light).

The match took place at Indore, not one of India's more exciting cities but certainly a place with a great sense of cricket history. Here, on the old ground, the state of Holkar once scored 912 for eight declared against Mysore in the first post-war season, with six of their team recording first-class centuries. Denis Compton once scored a double hundred for Holkar and the scoring feats of C.K. Nayudu are forever recalled in the form of a large statue of this great player essaying a somewhat airy-looking late-cut. Elsewhere, not far from the hectic centre of Indore, a 25-foot-high concrete cricket bat, with all the autographs of Ajit Wadekar's successful side to England in 1971, bears testament both to a notable achievement and to the fanatical following for the game on the sub-continent. Would Hove, one wondered, erect a similar edifice in honour of Greig's team?

MCC's opponents at Indore were the Ranji Champions, Bombay, and although the tourists scored 308 for four in 100 overs on the first day against a useful spin attack led by Shivalkar (left-arm orthodox) and Zarapkar (off-spin) the fact that four batsmen scored half-centuries served only to complicate the selection for the final Test. Better late than never, Miller was given the chance of a big innings by being sent in third but in the first innings failed to take it, coming in after a long opening stand between Brearley and Woolmer. Batting was not easy on a pitch which occasionally caused the ball to bounce awkwardly or stop suddenly but both Woolmer and Brearley played some pleasing strokes. Fletcher made 65 not out without ever really finding his true form and Randall's 61 not out was memorable only for a sudden explosion of fine shots at the end of the day. It was enough to make sure that he retained his Test place, especially since Barlow was dismissed for 26. But at least the latter, like Fletcher, refound some sort of touch and confidence.

Bombay replied with a dismal piece of batting before a Sunday crowd of 25,000, with Gavaskar failing and no one else having the ability to master the MCC attack. Selvey, Old, Woolmer, Cope, Miller and the lightly bowled Underwood all performed to the high standards one had come to expect from this MCC side in the field, and only the left-handed Mohanraj, with a painstaking 76 not out, gave the locals anything to celebrate.

The dullest match of the tour became even grimmer on the last day, despite some good MCC batting in the morning when Miller stole the show with a mature and typically composed 52. Now there was real substance to the talk of his being thrown into the deep end at Bombay. Set 220 to win at a fraction over a run a minute, the national champions proved hardly worthy of their name, Solkar spending three hours over 34 not out as the match died a particularly slow and painful death. The large crowd once again had Randall's outfield antics to be thankful for, although Cope, Yorkshire from head to toe, strove hard to win their interest away from the preposterous 'Arkle' (so called because, like that great steeplechaser, Randall's energy seems boundless) and towards his own wholehearted attempts to winkle out stubborn batsmen. His reward came when, soon after stumps had been drawn to everyone's relief, he was presented with a beautiful piece of ivory as the bowling prize.

So, back to Bombay for the final encounter: that huge, cosmopolitan city with any number of five-star hotels and cinemas, golf-courses, handsome Victorian buildings, and a much more ancient culture lurking in corners for anyone who wants to look for it. None of Bombay's tourist attractions is more impressive than the sixth-century cave carvings of Lord Siva, hewn out of solid basalt on Elephanta island. Lord Curzon was responsible for their re-storation after the Portuguese – fervent Catholics – had treated them with less respect, so here at least the British are thanked for what they did.

Modern India has two faces, and nowhere are they more clearly revealed than in Bombay. One's first impression is of a thriving, affluent port and commercial centre. Where else in the world would a new television centre be constructed with such a preponderance of solid marble? This indeed will be a proud legacy for future generations: a skyscraper not of glass and concrete but of the beautiful cool rock that has been the making of so many wonderful Indian buildings from the Taj Mahal onwards. Yet one only has to lose one's way, as I did one day, to stumble across the hidden sores of the city, the bustees – those villages of filth scarring the side streets and marshy wastes, desperately overcrowded, smelly, disease-ridden. The old and the new India are uneasy bedfellows. The beach at Juhu, ten miles outside the city centre, is as beautiful a stretch of palm-fringed golden sand as one could wish to find anywhere in the world, yet it is defiled for the visitor by hundreds of Indians defecating on the edge of the sand every morning. Thirty years ago the water was blue. Now it is grey with oil and human pollution. The mayor's message to his city, glaring down from huge red-and-green posters on the side of the road, reads: 'Clean

Bombay, green Bombay.' Good luck to him.

There is nothing poor or deprived about the cricket facilities at Bombay. The Wankhede Stadium where the fifth Test was played is a magnificent modern construction with white-painted wooden seats giving it a much more comfortable and smart appearance than the concrete and bamboo which dominate the other main stadiums of India. Not a quarter-mile from Wankhede another fine ground, the Brabourne, lies idle save for a few proposed greyhound meetings, some amateur athletics, and the matches played by the Cricket Club of India. As mentioned in Chapter 2, a financial disagreement between the CCI and the Bombay Cricket Association led to the building of the Wankhede, which takes its name from the prominent politician and senior cricket administrator, S. K. Wankhede.

The preliminaries to the Test were somewhat bizarre. England named an unchanged eleven on the day before the match, the selection committee flinching from experiment and eschewing any special planning for the future. Miller was officially stated to be unfit because of a pinched nerve in his back, but had he been a recognised member of the side the minor injury would probably have been overlooked. Announcing the decision Greig said he hoped that Miller would be allowed to go in third for Derbyshire the following season – a strange statement in that it had mainly been the initiative of Derbyshire's captain, Eddie Barlow, which led to Miller being noticed by the England selectors in the first place. Barlow had made Miller go in at number four and had given him much more bowling than he had ever had before. If Greig really believed him to be a potential England number three he now missed a golden chance to test his theory.

Instead England's tour selectors decided on a change in the batting order with Randall and Fletcher swapping places at three and four, Greig moving up to five, Knott to six and Tolchard dropping to seven. Then, on the morning of the match, Old dropped out of the game with a mysterious back complaint which Bernard Thomas was unable to diagnose, and the theory that some of Old's illnesses are psychosomatic was aired again. It would have made a pleasant change if he had proved fit to play through an entire series for the first time in his career. His replacement was not Woolmer, who would have added strength to the batting and been a serviceable third seamer, or Cope, who would have had a pitch far more suited to himself than to a faster bowler, but Selvey. Like

Cope and Miller, the only players on the tour not to play a Test in India, Selvey had soldiered on with determination and without complaint, but his selection now must have been almost as big a surprise to him as his original one for England the previous season. A factor in the decision was that Lever was still suffering stomach pains after a bad night.

India named an unchanged side and for the third time in the series Bedi won the all-important toss. There was less excitement this time, however, both because the stadium, which holds 47,000 people, was only three-quarters full and because news was filtering round the ground that India's genial and much-respected President, F. A. Ahmed, had died earlier in the morning. The two teams stood in the centre of the arena and the crowd stood quietly for thirty seconds as the flags on the scoreboard slid to half-mast.

The strong breeze fluttering those flags was the sole consolation for England as they took the field. The first few overs confirmed their worst fears about the pitch, on which two years previously West Indies had scored over 600 runs in their first innings and India, earlier this same season, had made 399 against New Zealand. A few balls from Willis were enough to confirm that the pitch was slow, low, flat and true: ideal for a patient run accumulator like Gavaskar. How Amiss must have envied him as he got into his stride with an on-driven four off Lever in the second over and settled in with the help of four overthrows from a Randall throw that just missed the stumps. Gaekwad was the recipient of a similar piece of good fortune and by the end of the first hour India were riding high with 49 for no wicket from twelve overs.

But with the help of the breeze and, after ten overs, a replacement ball for the new one which almost inevitably had gone out of shape, Lever began to get some movement in the air and had his first reward for determinedly keeping the ball up to the bat when Gaekwad went to clip him off his toes and spooned a gentle catch to mid-wicket. In the same over Lever appealed confidently for an l.b.w. as Surinder Amarnath went across his stumps to leg-glance, but the ball hurried away off his pads over a speedy outfield for four leg-byes. Lever was making light of his stomach upset and was now warming to his work.

The cricket took on a new bite. Selvey, who earlier had tended to overpitch, bowled a testing over to Gavaskar, but the latter countered by hooking Lever to square-leg for four and then cover-driving him crisply – only to see Randall sliding to his left to cut the ball off. At the other end Surinder looked neat, positive, alert, but vulnerable.

Fifteen minutes before lunch Underwood came on and bowled a relatively slow, teasing over to Gavaskar which, needless to say, was a maiden. At the other end Greig introduced himself. Much would depend on his unpredictable bowling; having taken the decision to leave out a third spinner he had to perform like a front-line one himself, or England's attack would be badly lopsided. Surinder hit him confidently through the covers as he overpitched in his first over, then repeated the shot less convincingly against Underwood. At lunch India were 83 for one with Gavaskar on course for his tenth Test hundred.

The way Underwood turned the ball after the interval was as ominous for England as the score. He twice appealed against Surinder for l.b.w.'s and when he had scored 34 Surinder drove only inches over the bowler's head. But if he lived a little dangerously he never missed a scoring chance, punching the ball away through the covers or down to third-man with a relish that put one in mind of Kallicharran.

Willis bowled a second innocuous spell after lunch – conditions could hardly have been worse for him – but Lever again bowled beautifully, swinging the ball more than anyone else and right on target. Gavaskar suddenly looked less confident, but it was at the other end that the wickets fell, first when Surinder was bowled playing back with an angled bat to a ball of good length which kept a little low, and then, one over later with the score 122, when Viswanath checked a drive and was caught by Lever off his own bowling.

Both the left-handers deserved their success, but the pressure came off Gavaskar and Patel when Greig made a double change, himself for Underwood and Selvey for Lever. Patel hit Selvey's first two balls, both half-volleys, for fours on either side of the wicket and the spell was broken. In defence of Greig, it was, despite the breeze, an afternoon of remorseless sunshine, and changes had to be made at some point. But Lever, who had bowled only five overs in his afternoon spell and was not looking distressed, would surely have gone on longer, tummy pains or not, and Underwood, with a wicket under his belt, would certainly have done so.

Patel's two opening fours were just a beginning. He and Gavaskar took 51 off the eight overs which Greig and Selvey bowled before tea, by which time Patel had hit eight fours in his 38, six of them off Selvey who on this pitch was money for old rope.

Patel was in truly brilliant form. Willis and Knott thought they had him caught down the legside in the over after tea but the umpire disagreed, and he continued to flash and sparkle in the sunlight as the crowd grew increasingly excited. The leg-glance off Willis with which he reached fifty in 54 balls, 40 of his runs coming in boundaries, summoned forth a roar evocative of a winning goal at Wembley, and no less a one greeted Gavaskar's cover-driven four next ball which raised the 200. Greig must have pinched himself in disbelief. Was this really India, 1977, or the Oval, 1976? Was it really Patel and Gavaskar, or Richards and Greenidge?

England's captain anxiously sought advice from Brearley and more obviously from Fletcher, who as usual was at the heart of every tactical talk. The solution was to resort to Underwood and Lever, only now the latter bowled off a short run and the aim of both was containment rather than attack. The over-rate slackened still further. England were already in a hole, and although they continued to field with skill and spirit (none more so than Tolchard) they clearly knew it. Bravely Greig continued to play to the gallery, but there was an element of whistling in the dark about his apparent gaiety. The England batsmen must have already been steeling themselves for an extension of the defensive tactics which were now perforce being adopted by the bowlers.

Patel would not be tied down: he continued to cover-drive and especially to on-drive with wristy certainty, whilst Gavaskar, his moments of doubt now forgotten, ground on remorselessly to his hundred, driving anything overpitched with remarkable power. Ten minutes from stumps he reached his goal, his second Test hundred against England. Of his nine previous Test centuries only one had been scored in India, against New Zealand earlier this same season at the same Wankhede Stadium.

But there was a final moment of consolation for England on a day which had belonged entirely to the home team from the moment the fateful coin was spun. Off the penultimate ball of the day Patel moved out of his ground to stun a ball from Greig. It spun a few inches behind Patel on the offside, and with devilishly quick reactions Knott swept the ball on to the stumps before the batsman could get his bat back.

It had been a brilliant innings of 83, the best of many good ones Patel had played in the series, and a first-day score of 261 for four off only 72·5 overs represented a fine performance, although it was little more than India might have hoped or expected having won the toss on such a pitch. England's two left-handers, Underwood and Lever, emerged from the day with enhanced credit and the fielding never wilted, but the sting of Willis had been drawn by the dullness of the brown turf, Greig had bowled some loose overs before tea and the unfortunate Selvey, asked to play at the last moment in conditions which could hardly have suited him worse, had been savaged for 80 runs in fifteen overs.

India's favourable position was underlined next morning when the turn became notably sharper for the spinners. England got the start they needed when Underwood held on to a rasping return drive from Gavaskar in the third over of the day. Now, although the new ball was at last due, Greig could attack – he is a much better off-spinner when he can do so: the sight of close fielders seems to improve his control – and it was he who bowled Yajuvendra Singh on the back stroke with a ball not far short of a good length which turned an ominously long way. The dangerous Kirmani might have been dismissed soon afterwards if Underwood had been able to cling on to another caught-and-bowled chance. Kirmani, however, had hit the ball even harder than Gavaskar and instead of a catch Underwood received a painful winding in the solar plexus.

After an hour India had progressed by only 26 runs and had lost two more wickets, but one felt now that the match would be decided not by a sudden collapse of the tail or by any tail-end heroics: instead the crunch would come when England began batting. As though to underline this, Underwood took two more wickets before lunch. Kirmani was caught behind trying to force another fairly sharp turner off the back foot, and Prasanna, after hitting two loose balls from Greig for successive fours, was bowled by the arm ball, further proof of Underwood's versatility. In truth the innings should have been polished off by lunch with no need of the new ball, but Tolchard, the best of a moderate bunch of short-leg fieldsmen, missed two chances, both of them very sharp, one off Underwood, the other off Greig. The latter kicked the ground in frustration.

Greig again withheld the new ball after the interval and with the third delivery of the afternoon he had Ghavri l.b.w. as he aimed furiously in the direction of mid-wicket. Bedi and Chandra gave the crowd the entertainment all last-wicket partnerships (especially between these two) ought to, before Lever came back to hit Chandra's stumps with the new ball and the first straight ball he bowled.

India's last seven wickets, six on this second day, had fallen for the addition of only 77 more runs, and whilst their score of 338 was a formidable one which went most of the way to insuring them against defeat it was not quite big enough for their peace of mind. Underwood's bowling had been masterly, and the policy of keeping him fresh for the Test matches was paying off handsomely.

Knowing that a major reply was essential England naturally began with extreme caution. The preliminary overs by Ghavri and Gavaskar were safely negotiated although Brearley revealed his nervousness with some taut, unsynchronised strokes. Bedi came on in the sixth over of the innings but for the first time in the series neither he nor his fellow spinners could achieve an early break-through. The realisation that after living on our nerves for so long we might at last be about to see one of those Tests of our boyhood, when batsmen used to make bowlers toil for hours in hot sunshine, dawned gradually. But the change from tentativeness to assurance came quite suddenly by means of four fine shots from Brearley.

All tour he had striven without success to find the smooth effortless form of that first double hundred in Poona. Now his silken touch came back and it was as if the doubts and misfortunes surrounding much of his batting since had never been. First he hooked Ghavri with clinical certainty to end the pretence of this spirited but very ordinary opening bowler to be an oriental Tyson or Thomson (though, to be fair, he had dismissed Amiss round the corner with a popper in the last match and his stock ball, a short rising delivery aimed at the chest, had to be watched carefully). Next Brearley persuaded a half-volley through the off-side field with pinpoint accuracy. In the next over he moved a pace down the wicket to on-drive Bedi between the stumps and mid-on, a shot warmly and generously applauded by the bowler, before square-cutting a short ball just backward of cover for four more. This time Bedi wrung his hands in anguish. This was a pitch on which the short ball and the overpitched alike could be punished with confidence. The pace of it was slow and the bounce even, and it was this latter point in particular which made it so much more friendly to batsmen than those in other matches. Moreover Underwood and Greig, by pushing the ball through, had achieved a faster turn than Bedi and Prasanna.

By tea England had reached the haven of fifty without loss. Soon Brearley and Amiss passed the highest opening stand by either side in the series and when Brearley reached his own fifty, forty minutes from the close, he had hit eight fours to Amiss's none. By stumps he had extended his boundaries to eleven, almost entirely made up of smooth and pleasing cover-drives, and England were 99 for no wicket.

Amiss had played one of his stickiest innings, a typically valuable and gutsy effort but one which became less free and more introspective as the shadows lengthened. He was missed when 20, a very wide snick off Prasanna which Kirmani did well to get his gloves to, and towards the end he was missing full-tosses and wide legside balls. Those runs might in the long term have proved valuable. But he was still there at the end of the day, and that was the most important thing.

Because the funeral of the Indian President was taking place on Sunday, 13 February, the rest day in the Test was held on that day instead of after the third day of the game as normal. So for once the cricketers had a Sunday rest and plenty of time to think about the interesting state of the game. The odds had shifted during the second day from a likely Indian win to a likely draw, but no one was quite sure what the effect would be of a baking in the sun followed by the mowing of the pitch authorised by the playing conditions for the third day. If either of these two factors were to add pace to the wicket India's spinners might in an instant become unplayable terrors again.

Brearley began Monday's play in the same vein as before, turning Prasanna's first ball round the corner for two and continuing to look for and to acquire runs in a way which at once looked busy yet unhurried. Amiss, so sticky during the first stage of his innings, soon got into gear when he resumed with a wristy flick through mid-wicket off Prasanna. But it was the off-spinner, starting with three short-legs, who turned the ball most dangerously.

If the pitch had indeed gained a little in pace it was Chandrasek-har who ought perhaps to have taken most advantage of it, but he was in one of his perverse moods. Brearley greeted him with the subtlest and finest of leg-glances, only to see the four runs which would have taken his score to 82 transformed into leg-byes by the umpire. Brearley's tension as a first Test hundred loomed was plainly evident in the way that he stalked about the crease to get over his disappointment, before composing himself again and facing the bowler with the exaggerated high backlift which precedes his actual stroke.

It was Amiss, however, who got most of Chandra's wild deliveries. He smacked a long-hop to mid-wicket for four, then repeated the shot with equal force, this time the ball carrying to the boundary after glancing the dark mop of curly black hair on the head of Yajuvendra at short-leg. This brought Amiss to 50 after three hours and forty minutes of struggle. All his fours had come on this third morning, but although he received two successive full-tosses from Chandra he could not add to his score.

Bedi, sweat staining his blue patka black on the part of the cloth which covered his forehead, came back in Chandra's place and when the last ball of his first over popped it carried off the top outside edge of Amiss's bat via Kirmani to Viswanath, who held a fine, low left-handed catch at slip. The breakthrough had come at last after an opening stand of 146, the first century opening stand for England since Wood and Edrich had scored one against Australia at Lord's in August 1975.

A crucial period had been reached and England now had two pieces of luck of the kind they had not been granted at Bangalore. Randall was so eager to get in that he was on his feet at the pavilion gate even as Amiss took his first stride back from the wicket. But he had to wait for the best part of five minutes whilst drinks were taken, England having scored 47 in the first hour off seventeen overs. Then, after a protracted setting of his field and an especially fastidious placement of the close catchers, partly of course to draw out Randall's agony, Bedi at last bowled him his first ball. 'Arkle' pushed out at it and Viswanath fell forward to catch the ball, instantly claiming the wicket with support from all around him. Randall looked indignant and stood his ground, explaining later that the ball had come off his pad. Certainly umpire Rao stood motionless. He was probably correct, although perhaps the gods were righting here the wrong done to Randall when he was adjudged caught at short-leg in the previous Test. Now he looked more than ever like an expectant father outside a maternity ward, pacing about, adjusting his cap, fiddling with his pads, looking up at the sky, and generally giving the impression of a nervous wreck.

If Randall were to settle he needed help from his partner. But Brearley, in the very next over, played an indeterminate pick-up shot off Prasanna and the ball carried out to the right of Gavaskar who, after an agonising dive and juggle, dropped it. Brearley then was 87, and much nervous, tense, exciting cricket followed, with Bedi bowling teasingly well but Randall hitting him with excellent timing in between playing and missing outside the off-stump.

These two were together at lunch, but England's comfortable-looking score of 170 for one was deceptive. Their batting, especially in the second hour, had been anything but reassuring, and this was not surprising since the surface of the pitch was starting to go in places, and both Bedi and Prasanna had bowled beautifully.

The picture soon changed in the afternoon as three England wickets went down for 31 runs. The deserving Prasanna took the first two. Randall went ten minutes after the interval, falling to a rather weak shot off a shortish ball which he steered precisely to Gaekwad at short mid-wicket. It was a disappointing end to an innings which was developing promisingly, and meant a great opportunity missed by Randall. No one was any wiser about his true potential as a Test player. It is worth repeating that he received little encouragement from Brearley's struggles at the other end. It was sad that an innings which had been so fluent for most of its course should have become moribund after Gavaskar's missed chance. Though Brearley batted for eighty minutes after that he added only four more runs before, in the over after Randall's demise, he moved out of his ground to stun Prasanna's spin and was beaten in the air and stumped with a flourish by Kirmani. England were 190 for three with Fletcher and Greig together and the innings, like the match, at a crucial stage. These two seemed to have the situation in hand, and Fletcher at last appeared to be settling down to play a decent innings when he quite legitimately shaped to pull a short, fast ball from Chandra. It bounced higher and came on faster than he had expected and he was caught off the top edge by slip running back. Chandra had got away with any number of loose balls, and there were more to come, but Prasanna wheeled on through the hot afternoon with a stamina which made fools of those who had said at the start of the series that he had become too tubby with advancing years.

Greig once again met the crisis with a commanding innings. With him there was no hasty prodding or unorthodox attacking shots of the kind that Knott now used to try to unsettle the bowlers' length. He simply stood up straight and played each ball calmly on its merits, scoring mainly off the short balls with strokes of controlled power, but once stepping out when Prasanna flighted a ball higher to hit it straight back over his head.

Knott swept and dabbed with mixed success until, when he had reached 20, he missed another intended sweep off Bedi and Gavaskar claimed a catch at point. Bedi and all the close fielders shouted an appeal as well and when umpire Rao turned them down there were scenes of bad-tempered dissension by the fielders and loud booing accompanied by the throwing of hundreds of red cardboard hats from the crowd. It was all very unsavoury and the standards of sportsmanship with which the series had begun were seen to be slipping fast.

England were 247 for four at tea, but again they suddenly slipped back after the interval. With the second ball of the evening session Chandra bowled Knott as he went back and the ball hurried through low. Tolchard came in and for a few minutes made everything look very easy. He was undone by an obvious yet nonetheless intelligent ploy. Prasanna saw the batsman dancing down the pitch a fraction before he released the ball and fired it well wide of the leg-stump. Tolchard, several feet from the safety of his crease, made a vain lunge, then turned to see Kirmani exultantly sweeping off the bails. Thus were England, still a long way short of India's 338, reduced to their captain and his tail which, with Old not playing, was a longer one than usual.

J.K. Lever, the first 'rabbit' from the hutch, had already proved several times that his temperament and technique were not to be underestimated, and he did so once again. Greig knew that he could not take liberties and get away with them but half-an-hour from stumps he swept Bedi away to square-leg with a splendid flourish for his seventh four. It took him to fifty after two hours and forty minutes of responsible batting which had kept his side very much in the game. But well though he had despatched the bad balls he had never taken control, especially of Prasanna whose figures throughout the day had been outstanding. He bowled for 75 minutes in two morning spells of 8-1-20-0 and 9-4-7-0; bowled throughout the afternoon taking two for 17 in fifteen overs, six of them maidens; and came back for more in the relative cool of the evening, his final spell earning him one for seven from seven more guileful overs.

England began the fourth day with four men left, 53 runs behind. In theory, with three-fifths of the game gone, a draw was the most likely result. But the pitch was now taking so much spin that a positive result was very much on, and since England had to bat last with the pitch at its worst it was India who held the advantage.

Bedi soon underlined the point. After Greig had sliced Chandra's warming-up long-hop for the first four of the day Lever was well caught at point off a sharp turner in the second over. In all he had batted 85 minutes for seven runs and the time used up was very helpful to England. Bedi did not take so long to get rid of

Above Yajuvendra Singh, playing in his first Test match, held seven catches at Bangalore and in doing so equalled two world Test records. Here he has caught Randall off Prasanna in England's first innings, another disputed decision.
Below Brearley's highest Test innings (91) ends at Bombay when he advances down the wicket to Prasanna, misses and is stumped by Kirmani

Above Fletcher sweeps Prasanna for four during his invaluable innings of 58 not out in the second innings at Bombay.
Below Tony Greig – in familiar style – hits out at Bedi in the final Test. Bedi was hit off the back foot more often than in previous series.

Underwood, who is a quicker scorer but less patient than Lever and who soon took the bait of a flighted ball on his leg-stump. Bedi's intention was probably a catch in the deep but Underwood missed, so that was that.

Selvey, incidentally playing only his third innings of the entire tour (and one of these had been nought not out), was almost caught off his first ball from Bedi and the sight of this decided Greig that he must now farm the bowling and garner what runs he could. Has there ever been such an entertainer as this mountainous man? He moved a massive step down the pitch to hit Chandra back over his head for a four which was inches from being a six, then sneaked a single off the last ball of the over with a snick off the inside edge, running backwards down the wicket to take on Bedi. The latter spread his field wide and the challenge was accepted at once as Bedi flighted a ball which Greig hit mightily into the second tier of the stand at long-off. From the Nursery End at Lord's the ball might have landed amongst the members in the pavilion library. Bedi called up Prasanna to relieve Chandra and as Prasanna went through his arm exercises Greig imitated him. The crowd missed this little joke, but they were enjoying it all quite as much as England's captain. However, it was tubby little 'Pras' who had the last laugh. His fifth ball kept low and as Greig made room to push a single to keep the bowling the ball evaded the bat and hit the leg-stump. Selvey scored five before Willis pushed out at Bedi and looked disappointed to be given out caught at point by Gavaskar. In seven overs Bedi had taken three for 13 and England's last four wickets had fallen in under an hour of this fourth morning for just 32 more runs.

India's lead was 21. England would have liked at least that sort of lead themselves, but they knew their task now: to bowl India out cheaply. The heat haze – or was it a sea fret? – which had laden the atmosphere when play began, had cleared when Willis and Lever began bowling, and there was no discernible swing. Indeed but for some brilliant ground fielding, with Randall, Underwood and Amiss all making marvellous stops, the score might have been more than ten for no wicket when Underwood and Greig came on for the sixth and seventh overs of the innings.

One wondered whether Greig might not have held himself back a while longer and used Willis and Lever at least a little more. At any rate, although Underwood at once got the ball to turn past the outside edge, Gavaskar was in devastating form, pulling and cutting anything short with the strength and timing of a boxer aiming a short-arm punch. Too much from Greig *was* short of a length, and even Underwood allowed Gavaskar to get on to the back foot more than he would have wanted.

At lunch India were 34 for no wicket and Gavaskar and Gaekwad had exactly doubled that score before Underwood finally broke through after India's highest opening stand of the series. Both the openers played very well but both also needed luck, as anyone would against a top-class spinner on a pitch turning as much as this one now was. Gaekwad, for instance, drove Underwood in the air only a yard or two short of Greig at extra-cover, and later Gavaskar, who had now forced Greig to take himself off and bring on Lever in a defensive role, would have been caught off his glove if Knott had not slipped. In the same over Gavaskar was denied a certain four when a furious cover slash was superbly stopped by Randall, who celebrated by catching his cap in the middle of a cartwheel.

India's lead was 89 when Gavaskar moved out to drive Underwood without quite getting to the pitch of the ball and skied it high over Willis at mid-off. One of the safest fielders in the England side made no mistake, running back and catching the ball in two hands, facing away from the wicket. Once the first wicket had been taken others followed quickly. Surinder Amarnath soon settled in to play another perky, positive and useful innings but Gaekwad went in Underwood's next over as he was drawn out of his ground, saw the ball turn away to the off and watched Knott whip off the bails. Two overs from Underwood later Patel apparently snicked the ball on to his boot and was caught in the gully. Patel looked angry and the crowd needed no further cue. Prolonged booing broke out and again the red cardboard hats came flying out. Although the crowds at Bombay were – with the series decided – the smallest (averaging less than 30,000 a day) they were also, by a fraction, the most excitable.

At tea India were 88 for three and soon afterwards Viswanath was out to yet another loose stroke, hitting Greig to Lever at mid-wicket, exactly as he had done in the second innings at Calcutta. There, however, England's progress ended for a while. Surinder hit anything off a good length with admirable decisiveness and Yajuvendra Singh, by dint of some fine shots interspersed with extraordinary good luck outside his off-stump against Under-wood, stayed with him. England appealed confidently for a catch by Knott in the course of three successive balls which beat Yajuvendra, but the latter signalled that his bat had touched his pad rather than the ball and it was good to see the umpire's decision accepted with good grace. Unlike the Indians the day before, England's team continued on the whole to resist the contagious histrionics which have become so prevalent in Test cricket all over the world. For this Greig, a sinner rather than a saint so often in the past, deserves most of the credit. On the other hand India, with the series lost, were under greater pressure.

The sixth-wicket pair added 44 important runs, although Bedi would have wanted them to come more quickly than they did. But no liberties could be taken with Underwood, who kept going with marvellous stamina and accuracy from the pavilion end, all the time threatening to take another wicket, and Lever contributed a typically disciplined defensive spell at the other end. He was succeeded by Greig, whose bowling in the afternoon was a good deal tighter but who must have wished in his heart of hearts that he had Cope or Miller to call upon.

The last wicket of the day came in an unexpected way. Yajuvendra hit Underwood hard into the covers and at once called for a sharpish but distinctly possible single. But the sight of the menacing Randall moving in on the ball dissuaded Surinder from accepting and he refused to budge from his crease. Randall so often creates a run-out chance without completing the execution but this time he was lucky; he threw to the bowler's end, the wrong one, and Underwood in turn threw the ball to Knott, who took off the bails before Yajuvendra could complete his return sprint. He had, however, played his best innings for India and perhaps done enough to earn a place on his country's tour of Australia the following year. He was certainly not lacking either temperament or confidence.

One could hardly have wished for a more promising position, from a spectator's viewpoint, than the one which prevailed at the start of the final day of the series. India, 161 runs to the good with five wickets left, held most of the aces but England's hand was far from hopeless. Whatever happened early in the day their batsmen were bound to be put to a severe test.

It was India's turn first and they made their intentions plain enough from the first ball. They were after quick runs and Surinder and Kirmani were an ideal pair to seek them. Twice in the first over there were near run-outs as five runs were stolen off Lever who, until

then, had conceded only 13 from eleven overs. Then, in
Underwood's second over, Kirmani, four not out, opened his
shoulders to drive and Randall at extra-cover circled under a
straightforward skier. Instead of taking it simply in front of his
chest in the time-honoured manner – I always think of H.A.
Pawson demonstrating the correct method in the old *MCC
Coaching Book* – he slipped on to his back at the last moment and
the ball popped out of his hands.

The unworthy suspicion crept in that England might be thinking
only of a draw, and that the longer India batted the less batting
England would have to do. But when Kirmani, after one skilful
squirt for four off a Lever half-volley past a non-existent slip, hit
another skier in Underwood's next over, Greig made no mistake
with the catch this time. It was Underwood's 28th wicket of the
series and he thus passed Fred Titmus's record by an English
bowler for a series in India, set during Mike Smith's tour in
1963–64.

Surinder Amarnath, whose return to the Indian side had
coincided with their revival, soon made up for Kirmani's fall by
pugnaciously square-cutting Underwood to the cover boundary,
then lifting Lever over mid-off for his sixth four to bring up his fifty
in two-and-three-quarter hours. The cardboard hats rained over
the wire-meshed fence on to the outfield and the boos started again
when Greig extended the hiatus by asking the umpires to inspect the
ball lest it should have gone out of shape. Greig has never been one
to apply the manual of gamesmanship at all furtively and when a
little while later a blue-shirted spectator came on to shake him by
the hand England's captain was only too happy to pass the time of
day with him before ushering him off the field. Bedi's thoughts
would have been worth reading, but as an expert at public relations
and master of gamesmanship himself he had qualified with almost as
good a degree as Greig's.

Surinder's fine innings came to an unfortunate end when Ghavri
refused a run to Underwood at wide mid-on and Underwood's
return to the bowler's end ran him out. India had not gained much
for the future from this series, but Surinder's name could already be
written down with confidence for the tour of Australia.

The hectic pace of the morning's cricket hotted up still further
now. Ghavri turned Underwood to Fletcher at leg-slip and
'Deadly' leapt up and down three times like an excited schoolboy,
for he had now taken five wickets not just for the first time in the

series but also for the 100th time in his first-class career. Moreover, he had now equalled Richie Benaud's haul of 248 Test wickets. Only Statham, Trueman and Gibbs lay ahead of him.

England's other left-handed hero, of course, was the faithful 'J.K.' and it was he who with two straight yorkers, one l.b.w. and the other bowled, ended India's innings. In 75 minutes and 12·4 overs five wickets had fallen and 52 runs been scored. England needed 214 to win in five minutes over four hours. The din in the stadium, the tension in the air, was already too much for those of a 'weak or nervous disposition'. And it could only get tenser and noisier. England chose the light roller and Amiss and Brearley opened with 35 minutes to bat before lunch. The extraordinary passions aroused by a close cricket Test in India were quickly evident. Ghavri and Gavaskar bowled a token over each. But Gavaskar's sole intention, it seemed, was to follow through down the wicket and rough it up for the spinners. He had got away with a similar shoddy practice at Bangalore but Amiss hotly pointed it out to the umpires this time and Gavaskar was warned to stop it. The wicket was tricky enough as it was. England were 17 for no wicket at lunch and 34 when in the nineteenth over Amiss pushed out at Bedi, for once did not stifle the sharp spin, and was caught at slip off the outside edge.

Bedi may have been unlucky not to have got Amiss l.b.w. with the arm ball a little before this, but equally Prasanna may have been lucky to get Brearley, given out caught by Yajuvendra Singh at very close forward short-leg, four runs later. Under three hours now remained, but the Indian spinners were getting the first scent of victory. It soon wafted away again as Randall and Fletcher, youth and experience, took over England's helm.

Both played judiciously and well. Fletcher this time resorted to nothing ungainly and the turning-point for him came when Chandra replaced Bedi at the pavilion end in mid-afternoon and bowled three successive offside long-hops, which Fletcher cut with rapier force to different parts of the cover boundary. This was the real Fletcher, too seldom seen in Test cricket, the players' Fletcher respected inside the game as a skilled and canny cricketer. All the natural ability and the experience which his fellow selectors had backed to come good sooner or later was doing so now. Not before time, perhaps, but still at the time when he was most needed. His three fours took him into the twenties and England into the sixties, but Chandra had to come off, and indeed to go off the field for a while for treatment to a strained leg muscle, and against Prasanna and Bedi there were no easy pickings.

Randall, indeed, was reduced to all-out defence, but he looked a good deal more at home than in the first innings and it was a surprise change by Bedi which undid him. Ghavri was called up to bowl Underwood-style orthodox spin and he had Randall caught behind with one that turned and lifted in his first over. Randall had batted for 83 minutes and the value of his innings was more than its sum. Greig hit the first ball he received from Ghavri firmly through the covers for four and the heat gradually went out of the situation. At tea England were 92 for three and when the last twenty overs began they still needed 103 to win. In a Gillette Cup match, or if the series were still to be decided, they would from this point have had a go, and indeed might have expected to win, but they could hardly be blamed for making a draw the first objective. Bedi said later that he was anxious about the possibility of an England win at this stage, but the last English hopes of a glorious victory departed when Greig opened his shoulders to hit Ghavri in the third of the last twenty overs and was calmly and skilfully held by Bedi running back from mid-off. Greig walked back with boos ringing in his ears and a bemused look on his face. After all he had done for crowds around India, and all the compliments he had paid them, he must have felt for a moment that he never wanted to return.

He must also have felt very annoyed with himself, more so when Ghavri, suddenly a potential matchwinner, got a ball to turn behind Knott's legs to knock out his middle stump in the fifth over of the last twenty. A game which had been on the verge of going to sleep was suddenly pulsatingly alive again, and the team with winning ideas was once again India. The crowd's din, echoing from the tin roof of the stands all round the stadium, was deafening. But Fletcher was looking less and less likely to get out, playing his defensive strokes with the bat almost parallel to the ground, and he now found in Tolchard a nerveless and assured partner and an equally shrewd player of the turning ball. Tolchard even dared to follow through with his front-foot strokes, occasionally piercing the covers, and he generally played so well that one wondered what he might have achieved if he had gone in at number five when victory was still possible. He might have been out, three overs from safety, but Kirmani failed to provide Prasanna with the legside stumping he had achieved in the first innings. Yet the most skilful 'not-out merchant' in the MCC party just missed another star against his name when Ghavri, returning after two better but still innocuous overs from Chandra, had him caught close on the offside. Ghavri then ended the match and the series by persuading a carefree Lever to go for a big hit off the last ball and having him caught by Patel at cover. So, in somewhat unlikely circumstances, Ghavri achieved his best Test figures. Bedi, the man India looked to as their main executioner, had bowled only two overs after tea. He was, he said, mentally and physically exhausted. But it had been a collective failure by the Indian spinners. Chandra, disturbed by his leg injury, had been a negative force, and Prasanna, well as he had bowled again, had lost the extra nip which had brought him success in the first innings. Fletcher's technique, flawless to the end, and his determination to justify his presence in England's team, had denied him all the way.

So, at last, it was all over. Fletcher returned, with his face red and beaming, to the embraces of his colleagues. The speeches were made in front of the pavilion before a crowd who had got more than their money's worth on the final day. England's team collected the majority of the various prizes and Greig added 5,000 rupees to the team pool as 'Man of the Series' on top of the 10,000 awarded for the winning of the series itself. For the final time he led his team on a lap of honour, and there was no booing now. Then, back at the Taj Mahal Hotel, Ken Barrington and his team gave a party to thank as many as possible of the hosts who had treated them so generously over the three months that had elapsed since their first stop in Bombay. Any heat-of-the-moment bitterness was forgiven and the two teams mingled happily. For some MCC players the evening finished with a visit to the *Queen Elizabeth II*, moored close to the Gateway of India in the middle of its world cruise.

As with MCC, the massive liner's next port of call was Colombo, the steaming capital of the tropical island of Sri Lanka.

Chapter Eight
POST-MORTEM

Greig's tour de force was complete. It was difficult to recall now the dismal facts surrounding his side at the outset. England had not won a Test for the best part of two years. They had never won under Greig. They had won only two Tests on Indian soil since Douglas Jardine's tour over forty years before. And since that time they had not won a series. Nigel Howard's and M. J. K. Smith's teams drew; Ted Dexter's and Tony Lewis's both lost. The climate, illnesses, slow pitches, spin bowlers and sometimes even the crowds and the umpires had contrived to undo them all to a greater or lesser degree; it is also true that Greig's team was the first to be fully representative of England's strength.

The cricket played in 1933–34 can have borne little resemblance to the latest series. Field placings had altered completely and the fielding improved. Batsmen before the war had to contend, generally speaking, with outfielding less athletic and with close fielding less rapacious. The sight of a Yajuvendra Singh, hovering fearlessly at the batsman's hip pocket, would have elicited cries of 'the man's mad' in the old days. This, however, is just one extra pressure the modern batsman faces in India. It is difficult to believe, for instance, that crowds were quite as noisy in the past or so eager to yell an appeal every time a ball hit the pad of an opposition player. It is documented that in one match on his tour Jardine ordered one of his bowlers to wait until the unruly comments coming from the crowd had ceased. The biggest difference, however, is without doubt the deterioration of the pitches. This does most to explain why the typical match in India only a few years ago, a draw dominated by batsmen, did not once occur in the 1976–77 series. At Bombay it looked as though the wicket might last, but after two days it was affording all the spinners plenty of turn and only the fact that it became, if anything, even slower as the match proceeded enabled batsmen to survive for long in the later stages.

England's three-one win in the series was probably a fair

reflection not only of events but also of the true strengths of the two teams. India's batting was even weaker than England's and their bowling fatally lacked balance. Throughout the series Gavaskar and Patel were their most consistent batsmen, but the former, India's sole undisputed world-class batsman but a moody character, did not always bat in the way that the situation dictated (witness the way he sacrificed himself at Bangalore.) Patel is a talented player, but the really big Test innings contiues to elude him. Gavaskar often seemed to be fighting a lone battle until Surinder Amarnath came along in the last two Tests to add a considerable presence to the batting. Unlike the others Sharma was probably unlucky to play at the start of the series rather than at the end and he was never an easy man to get out. He had the honour of being the only Indian other than Gavaskar to score a hundred against the touring team, though not of course in a Test. The major batting disappointment was Viswanath, who played only one innings of substance and did not seem able to summon the necessary concentration to settle down to a long Test innings.

Of India's spinners it was Bedi and Prasanna who emerged with greatest credit, and the biggest reason for their failure to undo the England batting as effectively as they had four years before was Chandrasekhar's disappointing form. Of his 19 wickets in the five games, 14 came at Madras and Bangalore. The unpredictability was as great as ever, but the old devil was lacking. Prasanna finally proved, to all Englishmen at least, that he is a superior off-spinner to Venkataraghavan, that most likeable cricketer whose bowling lacks the masterly subtleties of his great rival. Greig said at the end of the series that Prasanna is the best off-spinner in the world, and it was hard to argue with his assertion.

Considering the cares of captaincy which would have worn out many another, Bedi had a remarkably good series with the ball, taking 25 wickets at 22 runs apiece and never being fully mastered. If he had found a short-leg of Yajuvendra's abilities earlier in the series he would have added further to that tally. Solkar's recall at Calcutta proved disastrous in this respect, which was another reason why MCC found batting against the spinners easier than it had been on the last trip when Solkar had been at his brilliant best.

Bedi's captaincy stood up well in the field, even in a losing cause. He manipulated his bowling skilfully and rarely missed a chance to apply pressure on a batsman. In a way his job was made easier by the very paucity of his seam attack; he had fewer combinations to play with than most Test captains. The same could be said of Clive Lloyd when operating in England with Roberts, Holding, Holder and Daniel. The difference is that Bedi is himself one of the bowlers in the equation, and he was never shy to use himself. He had a useful all-round cricketer in Ghavri to call on in three of the Tests but the younger Amarnath did not in this series measure up as either batsman or bowler. India desperately needed a genuine number six batsman and a genuine fast or fast-medium bowler.

As far as the number six position was concerned, Mankad was not this time given a fair chance and Vengsarkar was too inexperienced to take his. The latter was certainly the most talented young player MCC came across, and a season playing county cricket in England, even at 2nd XI level, would soon develop his abilities. It would be sad if he goes to Australia, finds himself out of his depth and subsequently loses his confidence. On the other hand the faster wickets there may well bring out the best in him.

Yajuvendra Singh will always recall his first Test match with great pride. From appearing a no-hoper with the bat in the early games against the touring side he developed all the time in the Test innings he played. He lacks neither courage nor confidence but has a good deal to learn yet.

Overall, Indian cricket followers and administrators cannot but be concerned, although it is easy to overdo the gravity of their situation. Much the same side as the one that lost to England did, after all, score 406 for four in the fourth innings to beat the West Indies at Port of Spain, and in the first part of the Indian season New Zealand were comfortably beaten. But the major weakness of the side, a lack of fast bowlers, remains, and so do the forces which hold back the development of the game in the sub-continent despite interest unequalled in any other country in the world, with the possible exception of Barbados. The two basic problems are the slow wickets which retard fast bowlers and therefore deny the batsmen practice against them, and the fact that there are so few first-class cricket clubs. In other words, despite the immense population of India, the selectors must choose from only a small group of players. This, more than anything else, is a social problem.

If Indian cricket took a half-step backwards in the three months of the MCC tour, English cricket made some solid gains. The most obvious was a new team spirit, which was partly the result of travelling together in a strange land, partly of good off-the-field leadership by Greig, ably supported by the other central figures –

Barrington, Brearley and Thomas – and partly of the success on the field. Of the thirteen matches played MCC won four, lost only one – the fourth Test – and drew the remaining eight.

From the first day to the last Tony Greig was the central figure. His successful tour four years before had given him a head start with the Indian public and throughout the tour his handling not only of the crowds but also of the media was masterly. Crowds never seemed to tire of his gestures to them, sometimes paternalistic, sometimes humble, always smiling and reflecting the extraordinary energy and enthusiasm of the man. There was usually a double purpose behind his performances. Greig is a natural entertainer and he enjoys making crowds laugh; but he also knew that England's chances could only be enhanced by having the crowd, if not exactly on his side, at least not hostile.

His handling of the umpires was equally tactful and diplomatic. He began by saying publicly that Indian umpires were on the whole as good as any other umpires in the world, and he went out of his way to be polite to them. Every cricketer soon learns that this is the only way to be. Perhaps MCC were fortunate in that their tour followed hard on the heels of New Zealand's, and New Zealand had reacted angrily to what they considered unfair treatment by the umpires. MCC, as a result, were favourably compared to their predecessors. Greig told his team that they were not to appeal unless they thought a man was out, and that they were not to show dissension if they did not like a decision given against them. It would certainly not be true to say that these rules were universally obeyed but, generally speaking, they were kept well in mind. It was an example which all Test sides should follow. Indeed no international cricket conference these days passes without some piously expressed hope that dissension will be stamped out. Not only is polite treatment of umpires, who for little thanks or monetary reward do one of the hardest jobs in sport, good manners and therefore good for the image of a game which is in danger of becoming tarnished by commercialism, but also there can be little doubt that England's policy gained them, on the whole, unbiased umpiring. Only at Bangalore could they claim to have been unfairly treated. If the occasional bad decision was made in the other Tests India were equal sufferers. On the other hand the Indians, especially as the series went on and the pressure on them mounted, tended to react less subtly when they disagreed with a decision.

Greig is well aware of his responsibilities as a major figure in the

game and he is always happy to make himself available for
interviews with those whose typewriters and microphones enlarge
his reputation in the public eye. Perhaps there were some cynics in
his team who felt that journalists paid too much attention to him
and that he hogged too much of the limelight. They may have had a
point, but if Greig is a shrewd enough businessman to know that
public self-promotion is a kind of free advertisement for his various
off-the-field interests he is also a godsend to journalists. Incidents
on the field which in the days of old might have been interpreted by
guesswork from the press box can now be verified or explained by
direct reference to the captain.

On the field Greig still has much to learn about tactics. He
recognised this by relying heavily for advice on his two main
lieutenants, Brearley and Fletcher. There were times when one felt
that he had two vice-captains and although there was no jealousy
on Brearley's part I felt this was another good reason why only one
of them should have been on the tour. If Greig did not take so many
odd decisions as he had against the West Indies he did not always do
the orthodox thing, which nine times out of ten is the best course. At
Bombay, for instance, he took the pressure off the Indian batsmen
at a stroke by replacing Lever and Underwood, who were very
much on top, with Selvey and himself, who in a few loose overs
transformed the atmosphere and course of the whole day's cricket.

Test cricket is all about pressure, and Greig understands this
instinctively. It is difficult to think of a player who both with bat and
ball strives so immediately and constantly to establish his presence,
to let his opponents know that he is the master and that he is going
to dictate the terms. It is all the stranger therefore that on occasion
he still tends to take the defensive course. On the whole, however, he
led his team very well in India, and his dogged adherence to the
theory that, since Indian batsmen play seam bowling with less
confidence than they do spin, he should rely mainly on a three-
pronged seam attack, proved correct except during the fourth and
fifth Tests when an extra specialist spinner would have improved
the England attack. This was especially true at Bombay when Old
dropped out on the morning of the match and should not have been
replaced by Selvey.

As far as his own cricket was concerned Greig can be proud of the
part he played despite all the daunting strains of being captain on
possibly the most arduous of all tours. His batting in the minor
matches was calculated only to entertain. After a superb exhibition

of hitting at Poona his attempts to give the crowds the 'sixers' they so adored, and indeed expected from him, were generally less successful, but his generous and exhibitionist nature put the interests of the public before any private wish to get serious batting practice. In the Tests his mood switched as if by magic and for once he did not play a single irresponsible innings. This suggested a new maturity, of which the clearest example was his self-denying hundred at Calcutta. At Delhi he helped to rescue England when he came in at 65 for four and at once made batting look an ·easier business; at Madras he shared a crucial stand in the middle of the innings with Brearley; and it was with Brearley again that he ensured a solid England reply to India's highest total of the series at Bombay. The captain's only first-innings failure was at Bangalore, which also happened to be the scene of England's sole defeat.

Greig's decision in the final Test to go in one place higher, at number five, was, one hopes, a guide to the shape of things to come. As the scorer of eleven Test hundreds he bats too low at number six. Equally the side would be better balanced if he were in future to bowl rather less and to consider himself a shock bowler, coming on like a Ted Dexter or an Eddie Barlow to break a partnership or tie up one end for a while, rather than as a stock off-spinner as he does at present. The brilliant inspirational performance he produced at Trinidad when he undid the West Indies with thirteen wickets in the match has turned out to be one of cricket history's freaks. He is a very useful off-break bowler but not as good as that match-winning performance suggested. The loop to his flight which deceived so many good players on that occasion has not appeared very often since. He certainly did not fail as a spinner in India, but ten wickets at 33 runs apiece in the series confirmed the impression that England would be stronger if Underwood had the support of a specialist spinner of the requisite class. Since Cope did not play in the Tests and Greig appeared not to consider Miller seriously as an off-spinner one was all the sorrier that Edmonds was not on the tour. In 1977 England's selectors would have to make up their minds whether Edmonds and Underwood, both left-arm spinners, could operate successfully together or whether there is an off-spinner good enough to allow a more balanced spin attack. If Cope or Miller had been chosen instead of Selvey at Bombay they would have had more evidence to guide them.

The greatest gain of the tour was the formidable combination of Willis, Lever and Old. It was a tremendous help to the team that

Willis remained fit throughout once he had shaken off his early illness. He was tenderly and wisely used by Greig in short bursts, and even on the slow pitches on which, with the exception of Madras, the Tests were played he bowled genuinely fast. In addition to his wholehearted bowling, his reliable fielding and occasional useful innings were welcome contributions. With his long brown bushy hair, his slow southern drawl and deep voice, he is a genuinely funny man. At cocktail parties even the most pompous High Commission man or high-level cricket official, alarmed at first by his casual, apparently rather weird manners, is eventually disarmed by his idiosyncratic charm. In a way he is the successor to Freddie Trueman in this respect. He has certainly offended one or two people with his offhand manner and occasional tactless gesture (when the Bombay crowd started throwing orange peel at him he put his hands under his arm-pits and walked about like a monkey) but a team needs someone to make them laugh, and with Randall and Willis this one was well served. He is also a kind-hearted colleague when things have been going badly for a fellow-player.

The great find of the tour was his new-ball partner John Lever. The mystery is that no one appreciated during his several seasons of consistent success for Essex that he was a bowler capable of performing with equal success at the highest level. All the virtues he had shown in county cricket were evident on this tour: stamina, accuracy, self-discipline, determination, commonsense. At Delhi he showed something else, a devastating late swing. It is possible that he will never produce a performance quite like the one which removed the first four Indian batsmen in that never-to-be-forgotten second evening at Delhi. On the other hand, it is probable that he will continue to bowl steadily and effectively for England for several years. He never bowls badly and is always likely to take a useful wicket. Moreover, he is a brilliant fielder, a capable and sensible batsman and a quiet, level-headed character who came through the mud-slinging which followed the Vaseline affair with enhanced credit. Lever's success in taking 26 wickets in his first Test series both delighted and surprised him. He is well aware that Australians will not fall to him as easily and softly as the Indians sometimes did.

Chris Old was the third of the seamers, and his last-minute withdrawal from the team at Bombay emphasised his value to the team, despite his modest figures in the first four games. The fact was that as he was not given the new ball he did not get so many opportunities to shine. But he played an extremely effective supporting role, always working up a good pace, always pitching the ball well up and keeping a tidy off-stump line. Like Willis, he has learned a good deal from less happy tours of the West Indies and Australia. Also like Willis, he remained much fitter than on previous tours, which made his minor back injury at the end of the tour all the more irksome. There was no sign of trouble from the knee injuries which had originally threatened to prevent his touring.

Old's batting was, on balance, a disappointment. He made one spectacular hundred against North Zone but in the Tests did not play a big innings. It is well-known that he plays spin better than pace, so he missed a big opportunity to justify his billing as a genuine Test all-rounder. But his fielding close to the bat was excellent and played no small part, along with Greig's equally reliable slip catching, in England's successes. The odd seamer out, as it were, was Mike Selvey, who was praised by Greig after his disappointment in the fifth Test as a 'bloody wonderful tourist'. Although quite unsuited by Indian conditions he bowled very well on the whole, and kept on trying without a word of complaint.

The most successful bowler, in the end, of course, was Derek Underwood. He had the best of many good tours for MCC abroad and set a new record for an England bowler in India as well as equalling Fred Trueman's haul of 29 wickets, the best for England in any series between the two countries. Underwood's secret on this tour was that he was kept fresh for the important matches. He is half the bowler he can be by the end of a season in England because all his work for Kent in knockout and three-day cricket and all his labours for his country as well make him become stale. He is such a mechanical bowler that he will never let anyone down, no matter how tired he is, but future MCC teams, to get the most out of their greatest asset, would do well to follow the policy used in India. After the first Test in Delhi he bowled only thirteen overs outside the Tests. Hence, in the important matches he was deadlier than ever. It will be a major surprise if, by the next time an MCC side goes to India, Underwood has not become the biggest wicket-taker in Test history. He remains the most dependable slow bowler in the world.

Unfortunately a combination of circumstances plus a certain lack of imagination on the part of the tour selectors meant, as already metioned, that he was no nearer getting a suitable spinning partner. Geoff Miller had so little bowling that no one was any wiser about him, except that those who did not know him discovered an amiable, unflappable character with a philosophical approach to life and a dry sense of humour. Like Selvey, he never uttered one word of complaint, not even after the match at Gauhati when Greig unintentionally insulted him by coming on himself in the last twenty overs to bowl seamers on a glaringly obvious spinners' pitch soon after giving Miller a cruelly belated bowl. At least at the end of the tour Miller was allowed a real chance as a batsman when he opened the batting in the four-day unofficial Test in Colombo. He scored 56 and played in his own calm, undemonstrative manner. In India he had gained useful general experience and if his ability to be a genuine Test all-rounder was still in doubt his temperament was not.

Geoff Cope must have wondered how he managed to go through a tour of India, the land of spin, without playing a Test. In the minor matches he did what was asked of him and once or twice a bit more. He is not a world-beater, but he is a very accomplished performer, a dour, single-minded Yorkshireman from head to toe. He would give everything to play in a Test match for England, and he was unlucky not to do so when Old withdrew at Bombay. Like Underwood, his greatest assets are accuracy and dedication to his craft. So long as his action continues to satisfy umpires he has ten years' cricket yet in which to fulfil his dream and when his chance comes he will not let England down.

Every game of cricket is a serious one for Cope. He cannot ever give anything other than a hundred percent. At times he was angered when his team colleagues took it easy in the minor matches while he strove to force his way into the Test team. But off the field he likes to behave in the Yorkshire tradition of characters. Early in the tour an Indian said to him at a cocktail party how much he admired the caves he had seen near Rotherham. 'They're not caves,' said Cope in broad Yorkshire dialect, 'they're coal mines.'

The satisfaction Greig must have felt as he manipulated his bowling attack was tempered by near-despair as England's batting failed to convince for yet another series. One has lost count of all the collapses England has suffered over the years since the departure of May, Barrington, Graveney, Dexter and Cowdrey, the most distinguished of England's post-war middle-order batsmen. No one has yet superseded them and the three most prolific players in England remain opening batsmen – Boycott, Amiss and Edrich. Boycott did not go to India for his own reasons, which have kept him out of Test cricket for three momentous years, and Edrich did not do so because of his age rather than his ability. It was quite right that he should not have gone because the need to find a long-term answer to the basic problem of all recent English sides was desperate after the drubbing handed out by Lloyd's West Indians.

In the circumstances a great deal depended on Dennis Amiss and he responded magnificently. It seems his destiny always to have to prove something to somebody and even after India Amiss faced a new challenge from the one set of bowlers in the world he had not yet succeeded against: the Aussies. But he had every right to be satisfied with himself after his second visit to India. The first time there he had been overwhelmed by India's high-pressure spin attack, backed up by close fielders and roaring crowds, and he had lost his place after three games in which he averaged only 15.

After a laboured start in the warm-up matches on his second tour there were those who thought he might fail again. But in the Tests he had the all-important good start, his 179 at Delhi being easily the highest knock of a very low-scoring series. In one sense it was not a typical Amiss innings. He batted all day for his first 109 and there was no more important dropped catch in the series than his life from Patel off Bedi when he had scored 92. It made the difference between a respectable and a commanding English score and it set the pattern for the next few games. Amiss never broke loose in that innings, or in any other thereafter. Apart from the occasional flurry of cover-drives and wristy flicks off his legs against India's moderate seamers he seemed to be fighting a grim, uphill battle much of the time against Bedi, Chandra and Prasanna. Never once did his respect for them diminish or his concentration against them waver. Once again one remembered the way that the Indian spinners had bowled at him in a net in simulated Test match conditions after his failures four years before and how his Test fortunes had immediately improved on the subsequent tour of Pakistan.

Quite apart from that first escape which allowed him to score his eleventh Test hundred, Amiss had more than his share of luck at times in the series, just as he had had a great deal more than his quota of unplayable balls and brilliant catches in Australia on the last MCC tour. Close l.b.w. decisions more often than not went his way, and strokes turned on the legside narrowly evaded the grasping fingers of the short-leg fieldsmen. But nothing can dilute one's admiration for the way in which he grafted his way to success with a carefully thought-out technique to counter the turning ball, based on a firm, low, forward defensive with cocked wrists and bat angled almost parallel with the ground, or for the manner in which he met all bowlers with characteristic concentration and unde-monstrative determination. As a close family man Amiss was one of only a few members of the side not joined by his wife at some stage in the tour, and he felt the four-month absence from home strongly. Nor did he ever look really fit after suffering 'flu during his long innings in Delhi. But the man who always has something to prove can tick off another score as settled.

After Greig the next most dependable batsman was Amiss's longstanding friend, the redoubtable 'Knottie'. For sheer brilliance his 75 at Delhi and his 81 not out at Bangalore stand out as two of his greatest Test innings. Indeed, because of the circumstances in which it was played, with the game at the crossroads when he came in to bat at 125 for five, that first innings may well have been the best of all the fine attacking innings he has played for England. It was the only time in the series that a batsman really took the opposition bowling apart until Patel came near to doing so for India in the last match. Knott made 75 out of 101 on that opening day of the series and proved to his fellows that Bedi and company were not what they had sometimes seemed during the previous trip: unplayable. Later in the series Knott's desire to counter orthodox spin with unorthodox attack sometimes led him to take unnecessary risks; there were times when he seemed obsessed by the sweep, especially against Bedi. The latter may have been infuriated by the batsman's audacity but every time Knott swept he knew there was a chance of a top-edged catch and he eventually had him caught in this way at Madras. On balance there were too many close shaves and too few boundaries for the policy to have more than a limited success, but it meant that Bedi nearly always had to post three men for the Knott sweep in various parts of the leg-side and at least one of them on a turning wicket would normally have been placed close in on the off. Knott's tactics meant that one danger man was therefore kept at a safe distance. As a wicket-keeper, Knott excelled even by his own high standards. He missed only one chance that I can recall and was central to the overall success of England in the field.

If Amiss and Knott had luck more often than not on their side, Mike Brearley definitely did not, though he put the record a little straighter with his 91 in the last Test which helped boost his series aggregate to 215 and his average to 25. At Madras he seemed destined for his first Test century when he swept a ball firmly against short-leg's head and was caught and bowled off the rebound.

Brearley is likely to be a useful man against the Australian fast bowlers. He has already proved his courage and there is nothing much wrong with his technique, which is upright and straight, or with his concentration. He is the most assiduous of run gatherers and he never resorts to the brutish or the unorthodox. Yet it is difficult to judge him as a player in the highest company. The freedom which marked his glorious innings at Poona, when strokes flowed from his bat like silk from a conjuror's top pocket, came back only once again, during the second phase of his 91 at Bombay, his highest Test score. This was an innings of stages, beginning with taut, nervous-looking jabs, developing into smooth, effortless control, then suddenly becoming lost again in a mist of doubt and defensiveness. At the moment it often seems that unless he can play a good stroke early in his innings he is not going to settle. Such is his calculated approach to the game which he loves as a challenge more intellectual than physical, that he will probably find a way to overcome this restrictive tightness. He shares with Colin Cowdrey and Dennis Amiss a proneness to periods of sticky introspection. From time to time he brought his intellect to bear upon a game of cricket in an unexpected way. At Nagpur, disgruntled by frequent and outrageous appeals, he told one bowler at the end of an over: 'It's not that I mind your appealing occasionally – it's the degree of conviction I disapprove of.'

Batting was his main job and preoccupation in India, but Brearley played important roles too as vice-captain and close fielder. He took over from Fletcher at first slip where he proved a very reliable catcher. As vice-captain he was content to play a quiet back-up role, giving Greig advice only when he was asked for it. There were times when one wished he had been more forthright, but as an admirer of Greig and a potential threat to him as captain if things had gone wrong he had no intention of overstepping the limits of his brief. After his ups and downs as prolific undergraduate batsman, failed MCC tourist (in South Africa), disillusioned county cricketer, highly successful county captain, and now partially successful Test batsman it will be fascinating to see how his career develops in this final stage. When 1976 began he had only an outside chance of ever playing for England. 1977 will probably establish his true worth as a Test cricketer.

One man whose career at the highest level is unlikely to go further is Roger Tolchard. Yet no one on the tour performed with greater efficiency. His role as deputy wicket-keeper to Knott was largely incidental. Tolchard had proved on his previous trip to India that he was an outstanding player of spin bowling with his nimble footwork, quick eye, organised technique and ability to play the ball unusually late. This time his success suggested that if England's selectors had seen him as a batsman rather than as a wicket-keeper-batsman on Tony Lewis's tour England might have won then as well. It was Tolchard's memorable first innings at Calcutta, his 67 runs worth at least a century in other circumstances, which gave England the nerve to achieve the most important of their Test wins.

Two injuries to his right hand reduced his effectiveness thereafter, but he can look back with great pride on the high point of his career. He was very useful in the field, too, the best man that the touring party possessed in the suicidal short-leg position, and speedy and fearless anywhere else.

It was from Bob Woolmer that Tolchard took over a middle-order batting place and the fact that he did so was a disappointment not just to Woolmer but to the many followers of English cricket who saw in Woolmer the natural successor to Cowdrey, a graceful 'touch' player of true class. After India painful doubts surrounded Woolmer: was he too nice a man for the rough-and-tumble of Test cricket? Was his technique, never right back in defence, only rarely right forward, tight enough in the highest company? Was he dedicated enough? Was he a thirties and fifties man rather than a player of big innings who could concentrate and discipline himself for long periods? On the evidence of India all these questions would receive the wrong answers. Yet, although the memory of his 149 at the Oval against Thomson and Lillee was beginning to fade, that innings had in itself shown that he could be tough enough, that his technique could stand a searching test and that he could indeed concentrate for long periods. So Woolmer rightly saw no reason for despair. 'Of course I'm disappointed,' he said, looking back on his three months in the country of his birth. 'But if I was ever lucky enough to return I know I would do better. I probably thought that runs would come too easily. I did not graft enough. Every player has setbacks like this at some time. Perhaps it is no bad thing. Perhaps after a season like the one I had for Kent in 1976 you begin to think you are a better player than you really are.' There were those who thought that Woolmer was not worried enough by his relative failures in India. But these were hardly the words of a self-satisfied man. On the contrary, they represented a sensible realistic attitude.

Especially on slow wickets his technique needs tightening up, but the ability is still there and 'Wobbler' Woolmer should come again. By the end of the tour he believed that he would like to settle down as an opening batsman. Whether his wish would immediately be granted, however, was doubtful, because Brearley and Amiss were looking the most dependable of the many different opening pairs England had fielded over the last few years, despite the decision to demote Amiss in the order against Australia at Melbourne.

Another player who would undoubtedly do better if he returned to India is Derek Randall, the great character of Greig's team, who did so much towards making this MCC side one of the most popular to have toured anywhere. His fielding was always brilliant and if he can practise his throwing so that he hits the stumps (à la Bland of South Africa) more often than he misses he will be a terror as well as a deterrent to batsmen everywhere.

On and off the field his clownlike antics quickly became a legend. His batting still suffers from the restless, fevered air which he takes with him to the wicket, but as he has gradually learned to settle down to big innings in county cricket so he will in Test cricket. If he can retain his place the staid, rather dull, efficient professional image of the Illingworth team will be followed by the less reliable but more entertaining one of Greig's. Randall's promise as a batsman was clear, and he fulfilled it for the first time to the immense delight of the spectators – and his team-mates – in the Centenary Test.

Graham Barlow was the other batsman who went to India with a reputation as an entertainer and a label still marked 'young hopeful'. He began the tour wonderfully well with two hundreds which showed all his virtues: confidence, a willingness to dominate, a wide range of full-blooded shots and a typically cockney chirpiness. Unfortunately the next few weeks were to show his failings: a tendency to be impatient and a certain looseness of technique. But he described his tour to India as the best thing in cricket which had ever happened to him, and he was certainly no overall failure, with a tour average of 44 from a mere nine innings. After losing his place following the second Test he was allowed only two more innings in India. But in Sri Lanka he made up for lost time with another century in the unofficial Test. He is always, however, likely to be a vulnerable batsman, one who gives the bowlers a chance. As such he was not Ken Barrington's ideal sort of player. But a good Test side needs its grafters and its players of flair.

Barlow's left-handedness is on his side, as is his athletic fielding. He may well develop into an English Doug Walters, a man who, with strong players around him, will score his runs fast enough to enable Test matches to be won. I hope he is not written off by un-adventurous selectors as a 'flash Harry' because he is a good deal more than that.

England's batting line-up was completed by Keith Fletcher, who came home no less an enigma than he had left. Only in the first match of the tour, with a sparkling, carefree hundred, and in the last with a typically stubborn, gritty back-to-the-wall innings did he justify his selection for the tour. It is a moot point whether, overall, the choice was vindicated. Certainly his experience of Indian cricket was valuable to the other members of the team, especially his great friend Tony Greig, and certainly he was most unlucky to be injured on Christmas Eve and to miss two Test matches as a result. On the other hand we shall never know whether David Steele would have served England as well against spinners in India as he had against fast bowlers at home, and the presence of both Fletcher and Brearley in the team meant one less place for a younger player who might have gained valuable experience for the future.

In the end, however, the selectors will point with justification to the result of the series, a solid and reassuring win for England. No one went home a failure and although cricket in India is quite unlike Test cricket anywhere else these days the future may be faced with more confidence. The emergence of Randall and Lever had an important side-effect in improving the standard of the England fielding. This was undoubtedly one of the sharpest fielding sides England has ever had. I hope the selectors have learnt the lesson that young athletic fielders can lift their bowlers and make a tremendous difference to the morale of a side.

From an onlooker's viewpoint cricket in India was a fascinating departure from the increasing trend in Test cricket towards rule by the brute force of fast bowlers. It is true that England's seamers were their main weapons, but they succeeded through good accurate bowling rather than by a barrage of bouncers. India countered with the spin bowlers who give Indian cricket its special charm and identity in a world where variety is more than ever welcome. Even when they were bowling much of the cricket was slow, and only when it suited him did Bedi step up the shamefully slow over-rate which both sides were guilty of. The average for the series was a meagre 13 overs an hour. Slow wickets, slow batting, frequent delays caused by balls going out of shape, sight-screens being moved, mirrors being flashed, drinks being taken, or captains making fastidious tactical field changes: all this was characteristic of a series when 250 runs in a day was a fast rate of progress in a five-and-a-half-hour day. There seems only one certain solution to a problem which gets worse all the time. That pusillanimous body, the International Cricket Conference, has shied away from fining the players, which has proved an effective remedy in English domestic cricket. The only alternative is to stipulate a certain number of overs per session with account being taken of stoppages for bad light, falls of wicket, etcetera.

Despite the sluggish nature of much of the cricket in India, it was only very rarely boring to watch. This was, after all, cricket in the mysterious orient, where five minutes are nothing against eternity.

Postscript
SRI LANKA AND
THE CENTENARY TEST

Sri Lanka, like India, had recently been under an official national emergency when MCC arrived, but the atmosphere after Bombay was altogether less frenetic. After the customary delay, an ancient 34-seater Avro propelled the team and some of their wives to Colombo. They arrived just in time to avoid a drenching from a torrential downpour and settled into a modern hotel on the edge of the Indian Ocean with the waves thundering dramatically against the sea walls. This was unmistakably the tropics: palm trees in abundance, lush foliage, copious frangipane blossom, and in the country areas men dressed only in sarongs.

The heat was far more intense than anything experienced in India and in the first match of the short tour, a forty eight-ball over affair at the Sinhalese Sports Club Ground in Colombo, MCC scored more than 200 without running a single three despite a lush, rough-grass outfield on which shots repeatedly pulled up just short of the boundary. Anyone who played an innings of substance – Woolmer, showing his best form of the tour, Amiss, Randall and Greig – came off with shirts stained black with perspiration. But it was an enjoyable match, which kept a crowd of some 20,000 buzzing cheerfully all day. The buzz became wild excitement for a time during a stand for Sri Lanka of 69 in twelve overs by Warnapura, a neat right-hander, and Mendis, in which many fine aggressive strokes were played, largely at the expense of the off-spinners, Miller and Cope. Underwood, Lever and Selvey saw to it, however, that there was no surprise result.

For their second game, against the Cricket Board's XI, MCC travelled 72 miles to the south-west tip of the island and spent two delightful days at Galle which, until a breakwater transformed Colombo as a port, was the main calling point for ships travelling between Aden and the Far East. Jardine's team had a match at Galle, a rather unfortunate one because the car carrying the captain and some of his team had so many punctures on the way that a game due to start in the morning did not begin until 2.30 p.m. It was altogether one of MCC's less happy visits to Ceylon because in another game, when Bryan Valentine was captaining, Nobby Clarke took it into his head to rough up the pitch with his boot whilst he was batting, an incident still recalled in local publications.

The main talk in Sri Lankan cricket circles these days, however, concerns the growing aspiration to be recognised as a full member of the International Cricket Conference, which carries with it full Test status. The one-day wins against MCC, the effort in the 1975 World Cup when Sri Lanka scored 276 against Australia (who nevertheless won the game comfortably) and most of all the victory at Colombo against almost the full strength of Pakistan in a four-day unofficial match the previous year were cited as evidence that Sri Lanka was now strong enough to hold its own against the best international opposition. Even the most loyal locals, however, admitted that a strong showing against Greig's side was essential if the case for inclusion was to have any chance of being carried at the next ICC meeting at Lord's.

Not the least of Sri Lanka's drawbacks is a lack of grounds suited to the staging of Test matches. Kandy, in the relatively cool tree-clad hills in the centre of the island, would be a delightful place for a Test, but the ground does not yet have a big enough capacity or the necessary facilities for a big crowd. The same is still more true of Galle, which had the atmosphere of a village ground. But for a lighthearted two-day game it could not have been a more charming venue. A good crowd fringed the ground, protected from the burning glare of the sun by parasols and umbrellas, and hundreds more spectators watched from the high stone ramparts of the fort which divide the ground from the magnificent blue-green ocean beyond. So long as its political situation is stable, Sri Lanka is the perfect holiday island but whether it will ever stage a long cricket tour depends on the development of the potential Test centres and on the breaking of a vicious circle which prevents the development of players who cannot get enough top-class opposition at home. Hopes of more tours, both home and away, are frustrated because money is not available to support them. But until the best Sri Lanka players become well enough known to attract crowds, their tours will not be financially viable anyway.

The match at Galle never got off the ground. Unless the island side had been very weak, which they certainly weren't, or the pitch very bad, there was no serious prospect of a finish in the allotted two days. The youthful Board XI acquitted itself well with the bat on the first day, when Cope took five wickets and Miller was unlucky not to have taken more than two; Houtersz, Wettimuny and Susil Fernando all played some good strokes; and the Sri Lankans fielded equally well on the second day when three MCC wickets were taken for 49. The Middlesex pair of Brearley and Barlow saved the visitors from any possibility of embarrassment, but there was no great excitement for an unsophisticated crowd who did not seem to mind any more than the players when three showers swept across the palm trees from the east and drenched the pitch. The final soaking was fatal and the game came to the same watery end as Jardine's match at Galle had done 43 years before.

The four-day international at the Colombo Oval later that week was altogether a more serious affair. The Sri Lankans knew that their ardent pleas for full membership of the ICC could only be answered in the affirmative if they played outstandingly well. MCC knew that they could not take the match lightly. Wisely they used the game to sort out some of their batting problems, resting Amiss and Brearley, who were both certain selections for the Melbourne Centenary Test, and giving Woolmer, Miller, Barlow and Randall the first four batting places.

Tolchard's job now was done, and the chances were that two of these four would play in Melbourne. If things went well there, the chances also were that England would start the summer with the same side against Australia. So there was much to play for, and this partly explained the dullness of the cricket on the first day, played out on a slow, bare pitch on a hot, sunny day before a sedate crowd of around 3,000. It was all very gentlemanly and peaceful after India. The open ground with its lush outfield and lack of concrete stands was like one of the smaller English county grounds. Miller and Woolmer began with a watchful, composed opening stand of 61 before Woolmer miscued a loose forward defensive stroke and was caught and bowled off D. S. De Silva's googly.

Miller batted in the way he usually does: very straight, very composed, but with no suggestion of exceptional class. He might twice have been caught and bowled before getting to a sticky but determined fifty in three and a half hours, finding himself hamstrung by the dead slowness of the pitch and the equally sluggish outfield. But he was stumped soon afterwards off the tidy off-spinner, Kaluperuma.

It was Randall who played the most fluent innings on the first day, timing the ball better than anyone, and he was just threatening to take full toll of an attack which had laboured over five and a half hours on a hot, humid day when he was beaten by a very good delivery from Opatha with the second new ball. Doubts about Randall's ability to adapt to the faster bowlers he would be facing in Australia and England over the next few months were raised by the fact that he was late into position to play this ball, which went through a gap so large between bat and pad that it appeared to miss the bat altogether.

Barlow was more fortunate, although he gave only one chance, a stumping one, in batting four and a half hours on the first day for 63. He grafted stubbornly, which may have been a point he was trying to make to those who believed he could not get his head down for long, and on the second day, when the outfield was noticeably faster and the strokes flowed more freely off the square, he carried on with greater certainty to a hundred in just under six hours. It was not one of his best centuries, but it was his third of the tour and it greatly improved his chances of playing in the Centenary Test.

The other main contributor on the second day was Greig, who brought the match to life with his own peerless brand of power hitting. In fifty minutes after lunch he hit five fours and three sixes, the first of them an immense lofted drive over the large scoreboard at long-off. The ball ended up in the garden of a local block of flats and it took some time to retrieve it. Once again, England's chief unofficial ambassador to the Orient had in a few minutes restored the image of his side. A local writer expressed the change of mood in colourful fashion: 'Suddenly the air was full of willowy jazz.' This apart, the MCC batting had been pedestrian, but then the Sri Lankans had insisted, quite rightly, on being taken as serious opponents and they could not have expected exhibition match batting.

Nor could they expect any mercy from the MCC bowlers, and they did not get it. It took six hours for Lever, Willis, Underwood, Woolmer and Cope to bowl Sri Lanka out but only for a short period on the second evening, when Dias and Warnapura played some good strokes, did they look likely to avert the possibility of a follow-on. Warnapura played the best innings, sensibly refusing to play at anything which Willis pitched short at him but getting into line when the ball was of good length or overpitched, and twice driving him beautifully through the covers. But Lever is a less straightforward bowler than Willis, and after beating Warnapura twice outside the off-stump he found the edge the third time.

Thereafter it was a grim and unequal struggle, punctuated only by frequent shouts of advice from the local barracker, well oiled by Sri Lankan whisky (called *arrack*) distilled from coconuts. He favoured a Mohammed Ali type of script, examples being: 'Cope, you're hoping against hope,' and: 'Tony, you've got the height, I've got the might.'

With his bowlers languid, weary and sore oppressed, Greig did not enforce the follow-on. As a result the last two hours' play made much more pleasant watching, with Miller, Barlow and especially Randall playing some glorious strokes in a golden summer's light on a wicket getting easier all the time. Miller's dismissal, l.b.w. to the determinedly hostile Opatha, as lively and aggressive a bowler as any in India, may have seemed purely incidental at the time. But it made it that much easier for the selectors to leave him out of the Centenary Test. There was very little to choose between Miller, Woolmer, Randall and Barlow, but Woolmer had difficulty picking up the line of the ball around his off-stump, and he was beaten a few times before being out caught behind.

The final day bordered on the bizarre. There was a record stand for Sri Lanka against an MCC side, a sudden collapse in which four wickets fell in 20 overs, an injury to two of the key men in the England team, and a final decision by the umpires to call off play because of bad light when the home side were again struggling to avoid defeat. The major part of the day was taken up by a four-and-a-half-hour stand of 163 between Anura Tennekoon and Bandula Warnapura. It was a disciplined piece of batting by both, and Tennekoon, who had centuries against India, the West Indies and a previous MCC side to his credit, underlined his quality. He is a very sound player, strong off his legs, and it was not just the floppy Sri Lankan cap on his head which made him look like an Australian Test batsman. Warnapura, on the day before his 24th birthday, needed luck against Lever early on and must have been close to being l.b.w., but his promise and ability were again apparent. It was only when Tennekoon called for a belated attempt to get the 309 runs Greig had set them to win that wickets started falling, Underwood and Cope taking two each before the new ball was called for.

Willis took a wicket with his first ball, but after one more over from Lever, with seven of the mandatory last fifteen eight-ball overs left, the umpires decided that a providential cloud was dark enough for them to intervene. Fletcher was captaining MCC for the last part of the match because first Knott and then Greig had sustained injuries. Knott was hit on the inside of his left knee by a sweep from Tennekoon and had to be carried off the field in pain. It was the first time anyone could remember his being taken off. Greig took over, using Knott's pads, which made him look like a giraffe in Wellington boots, but his light-hearted gesture turned sour when he severely bruised the middle finger of his left hand. Fletcher then took over the gloves and deputised very well, taking one brilliant diving left-handed 'catch' which was disallowed. The injuries to Greig and Knott were followed by Derek Underwood going down with fever on the eve of the final game of the short Sri Lankan tour, and the loss of England's three outstanding players proved too big a burden to overcome.

Everything was ripe for a Sri Lankan victory in the final limited-over match. An enthusiastic crowd of about 25,000 sensed this too and Tennekoon won an important toss, putting MCC in to bat on a damp pitch after the match had been reduced to thirty eight-ball overs following a heavy tropical storm the previous evening. MCC batted without any concerted plan, in direct contrast to their opponents who bowled to a general line outside the leg-stump with six men on the leg-side. This was a case of the professionals being outdone at their own sort of game, and MCC's total of 123, helped by a couple of dubious l.b.w. decisions at the end, wasn't enough. Thanks mainly to a bold attacking innings by Mendis, who was twice dropped, Sri Lanka deservedly got home with more than three overs to spare, despite a sudden loss of wickets as the target drew closer.

There was much rejoicing on the island and much talk at a cheerful farewell dinner party about the longed-for ICC membership. But the truth was that the four-day game, which MCC had dominated for three-quarters of its course, was a truer guide to Sri Lanka's likely fortunes in Test cricket than a win over a depleted, weary and makeshift side in a truncated limited-overs match.

It was beyond dispute that Sri Lanka had some very useful players who would become better still if they played more regularly against stronger opposition. But only Tennekoon really looked Test class, and only D. S. De Silva, Kaluperuma and Warnapura would at this stage have had a better than even chance of making an English county side. If the aspirations to Test match status were to be fulfilled, the game in Sri Lanka needed to be put on a more solid financial footing. There needed to be more three- and four-day cricket played on the island and the Sri Lankan government had to be prepared to underwrite tours which both at home and abroad would be certain lossmakers for some time to come. With their foreign exchange problems this was unlikely to happen. But the Sri Lankans are such friendly people that if their cricketers do join the Test match fold, they will certainly be welcome.

Between the sleepy, ancient, slightly seedy city of Colombo and the breezy, brash, ultra-modern city of Perth there can hardly be a greater contrast. Greig's team arrived in Australia desperately tired. They had played cricket for eight days out of their twelve in Sri Lanka, and after a delayed flight via Kuala Lumpur and Singapore they had a mere 24 hours to sleep off jet-lag before they found themselves in the field on a hot day against the Sheffield Shield Champions, Western Australia.

The arrival of the MCC team was overshadowed by a strong rumour that Dennis Lillee, Australia's greatest sporting idol, was about to withdraw from the team to tour England later that year. Ironically the arrival of Denness's side in Australia 29 months previously had coincided with Lillee's reappearance in first-class cricket after a long lay-off because of a back injury (it had stolen their thunder then too), and now tales of persistent back trouble and ominous 'no comments' from Lillee caused a sudden rash of stories on the day MCC arrived, to the effect that Lillee would be unavailable for England not just because of back worries but also because he wished to spend more time with his family in Perth; in addition there was the possibility of his signing a lucrative contract with a television firm. Lillee, of course, was front-page news in Australia. A documentary about his life was about to appear on television and a pop song about him threatened to become as popular as the one about Mohammed Ali.

But for the time being the storm blew over. Lillee suddenly denied the rumours and said he would be happy to tour England if he were selected and his doctor were satisfied that his back would stand the strain. The very next day he apparently proved his fitness and over the next ten drama-charged days in Australia the only people under strain when Lillee was around were the MCC batsmen.

Nothing, indeed, was more significant about the cricket which concluded the long and arduous tour than the confrontation between the two Dennis's – Amiss and Lillee. The latter had cruelly hounded Amiss since his tour of Australia in 1974–75, winning their duel by a wide margin and bowling him not just into strokeless submission but out of Test cricket as well. In thirteen first-class innings which Amiss played against Australia in the two countries before the Perth encounter, Lillee had taken his wicket eight times. Now Amiss was handicapped not just by Lillee's magnificent hostility and immense skill as a fast bowler but also by his own neurosis. For weeks before the match Amiss had turned at least part of his mind to his coming battle with Lillee, as conversation with him showed. Despite his great-hearted double-century against the feared trio of Holding, Roberts and Daniel and despite his consistent success as England's number one bat in India, Lillee's menacing, swaying, accelerating approach to the wicket and his glowering, sometimes near-diabolical face were already playing upon Amiss's nerves.

Sure enough, Lillee dismissed Amiss both times in the three-day game against Western Australia, for 9 and 29, although the latter score was deceptive because Lillee did not open the bowling in the second innings and it was only when he came on that the old Amiss frailties were revealed again. In fact there was considerable doubt about whether Amiss, with a leaden-footed attempt at a square-cut, had touched the ball off which he was given out caught behind. Any hope of his settling down and getting in some useful practice against his great bogey-man was stifled when he stopped Lillee in the middle of his run-up to point out that Charlesworth, fielding at short-leg, was moving as Miller was facing at the other end. Lillee's boiling point, whether deliberately calculated or not, is lower than any other Test cricketer's and he flung the ball down in fury after this interruption, bowling for a few overs like a man who had gone berserk.

If Lillee grabbed all the headlines from this game and MCC came close to losing in three days, they nevertheless got some useful batting practice on a pitch yards faster than any they had been experiencing in India or Sri Lanka. Brearley played well, especially in the second innings when, coming in late after damaging his hand in the first knock, he saved the side not by prodding but with polish and confidence. Randall also hit some gloriously timed strokes in the second innings before falling to a phenomenal catch by Clark off Malone, a strong and dangerous swing bowler who looked ideal for the tour of England. (So, too, did the 25-year-old batsman Craig Serjeant, a player of immense promise.) Woolmer made fifty in the second innings, although, having begun to play well again, one wished he had gone on to a really big score.

The two who particularly emphasised their claims to play in the Centenary Test were Barlow and Miller. The latter was intended to bat at number eight and was playing in the match only because Fletcher had chosen not to do so. But he had the chance to go in third as night-watchman when Amiss was out late on the first day, and in his short time at the wicket that evening and a much longer spell the next day he did enough in many people's view to justify a gamble being taken with him in the Centenary Test. He seems to be quicker than most to pick up the line of the ball and to position himself correctly. Equally important, he remains cool in the face of the sort of terrifying onslaught which Lillee in particular torments batsmen with.

Barlow, by scoring a well-constructed 60 in the first innings against Western Australia, merely confirmed the impression he had made in the four-day match in Sri Lanka: that he was ready to come back into the England side and do better. Yet when the tour selectors convened at lunchtime on the day before the momentous Centenary Test, all the native conservatism and caution of English professionals triumphed. Miller and Barlow, it was felt, were too raw for such a big occasion. Despite the general poverty of their batting in India, Fletcher and Woolmer were preferred on the grounds of their experience. In the favour of both players, it had to be granted, was the fact that they had scored major hundreds in recent matches against Australia: Woolmer at the Oval in 1975, Fletcher in the last match at Melbourne when Thomson was not fit and Lillee had broken down before Fletcher got to the crease. But the major surprise announced by Greig was not the omission of the two relative youngsters but the decision to ask Woolmer to open the batting and to place Amiss down the order at number four. Now the Lillee menace, which, of course, was real enough, was playing on everyone's mind—to the detriment of Amiss himself. He had been transformed as a cricketer from the moment that he became an opener for Warwickshire. Before this he had lost his place in the county side as a middle-order batsman. As an opener for England he had certainly had his failures, but overall he had been a prolific scorer. Against an attack more fearsome if less skilful or experienced than that of Lillee and Walker, who would be the main threats at Melbourne, Amiss had scored 203 at the Oval in the final Test against the West Indies. The mental pressure on him then had been just as great; he had been hit on the head by Holding earlier in the season and every eye was on him to see if he could re-establish himself as a Test batsman. Indeed if he had failed, by the public admission of the chairman of the selectors he would not have gone to India. Yet in focusing attention on him now Greig and his fellow selectors were putting still more pressure on him. The justification behind the decision was that Amiss would have a greater chance of getting a good start and going on to play a big innings if he was not confronted by Lillee when the shine on the ball was still new and glossy. But this presupposed a good start by England, and in the first innings at Melbourne they were to get a bad start and never to recover. In the second innings he faced a less taxing situation and batted well.

The remarkable story of the Centenary Test, which was watched by a mind-bending galaxy of famous cricketers, belongs not so much to the end of this long and successful tour by Greig's team as to the fight for the Ashes which was to begin in England three months later. The full story will be related in another book, but it would only be right to introduce it here.

The idea for the Test was first conceived by the former Victorian and Australian Test cricketer, Hans Ebeling, and it came to a more triumphant fruition than he could ever have imagined. In every way the occasion proved to be a dramatic success. The organisation by the Melbourne Cricket Club and the Victoria Cricket Association was excellent and a tremendous atmosphere pervaded the historic Melbourne Cricket Ground for the span of ten days. For the old players there were parties or dinners almost every evening, with the opportunity of endless reunions. For the current teams there was the satisfaction and honour of playing in a match which, in the end, turned out to be one of the best and happiest of all England v Australia Tests.

By an extraordinary coincidence the game ended in a 45-run win for Australia, exactly the same result as in the first Test one hundred years before. Australia's hero then was Charles Bannerman, with 165 out of a total of 245; this time it was a bowler, Dennis Lillee, who proved the matchwinner in an otherwise even contest, taking eleven wickets for 165 with tigerish, remorseless bowling before announcing on the last day of the game that, because of a stress fracture in his back, he would not be fit to tour England later in the year.

Lillee's fellow-Western Australian, Rodney Marsh, had an outstanding match too, becoming during the course of the game the new holder of the record number of victims in Tests by an

Australian wicket-keeper (surpassing Wally Grout's total of 187) and scoring one of only two centuries in the match. Apart from these performances there was a thrilling debut by 21-year-old David Hookes, a student physical education teacher from Adelaide, who stroked Tony Greig for five successive fours in an inspired spell of batting during his second-innings 56.

Despite this personal indignity Greig's tour ended on an appropriately high note. England lost the match, yet the margin of their defeat was negligible and by their performance on the first and final days they maintained the good impression they had made throughout the tour. On the first day Greig gambled by putting Australia in to bat and Willis, Old, Lever and Underwood bowled their opponents out for a meagre 138. Yet soon after lunch on the second day England had been torn apart by Lillee and Walker and failed by five runs to reach a hundred. 'After the first day I thought we *had* to get a lead of fifty or so, even if we batted badly,' said Greig later. 'I feared that all our good work in India was now going to be forgotten.'

The Queen, on her Jubilee Tour, was due to watch the Test on the last afternoon. Soon after tea on the third day, when Australia were a mere 53 for three in their second innings, it seemed she would be far too late to see a ball bowled in this historic encounter. Some of the former Test players with writing to do talked of sub-standard batting. But Marsh, Walters, Davis, Hookes, and a gallant McCosker, batting again after having his jaw agonisingly broken by a ball from Willis, carried Australia's innings into the fourth day and beyond 400. England were asked to score 463, 57 more runs than any Test side had ever made to win in the fourth innings. A courageous fight-back and a bold attempt to go for runs took them close to what would have been a sensational victory on the last afternoon, and not only was there no dishonour in defeat but there was even an element of heroism about it. Although Australia were saved in the end by the spin of O'Keeffe and the unyielding determination of 'Lillee the Lionheart', it was England's morale which ended higher. At last, one of the young batsmen the country's cricket-lovers had been yearning for produced a major innings in a critical situation. Derek Randall, the 'character' of the tour, whose timing and application through four months of arduous cricket had suggested that he must make his breakthrough one day soon, scored 174 and played brilliantly. It was a fitting ending. Within three months Randall and the majority of his colleagues would be taking the field for the Jubilee Test at Lord's. Everything pointed to a close and entertaining series between two young teams.

Australia's selectors, mourning the loss of their champion, Lillee, named Jeff Thomson, who was about to bowl for the first time for three months after dislocating his right shoulder in a collision with another fielder in a Test against Pakistan earlier in the season. Their party of seventeen included four other fast or fast-medium bowlers and only two spinners. Hookes was joined by two other potentially brilliant batsmen without Test experience, Craig Serjeant and Kim Hughes. Only three members of the team were over 30 years old. It was a typically bold Australian choice and the success of Randall was likely to persuade England's less adventurous selectors to encourage more young blood. Randall's success, together with Lever's throughout the tour, the effervescent spirit in the MCC team itself, and the new spirit of optimism in English cricket which the successes in India had created out of the 1976 depression, gave even more substance to the feelings of satisfaction and pleasure at being home again as we landed at Heathrow airport on a cool, sunny morning on 19 March.

Tony Greig had regretted making promises before, but he was confident enough that his side had turned the corner to make another one now. 'The loss of Dennis Lillee from the side which won the Centenary Test will cost Australia the Ashes this year . . . We have a few months to get over this long and exhausting tour before we do battle again and this time I promise the result will be different.'

Prophecy, Greig knows, is dangerous. But no one is more aware than he of the importance of psychology in cricket. He was already working to sow seeds of doubt in Australian minds and to bolster the growing confidence of his own team. The essential achievement of the tour, after all, had been to make English cricket believe in itself again.

MCC in India 1976/77

A statistical survey compiled by Patrick Allen

1 THE TEAMS

The MCC touring team to India

Players	County	Age on 15 Nov 76
GREIG, Anthony William (Captain)	Sussex	30
AMISS, Dennis Leslie	Warwickshire	33
BARLOW, Graham Derek	Middlesex	26
BREARLEY, John Michael (Vice-Captain)	Middlesex	34
COPE, Geoffrey Alan	Yorkshire	29
FLETCHER, Keith William Robert	Essex	32
KNOTT, Alan Philip Eric	Kent	30
LEVER, John Kenneth	Essex	27
MILLER, Geoffrey	Derbyshire	24
OLD, Christopher Middleton	Yorkshire	28
RANDALL, Derek William	Nottinghamshire	25
SELVEY, Michael Walter William	Middlesex	28
TOLCHARD, Roger Williams	Leicestershire	30
UNDERWOOD, Derek Leslie	Kent	31
WILLIS, Robert George Dylan	Warwickshire	27
WOOLMER, Robert Andrew	Kent	28
Manager		
BARRINGTON, Kenneth Frank	Ex-Surrey	45
Physiotherapist and Assistant Manager		
THOMAS, Bernard		

Their Indian Opponents

Players	State	Age on 15 Nov 76
BEDI, Bishen Singh (Captain)	Delhi	30
AMARNATH, Mohinder	Delhi	25
AMARNATH, Surinder	Delhi	27
CHANDRASEKHAR, Bhagwat S.	Kanataka	31
GAEKWAD, Anshuman D.	Baroda	24
GAVASKAR, Sunil M.	Bombay	27
GHAVRI, Karsen	Bombay	25
KIRMANI, Syed Mustafa H.	Kanataka	28
MADAN LAL, S.	Delhi	25
MANKAD, Ashok V.	Bombay	30
PATEL, Brijesh P.	Kanataka	24
PRASANNA, Erapalli Anantrao S.	Kanataka	36
SHARMA, Parthasarathy	Rajasthan	28
SOLKAR, Eknath D.	Bombay	28
VENGSARKAR, Dilip B.	Bombay	20
VENKATARAGHAVAN, Srinivasraghavan	Tamil Nadu	30
VISWANATH, Gundappa R.	Kanataka	27
YAJUVENDRA SINGH	Maharashtra	24

2 THE RESULTS

Match record of official MCC teams in India

Season	Captain	First-Class Matches			
		P	W	D	L
1926–27	A. E. R. Gilligan	8	6	2	0
1933–34	D. R. Jardine	16	8	7	1
1951–52	N. D. Howard	17	6	10	1
1961–62	E. R. Dexter	14	4	8	2
1964	M. J. K. Smith	10	1	9	0
1972–73	A. R. Lewis	11	2	7	2
1976–77	A. W. Greig	13	4	8	1
TOTALS		89	31	51	7

India v England in India

Series	Tests				Bombay			Calcutta			Madras			New Delhi			Kanpur			Bangalore		
	P	E	I	D	E	I	D	E	I	D	E	I	D	E	I	D	E	I	D	E	I	D
1933–34	3	2	—	1	1	—	—	—	—	1	1	—	—	—	—	—	—	—	—	—	—	—
1951–52	5	1	1	3	—	—	1	—	—	1	—	1	—	—	—	1	1	—	—	—	—	—
1961–62	5	—	2	3	—	—	1	—	1	—	—	1	—	—	—	1	—	—	1	—	—	—
1964	5	—	—	5	—	—	1	—	—	1	—	—	1	—	—	1	—	—	1	—	—	—
1972–73	5	1	2	2	—	—	1	—	1	—	—	1	—	1	—	—	—	—	1	—	—	—
1976–77	5	3	1	1	—	—	1	1	—	—	1	—	—	1	—	—	—	—	—	—	1	—
	28	7	6	15	1	0	5	1	2	3	2	3	1	2	0	3	1	0	3	0	1	0

3 THE AVERAGES

Test Match Averages

England—batting and fielding

	M	I	NO	Runs	HS	Av	100	50	Ct/St
D. L. Amiss	5	9	1	417	179	52.12	1	2	1
A. W. Greig	5	8	0	342	103	42.75	1	2	5
A. P. E. Knott	5	8	1	268	81*	38.28	—	2	13/2
J. M. Brearley	5	8	0	215	91	26.87	—	2	9
R. W. Tolchard	4	7	2	129	67	25.80	—	1	5
K. W. R. Fletcher	3	5	1	91	58*	22.75	—	1	4
J. K. Lever	5	8	1	122	53	17.42	—	1	5
C. M. Old	4	6	0	95	52	15.83	—	1	4
R. A. Woolmer	2	3	0	42	22	14.00	—	—	3
D. W. Randall	4	7	0	86	37	12.28	—	—	3
D. L. Underwood	5	7	1	71	23	11.83	—	—	5
G. D. Barlow	2	3	1	11	7*	5.50	—	—	—
R. G. D. Willis	5	7	2	19	7	3.80	—	—	3

Also batted: M. W. W. Selvey 5*

England—bowling

	Overs	Mdns	Runs	Wkts	Av	10wM	5wI	BB
J. K. Lever	149.4	29	380	26	14.61	1	2	7–46
R. G. D. Willis	135	25	335	20	16.75	—	2	6–53
D. L. Underwood	252.5	95	509	29	17.55	—	1	5–84
C. M. Old	88.5	20	201	10	20.10	—	—	3–38
A. W. Greig	131	28	336	10	33.60	—	—	3–64

Also bowled: M. W. W. Selvey 15-1-80-0; R. A. Woolmer 1-0-2-0

Test Match Averages

India—batting and fielding

	M	I	NO	Runs	HS	Av	100	50	Ct/S
S. Amarnath	2	4	0	180	63	45.00	—	2	—
S. M. Gavaskar	5	10	0	394	108	39.40	1	2	7
B. P. Patel	5	10	0	286	83	28.60	—	2	3
K. Ghavri	3	6	2	99	35*	24.75	—	—	1
A. D. Gaekwad	4	8	0	165	39	20.62	—	—	3
G. R. Viswanath	5	10	1	175	79*	19.44	—	1	7
S. M. H. Kirmani	5	10	1	167	52	18.55	—	1	5/6
P. Sharma	2	4	0	62	29	15.50	—	—	1
Madan Lal	2	4	0	51	17	12.75	—	—	1
Yajuvendra Singh	2	4	0	50	21	12.50	—	—	8
B. S. Bedi	5	10	3	81	20*	11.57	—	—	2
M. Amarnath	2	4	0	36	24	9.00	—	—	4
E. A. S. Prasanna	4	8	1	55	13	7.85	—	—	1
B. S. Chandrasekhar	5	10	3	20	6	2.85	—	—	1

Also batted: D. B. Vengsarkar 8 & 1* (retired hurt); E. D. Solkar 2 & 3; A. V. Mankad 0 & 4
S. Venkataraghavan 0 & 4

India—bowling

	Overs	Mdns	Runs	Wkts	Av	5wI	BB
E. A. S. Prasanna	232.4	79	389	18	21.61	—	4–93
B. S. Bedi	298	106	574	25	22.96	2	6–71
K. Ghavri	58	15	149	6	24.83	1	5–33
B. S. Chandrasekhar	194	40	537	19	28.26	2	6–76
Madan Lal	48	11	86	3	28.66	—	2–43
S. Venkataraghavan	34	6	94	2	47.00	—	2–94

Also bowled: M. Amarnath 29-7-56-0; E. D. Solkar 6-1-15-0; S. M. Gavaskar 5-3-2-0;
P. Sharma 4-0-8-0; Yajuvendra Singh 1-0-2-0; A. D. Gaekwad 1-0-1-0

First-Class Match Averages

MCC in India only

Batting

	M	I	NO	Runs	HS	Av	100	50	Ct/St
D. L. Amiss	10	16	1	762	179	50.80	2	5	3
J. M. Brearley	12	16	1	714	202	47.60	1	6	12
A. P. E. Knott	9	14	3	491	108*	44.63	1	3	21/2
G. D. Barlow	7	9	1	352	113	44.00	2	1	2
R. W. Tolchard	9	14	6	352	67	44.00	—	3	15
A. W. Greig	10	15	1	574	162*	41.00	2	3	11
D. W. Randall	12	18	3	515	142	34.33	1	2	8
G. Miller	8	7	2	170	52	34.00	—	1	3
C. M. Old	10	13	4	300	109*	33.33	1	2	5
K. W. R. Fletcher	8	13	3	333	118	33.30	1	2	6
R. A. Woolmer	8	14	0	380	60	27.14	—	2	5
J. K. Lever	10	12	2	150	53	15.00	—	1	6
D. L. Underwood	8	7	1	71	23	11.83	—	—	8
R. G. D. Willis	8	8	2	56	37	9.33	—	—	4
G. A. Cope	6	3	3	43	27*	—	—	—	1
M. W. W. Selvey	8	3	3	33	28*	—	—	—	3

7 catches were taken by substitute fielders

Bowling

	Overs	Mdns	Runs	Wkts	Av	10wM	5wI	BB
R. G. D. Willis	191.1	36	483	32	15.09	—	4	6–53
J. K. Lever	270.4	56	672	44	15.27	1	3	7–46
D. L. Underwood	328.5	130	638	36	17.72	—	1	5–84
G. A. Cope	236.2	91	448	23	19.52	—	1	6–41
C. M. Old	181.2	46	433	19	22.78	—	—	3–38
R. A. Woolmer	55	18	126	5	25.20	—	—	2–14
G. Miller	116	42	270	10	27.10	—	—	4–54
M. W. W. Selvey	171	51	433	13	33.30	—	—	2–17
A. W. Greig	172	33	504	12	42.00	—	—	3–64

Also bowled: D. L. Amiss 2-0-21-0; G. D. Barlow 1-0-2-0; K. W. R. Fletcher 15-4-55-1; D. W. Randall 5-1-14-0

MCC Tour of India, Sri Lanka and Australia

Full Tour First-Class Averages

Batting

	M	I	NO	Runs	HS	Av	100	50	Ct/St
G. D. Barlow	9	13	2	562	118	51.09	3	2	3
J. M. Brearley	14	20	2	888	202	49.33	1	8	14
D. L. Amiss	12	20	1	868	179	45.68	2	6	5
R. W. Tolchard	9	14	6	352	67	44.00	—	3	15
A. W. Greig	13	20	2	705	162*	39.16	2	4	16
D. W. Randall	15	24	3	822	174	39.14	2	2	9
A. P. E. Knott	12	19	4	563	108*	37.53	1	3	30/2
G. Miller	10	11	2	325	56	36.11	—	3	4
K. W. R. Fletcher	10	16	3	356	118	27.38	1	2	9
C. M. Old	12	17	5	325	109*	27.08	1	2	6
R. A. Woolmer	11	20	0	498	60	24.90	—	3	6
J. K. Lever	12	14	2	165	53	13.75	—	1	6
D. L. Underwood	10	10	1	94	23	10.44	—	—	8
R. G. D. Willis	11	10	4	62	37	10.33	—	—	5
G. A. Cope	7	3	3	43	27*	—	—	—	1
M. W. W. Selvey	9	4	4	56	28*	—	—	—	3

Bowling

	Balls*	Runs	Wkts	Av	10wM	5wI	BB
D. L. Underwood	2363	709	44	16.11	—	1	5–84
J. K. Lever	2128	898	53	16.94	1	3	7–46
G. A. Cope	1626	506	26	19.46	—	1	6–41
R. G. D. Willis	1656	740	37	20.00	—	4	6–53
C. M. Old	1494	624	28	22.28	—	—	4–104
G. Miller	776	314	10	31.40	—	—	4–54
M. W. W. Selvey	1252	616	19	32.42	—	—	3–81
A. W. Greig	1272	639	15	42.60	—	—	3–64
R. A. Woolmer	626	299	7	42.71	—	—	2–14
K. W. R. Fletcher	90	55	1	55.00	—	—	—
D. L. Amiss	12	21	0	—	—	—	—
G. D. Barlow	6	2	0	—	—	—	—
D. W. Randall	30	14	0	—	—	—	—

*8-ball overs were used in Sri Lanka and Australia.

4 THE SCORES

1st Match
MCC v West Zone *Poona, November 29, 30, December 1*

Match drawn

West Zone *First Innings*

D. B. Vengsarkar c Greig b Old	....	46
R. D. Parkar c Fletcher b Greig	....	25
R. V. Mankad lbw b Selvey	....	7
Y. Singh c Fletcher b Willis	....	16
*E. D. Solkar c Randall b Miller	....	57
R. Bhalekar b Willis	....	66
D. Parsana c Greig b Old	....	14
R. Jadeja c and b Willis	....	4
†V. Shetty b Willis	....	0
P. K. Shivalkar not out	....	1
U. C. Joshi lbw b Willis	....	4
Extras (b4, nb13)	....	17
Total	....	257

Second Innings

c sub (Barlow) b Fletcher	....	34
c sub (Barlow) b Greig	....	7
c Tolchard b Cope	....	14
not out	....	22
not out	....	2
(lb2, w1)	....	3
Total (3 wkts)....	82

Fall of Wickets
1 – 40 2 – 61 3 – 90 4 – 115 5 – 218 6 – 246 7 – 252 8 – 252 9 – 256 10 – 257
1 – 22 2 – 44 3 – 77

Bowling	*First Innings*				*Second Innings*			
Old	14	5	37	2	4	0	21	0
Willis	12.5	4	24	5				
Selvey	9	6	24	1				
Greig	19	4	74	1	3	0	22	1
Cope	22	8	40	0	16	10	8	1
Miller	11	2	41	1	11	5	20	0
Fletcher					4	1	8	1

MCC *First Innings*

D. L. Amiss lbw b Parsana	....	23
J. M. Brearley c and b Joshi	....	202
K. W. R. Fletcher lbw b Solkar	....	118
*A. W. Greig not out	....	162
D. W. Randall run out	....	0
†R. W. Tolchard c Mankad b Solkar	....	67
Extras (b2, lb7, nb4)	....	13
Total (5 wkts dec)....	585

G. Miller
C. M. Old
G. A. Cope   } Did not bat
M. W. W. Selvey
R. G. D. Willis

Fall of Wickets
1 – 50 2 – 342 3 – 369 4 – 370 5 – 585

Bowling				
Jadeja	14	1	32	0
Parsana	53	11	191	1
Shivalkar	39	6	133	0
Joshi	32	6	109	1
Solkar	22.4	2	65	2
Singh	2	0	22	0
Bhalekar	4	0	20	0

171

2nd Match
MCC v Central Zone *Jaipur, December 3, 4, 5*

Match drawn

MCC   *First Innings*

D. L. Amiss run out	60
R. A. Woolmer c Ansari b Ghattani	15
G. D. Barlow c Hans b Durrani	113
D. W. Randall not out	48
†A. P. E. Knott not out	16
Extras (b 4, lb 3, w 1)	8

*J. M. Brearley ⎫
G. Miller ⎪
C. M. Old ⎪
G. A. Cope ⎬ Did not bat
D. L. Underwood ⎪
J. K. Lever ⎭

Total (for 3 wkts dec.)....260

Second Innings

(2) lbw b Ghattani	36
(1) not out	108
(3) C. M. Old not out	2
(b 9)	9

D. L. Amiss ⎫
G. D. Barlow ⎪
D. W. Randall ⎪
J. M. Brearley ⎬ Did not bat
G. Miller ⎪
G. A. Cope ⎪
D. L. Underwood ⎭
J. K. Lever

Total (for 1 wkt dec.)....155

Fall of Wickets
1 – 29 2 – 138 3 – 223
1 – 126

Bowling	*First Innings*							
Ghattani	18	5	39	1	10	2	35	1
Ali	6	1	29	0	3	0	14	0
Deshpande	11	2	31	0	2	0	14	0
Ahmed	12	2	28	0	6	0	29	0
Sharma	16	4	42	0	1	0	8	0
Hans	21	10	44	0	7	1	29	0
Durrani	10	1	39	1	6	0	17	0

Central Zone   *First Innings*

M. I. Ansari b Old	0
V. Chopra c Knott b Lever	8
A. Deshpande hit wkt b Lever	64
P. Sharma c Underwood b Miller	23
Salim Durrani b Lever	9
*Hanumant Singh c Knott b Underwood	9
V. Nayudu b Cope	0
Gulrez Ali c Miller b Underwood	30
Kailash Ghattani not out	12
Hassen Ahmed not out	5
Extras (b 5, lb 2, w 1, nb 1)	9

Total (8 wkts dec.)....169
R. S. Hans did not bat

Second Innings

(1) lbw b Woolmer	9
(6) b Cope	13
(4) not out	41
(5) run out	1
(7) not out	36
(2) lbw b Lever	15
(3) c Knott b Woolmer	1
(lb 1, nb 3)	4

Total (5 wkts)....120

Fall of Wickets
1 – 0   2 – 17 3 – 65 4 – 87 5 – 111 6 – 112 7 – 133 8 – 160
1 – 19 2 – 21 3 – 25 4 – 26 5 – 51

Bowling	*First Innings*							
Old	2.3	0	5	1				
Lever	19	2	53	3	12	3	29	1
Woolmer	6	2	17	0	8	5	14	2
Underwood	23	13	23	2	10	4	17	0
Cope	26	12	52	1	9	3	19	1
Miller	11	9	10	1	9	5	16	0
Amiss					2	0	21	0
Randall					1	1	0	0

3rd Match
MCC v Board President's XI *Ahmedabad, December 7, 8, 9*

Match drawn

MCC *First Innings*
D. L. Amiss c Reddy b Prasanna		51
G. D. Barlow c Vengsarkar b Prasanna		102
D. W. Randall lbw b Ghavri		24
*A. W. Greig c Reddy b Ghavri		5
G. Miller not out		51
C. M. Old b Ghavri		2
†R. W. Tolchard not out		44

Extras (nb 5, w 1, lb 3, b 1) 10

J. M. Brearley
D. L. Underwood
M. W. W. Selvey   Did not bat
J. K. Lever

Total (for 5 wkts dec.)....289

Second Innings
(1) c Sharma b Ghavri		11
(3) not out		47
(4) c sub b Minna		1
(5) c Prasanna b Sharma		5
(2) J. M. Brearley hit wicket b Sharma		59
(lb 4)		4

Total (4 wkts dec.)....127

Fall of Wickets
1 – 103 2 – 174 3 – 187 4 – 193 5 – 196
1 – 24   2 – 105 3 – 110 4 – 127

Bowling	*First Innings*							
Ghavri	19	3	66	3	8	2	22	1
Burman	16	0	61	0	10	0	31	0
Prasanna	29	3	92	2	7	3	5	0
Minna	14	2	39	0	12	3	40	1
Sharma	11	2	21	0	8	0	25	2

Board President's XI *First Innings*
P. S. Chauhan c Tolchard b Selvey		6
D. B. Vengsarkar c Greig b Lever		0
P. Sharma c Tolchard b Selvey		111
Y. Singh c Tolchard b Lever		2
B. P. Patel c Old b Underwood		23
A. V. Mankad not out		51
K. Ghavri not out		0

Extras (b 4, lb 5, nb 11) 20

B. Burman
*E. A. S. Prasanna   Did not bat
†B. Reddy
A. Minna

Total (for 5 wkts dec.)....213

Second Innings
(2) lbw b Selvey		10
(1) lbw b Old		29
(3) c Tolchard b Old		21
(8) not out		7
(4) lbw b Underwood		16
(7) not out		32
(5) c Tolchard b Old		6
(6) B. Reddy c and b Underwood		16

Extras (b 1, nb 6) 7

B. Burman
E. A. S. Prasanna   Did not bat
A. Minna

Total (for 6 wkts)....144

Fall of Wickets
1 – 4   2 – 23 3 – 27 4 – 90 5 – 213
1 – 26 2 – 63 3 – 64 4 – 85 5 – 91 6 – 132

Bowling	*First Innings*							
Old	14	2	32	0	11	5	29	3
Lever	17	5	39	2	7	2	13	0
Selvey	12	5	21	2	11	1	30	1
Underwood	21	9	36	1	10	2	39	2
Greig	10	1	35	0	4	0	26	0
Miller	9	1	30	0				

4th Match
MCC v North Zone *Jullunder, December 12, 13, 14*

Match Drawn

MCC   *First Innings*

R. A. Woolmer b Shukla	57
*A. W. Greig c Chauhan b Bedi	53
J. M. Brearley st Raj b Bedi	65
K. W. R. Fletcher b Shukla	4
†A. P. E. Knott c Raj b Minna	71
C. M. Old not out	109
D. W. Randall c Goel b Bedi	8
J. K. Lever not out	0

R. G. D. Willis
M. W. W. Selvey   } Did not bat
G. Miller

Extras (b 7, lb 13, nb 2) ... 22
Total (for 6 wkts dec.)....389

Second Innings

(1) c Raj b Madan Lal	29
(2) c Raj b Madan Lal	3
(5) not out	54
(3) lbw b Shukla	23
(4) lbw b Shukla	11
(6) c S. Amarnath b Madan Lal..	37

(b 1, lb 3) ... 4
Total (for 5 wkts dec.)....161

Fall of Wickets
1 – 110 2 – 114 3 – 119 4 – 217 5 – 376 6 – 389
1 – 3   2 – 48   3 – 65   4 – 74   5 – 161

Bowling	First Innings				Second Innings			
Madan Lal	15	1	75	0	14.3	0	42	3
M. Amarnath	18	6	41	0	10	1	33	0
Bedi	15	4	38	3	5	3	8	0
Goel	13	2	66	0	10	3	31	0
Minna	9	1	46	1	4	0	22	0
Shukla	17	1	71	2	12	6	9	2
Chauhan	5	0	30	0	2	0	12	0

North Zone   *First Innings*

C. P. S. Chauhan c Knott b Lever	30
V. Sundaram b Woolmer	46
M. Amarnath c Randall b Lever	0
S. Amarnath c sub b Willis	30
S. Madan Lal c Selvey b Willis	1
V. Lamba b Lever	40
R. Shukla c Knott b Woolmer	0
†V. Raj not out	34
R. Goel lbw b Lever	3
*B. S. Bedi not out	10
Extras (nb13, lb2, b1)	16

A. Minna   did not bat
Total (for 8 wkts dec.)....210

Second Innings

c Knott b Lever	22
c sub b Lever	18
b Lever	0
not out	47
not out	34

(b1, nb4) ... 5

(3 wkts)....126

Fall of Wickets
1 – 47 2 – 48 3 – 96 4 – 102 5 – 131 6 – 131 7 – 191 8 – 195
1 – 36 2 – 36 3 – 44

Bowling	First Innings				Second Innings			
Willis	15	3	43	2	4	0	18	0
Lever	24	7	51	4	5	3	8	3
Selvey	24	5	54	0	5	2	12	0
Old	3	0	11	0	3	1	11	0
Woolmer	8	1	30	2	6	1	17	0
Fletcher	3	1	5	0	8	2	42	0
Randall					3	0	13	0

5th Match

INDIA v ENGLAND – First Test Match at Delhi: December 17–22

England won by an innings and 25 runs

England *First Innings*

D. L. Amiss c Sharma b Venkataraghavan	179
J. M. Brearley run out	5
G. D. Barlow c Amarnath b Bedi	0
R. A. Woolmer lbw b Chandrasekhar	4
K. W. R. Fletcher b Chandrasekhar	8
*A. W. Greig lbw b Venkataraghavan	25
†A. P. E. Knott st Kirmani b Bedi	75
C. M. Old c Viswanath b Bedi	15
J. K. Lever c Bedi b Chandrasekhar	53
R. G. D. Willis c Venkataraghavan b Bedi	1
D. L. Underwood not out	7
Extras (b1, lb5, nb2, wl)	9
Total	381

Fall of Wickets

1–34 2–34 3–51 4–65 5–125 6–226 7–263 8–357 9–363 10–381

Bowling				
Ghavri	14	3	50	0
Amarnath	8	2	12	0
Bedi	59	22	92	4
Chandrasekhar	33.5	6	117	3
Venkataraghavan	34	6	94	2
Sharma	3	0	6	0
Gaekwad	1	0	1	0

India *First Innings*		*Second Innings*	
S. M. Gavaskar c Willis b Lever	38	c Woolmer b Underwood	71
A. D. Gaekwad lbw b Lever	20	b Willis	11
M. Amarnath lbw b Lever	0	(6) c sub b Underwood	24
G. R. Viswanath lbw b Lever	3	c Knott b Greig	18
S. Venkataraghavan b Lever	0	(9) c Knott b Lever	4
B. P. Patel c Knott b Lever	33	(5) c and b Underwood	14
P. Sharma c Willis b Underwood	4	(3) c Fletcher b Underwood	29
†S. M. H. Kirmani b Lever	13	(8) c Lever b Greig	10
K. Ghavri not out	3	(7) not out	35
* B. S. Bedi c Greig b Old	0	b Lever	0
B. S. Chandrasekhar b Old	0	b Lever	0
Extras (lb4, nb3, w1)	8	(b3, lb8, nb7)	18
Total	122	Total	234

Fall of Wickets

1–43 2–43 3–49 4–49 5–96 6–99 7–103 8–121 9–122 10–122

1–20 2–110 3–133 4–153 5–163 6–182 7–190 8–226 9–226 10–234

Bowling	*First Innings*				*Second Innings*			
Old	12.5	0	28	2	4	2	6	0
Willis	7	3	21	0	9	3	24	1
Lever	23	6	46	7	13.4	6	24	3
Underwood	9	3	19	1	44	15	78	4
Greig					40	11	84	2

Umpires: J. Reuben and M. V. Nagendra. Toss won by England.

6th Match
MCC v East Zone *Gauhati, December 27, 28, 29*

Match drawn

MCC   *First Innings*

G. D. Barlow lbw b Doshi	35	
D. W. Randall b Bhattacharjee	55	
J. M. Brearley c Mukherjee b Bhattacharjee ...	5	
R. A. Woolmer c Mukherjee b Bhattacharjee .	8	
*A. W. Greig c Burman b Doshi	1	
†R. W. Tolchard lbw b Burman	53	
G. Miller not out	41	
C. M. Old not out	0	

G. A. Cope
M. W. W. Selvey } Did not bat
R. G. D. Willis

Extras (b5, lb9, nb1) 15

Total (6 wkts dec.)....213

Second Innings

c Banerjee b Doshi	61
lbw b Burman	6
c Banerjee b Burman	9
st Banerjee b Bhattacharjee	22
b Doshi	0
(8) c Banerjee b Doshi	6
(7) c Saxena b Bhattacharjee	0
(6) st Banerjee b Bhattacharjee ...	33
not out	0
not out	0

(b1, lb2, nb3) 6

(8 wkts dec.)....143

Fall of wickets
1 – 65 2 – 70 3 – 110 4 – 115 5 – 119 6 – 212
1 – 11 2 – 49 3 – 95 4 – 95 5 – 118 6 – 118 7 – 131 8 – 143

Bowling	First Innings				Second Innings			
Burman	14	2	37	1	19	3	49	2
Kakati	11	0	37	0	7	1	25	0
Doshi	33	10	54	2	23	8	35	3
Bhattacharjee	31	9	69	3	10	5	28	3
Nandy	1	0	1	0				

East Zone   *First Innings*

†S. Banerjee c Tolchard b Willis	1
P. Nandy b Willis	12
T. Raj b Willis	1
R. Mukherjee c Tolchard b Willis	62
R. Saxena b Selvey	10
*A. Roy c Brearley b Cope	8
B. Bharali b Cope	6
B. Burman not out	7
A. Bhattacharjee b Willis	6
D. Doshi c Randall b Cope	10
M. Kakati run out	5
Extras (b6, lb1, nb12)	19

Total....147

Second Innings

b Old	0
(5) c Brearley b Selvey	8
b Cope	3
(2) c Miller b Selvey	35
b Cope	1
(3) not out	45
(7) b Cope	15
(8) c Randall b Cope	0
(9) not out	8
(b6, lb11, nb4, w1)	22

Total (7 wkts)....137

Fall of Wickets
1 – 3 2 – 7 3 – 44 4 – 95 5 – 105 6 – 113 7 – 119 8 – 128 9 – 141 10 – 147
1 – 3 2 – 65 3 – 68 4 – 82 5 – 84 6 – 116 7 – 118

Bowling	First Innings				Second Innings			
Old	9	0	39	0	8	5	5	1
Willis	13.2	3	29	5	11	1	34	0
Selvey	6	4	21	1	8	0	17	2
Cope	12	3	39	3	23	6	55	4
Greig					1	0	1	0
Miller					3	0	3	0

7th Match
INDIA v ENGLAND – Second Test Match at Calcutta : January 1, 2, 3, 5, 6

England won by 10 wickets

India *First Innings*		*Second Innings*	
S. M. Gavaskar c Old b Willis	0	b Underwood	18
A. D. Gaekwad b Lever	32	c Tolchard b Greig	8
P. Sharma c Greig b Lever	9	c Knott b Willis	20
G. R. Viswanath c Tolchard b Underwood	35	c Lever b Greig	3
B. P. Patel hit wkt b Willis	21	lbw b Old	56
E. D. Solkar c Greig b Willis	2	c Knott b Willis	3
S. Madan Lal c Knott b Old	17	c Brearley b Old	16
†S. M. H. Kirmani not out	25	b Old	0
E. A. S. Prasanna b Willis	2	c Brearley b Underwood	13
*B. S. Bedi c Lever b Old	1	b Underwood	18
B. S. Chandrasekhar b Willis	1	not out	4
Extras (lb2, nb8)	10	(b2, lb4, nb16)	22
Total	155	Total	181

Fall of Wickets
1 – 1   2 – 23   3 – 65   4 – 92   5 – 99   6 – 106   7 – 136   8 – 147   9 – 149   10 – 155
1 – 31   2 – 33   3 – 36   4 – 60   5 – 70   6 – 97   7 – 97   8 – 146   9 – 171   10 – 181

Bowling	First Innings				Second Innings			
Willis	20	3	27	5	13	1	32	2
Lever	22	2	57	2	3	0	12	0
Underwood	13	5	24	1	32.5	18	50	3
Old	20	5	37	2	12	4	38	3
Greig					10	0	27	2

England *First Innings*		*Second Innings*	
D. L. Amiss c Kirmani b Prasanna	35	not out	7
G. D. Barlow c Kirmani b Lal	4	not out	7
J. M. Brearley c Solkar b Bedi	5		
D. W. Randall lbw b Prasanna	37		
R. W. Tolchard b Bedi	67		
*A. W. Greig lbw b Prasanna	103		
†A. P. E. Knott c Gavaskar b Bedi	2		
C. M. Old c Lal b Prasanna	52		
J. K. Lever c Gavaskar b Bedi	2		
D. L. Underwood c Gavaskar b Bedi	4		
R. G. D. Willis not out	0		
Extras (b5, lb5)	10	(nb1, lb1)	2
Total	321	Total (0 wkts)	16

Fall of Wickets
1 – 7   2 – 14   3 – 81   4 – 90   5 – 232   6 – 234   7 – 298   8 – 307   9 – 321   10 – 321

Bowling	First Innings				Second Innings			
Madan Lal	17	4	25	1	1	0	3	0
Solkar	6	1	16	0				
Bedi	64	25	110	5	1.4	0	6	0
Chandrasekhar	33	9	66	0				
Prasanna	57.4	16	93	4	1	0	5	0
Sharma	1	0	2	0				

Umpires: S. Rao and H. P. Sharma.   Toss won by India.

8th Match
MCC v University and Combined 'Under 22' XI *Nagpur, January 8, 9, 10*

MCC won by 143 runs

MCC   *First Innings*
D. L. Amiss c Azad b Minna	56
R. A. Woolmer c Ved Raj b D. Jadeja	49
*J. M. Brearley not out	76
K. W. R. Fletcher lbw b R. Jadeja	24
A. P. E. Knott c Ved Raj b Yog Raj	1
†R. W. Tolchard not out	19

D. W. Randall ⎫
G. Miller ⎪
G. A. Cope ⎬ Did not bat
M. W. W. Selvey ⎪
J. K. Lever ⎭

Extras (b4, lb5, nb3)	12
Total (4 wkts dec.)	237

Second Innings
(6) c Binny b D. Jadeja	6
(2) lbw b R. Jadeja	29
(8) c Vengsarkar b D. Jadeja	4
(5) c and b D. Jadeja	8
(1) b R. Jadeja	14
(10) not out	14
(3) c Vengsarkar b Minna	15
(4) c Ved Raj b D. Jadeja	3
(9) not out	16
(7) b Minna	17
(b2, lb3)	5
(8 wkts dec.)	131

Fall of Wickets
1 – 110   2 – 111   3 – 172   4 – 179
1 – 21   2 – 50   3 – 61   4 – 67   5 – 70   6 – 76   7 – 98   8 – 98

Bowling	First Innings				Second Innings			
Yog Raj	14	0	46	1	1	0	2	0
R. Jadeja	26	12	42	1	14	7	16	2
Binny	5	1	16	0	7	2	23	0
D. Jadeja	33	5	76	1	23	6	61	4
Minna	23	6	45	1	17	6	24	2

University XI   *First Innings*
*D. B. Vengsarkar b Miller	32
S. Akbar b Lever	4
V. Mohan Raj c Tolchard b Miller	32
R. V. Mankad b Cope	·1
K. Azad lbw b Cope	4
R. Binny c Tolchard b Cope	0
R. Jadeja lbw b Cope	15
†Ved Raj run out	1
Yog Raj c Amiss b Cope	10
D. Jadeja not out	7
A. Minna c Selvey b Cope	0
Extras (b8, lb1, nb6)	15
Total	121

Second Innings
c Randall b Cope	39
(6) c Lever b Miller	5
run out	8
c Woolmer b Miller	1
c sub b Miller	3
(2) b Cope	5
run out	1
c and b Miller	4
c Knott b Cope	15
lbw b Lever	13
not out	8
(b1, nb1)	2
Total	104

Fall of wickets
1 – 8   2 – 73   3 – 76   4 – 88   5 – 88   6 – 88   7 – 99   8 – 111   9 – 121   10 – 121
1 – 24   2 – 48   3 – 53   4 – 57   5 – 57   6 – 60   7 – 67   8 – 68   9 – 84   10 – 104

Bowling	First Innings				Second Innings			
Lever	7	0	14	1	8	2	19	1
Selvey	6	2	12	0	2	1	9	0
Cope	22.5	10	41	6	23.3	11	20	3
Miller	23	13	39	2	17	2	54	4

9th Match
INDIA v ENGLAND – **Third Test Match at Madras, January 14, 15, 16, 18, 19**

England won by 200 runs

England First Innings			**Second Innings**	
D. L. Amiss lbw b Lal	4		c Amarnath b Chandra	46
R. A. Woolmer c Gavaskar b Lal	22		lbw b Prasanna	16
J. M. Brearley c and b Prasanna	59		(4) b Chandra	29
D. W. Randall run out	2		(5) c Kirmani b Chandra	0
R. W. Tolchard not out	8		(9) not out	10
* A. W. Greig c Viswanath b Bedi	54		(6) lbw b Prasanna	41
† A. P. E. Knott c Viswanath b Bedi	45		(7) c Patel b Prasanna	11
J. K. Lever c Kirmani b Bedi	23		(3) c Amarnath b Chandra	2
C. M. Old c Amarnath b Bedi	2		(8) c Chandra b Prasanna	4
D. L. Underwood b Prasanna	23		st Kirmani b Chandra	8
R. G. D. Willis run out	7		not out	4
Extras (b5, lb8)	13		(b14)	14
Total....262			Total (9 wkts dec.)....185	

Fall of Wickets
1 – 14   2 – 29 3 – 31 4 – 142 5 – 162 6 – 201 7 – 209 8 – 228 9 – 253 10 – 262
1 – 39 2 – 54 3 – 83 4 – 83   5 – 124 6 – 135 7 – 141 8 – 169 9 – 180

Bowling	First Innings				Second Innings			
Madan Lal	21	5	43	2	9	2	15	0
Amarnath	14	3	26	0	7	2	18	0
Chandrasekhar	25	4	63	0	20.5	4	50	5
Bedi	38.5	16	72	4	13	3	33	0
Prasanna	27	11	45	2	22	5	55	4

India First Innings			**Second Innings**	
S. M. Gavaskar c Brearley b Old	39		c Woolmer b Underwood	24
M. Amarnath b Old	0		(3) c Woolmer b Underwood	12
G. R. Viswanath c Knott b Lever	9		(4) c Brearley b Underwood	6
A. V. Mankad b Lever	0		(7) c Old b Lever	4
B. P. Patel b Underwood	32		(6) c Old b Willis	4
D. B. Vengsarkar c Randall b Lever	8		(2) retired hurt	1
S. Madan Lal c Underwood b Willis	12		(9) c Knott b Willis	6
† S. M. H. Kirmani c Brearley b Lever	27		(8) c Brearley b Willis	1
E. A. S. Prasanna c and b Underwood	13		(5) c Brearley b Underwood	0
* B. S. Bedi c sub b Lever	5		not out	11
B. S. Chandrasekhar not out	1		b Lever	6
Extras (lb1, nb17)	18		(b5, lb1, nb2)	8
Total....164			Total.... 83	

Fall of Wickets
1 – 5   2 – 17 3 – 17 4 – 69 5 – 86 6 – 114 7 – 115 8 – 151 9 – 161 10 – 164
1 – 40 2 – 45 3 – 45 4 – 54 5 – 54 6 – 57 7 – 66 8 – 71   9 – 83

Bowling	First Innings				Second Innings			
Willis	19	5	46	1	13	4	18	3
Old	13	4	19	2	5	1	11	0
Lever	19.5	2	59	5	6.5	0	18	2
Woolmer	1	0	2	0				
Greig	4	1	4	0				
Underwood	17	9	16	2	14	7	28	4

Umpires: J. Reuben and M. S. Shivashankariah.   Toss won by England.

179

10th Match
MCC v South Zone – *Hyderabad, January 22, 23, 24*

Match drawn

South Zone   *First Innings*

V. Shivaramakrishnan run out	27
P. Ramesh b Lever	0
A. V. Jayaprakash c Greig b Selvey	6
G. R. Viswanath c and b Cope	49
B. P. Patel c Amiss b Miller	30
S. Abid Ali c and b Selvey	63
M. V. Narasimha Rao c Knott b Lever	32
*S. Venkataraghavan not out	6
B. Jyotiprasad not out	0
B. Meher Baba ⎱ Did not bat	
†B. Reddy ⎰	
Extras (b1, lb1, w1, nb12)	15
Total (7 wkts dec.)	228

Second Innings

c Greig b Selvey	2
c Greig b Lever	0
not out	37
(4) not out	64
(lb4)	4
Total (2 wkts)	107

Fall of Wickets
1 – 3 2 – 26 3 – 64 4 – 111 5 – 133 6 – 195 7 – 226
1 – 1 2 – 3

Bowling	First Innings				Second Innings			
Lever	14	3	42	2	8	0	24	1
Selvey	23	10	42	2	14	3	37	1
Cope	28	5	76	1	18	7	32	0
Woolmer	9	1	27	0	8	4	10	0
Miller	5	0	16	1				
Greig	4	0	10	0				
Randall					1	1	0	0

MCC   *First Innings*

D. L. Amiss st Reddy b Meher Baba	138
R. A. Woolmer c Shivaramakrishnan b Abid Ali	17
K. W. R. Fletcher c Reddy b Jayaprakash	1
D. W. Randall c Shivaramakrishnan b Abid Ali	142
G. D. Barlow c Abid Ali b Venkataraghavan	4
†A. P. E. Knott c Venkataraghavan b Jayaprakash	13
G. Miller lbw b Abid Ali	7
*A. W. Greig b Abid Ali	10
G. A. Cope not out	27
J. K. Lever c Patel b Meher Baba	0
M. W. W. Selvey not out	28
Extras (b6, lb4, nb4)	14
Total (9 wkts dec.)	401

Fall of Wickets
1 – 34 2 – 35 3 – 256 4 – 273 5 – 301 6 – 314 7 – 340 8 – 351 9 – 352

Bowling	First Innings			
Abid Ali	32	3	100	4
Jyotiprasad	8	0	26	0
Jayaprakash	21	3	68	2
Venkataraghavan	13	3	35	1
Meher Baba	34	5	92	2
Narasimha Rao	17	2	54	0
Patel	3	0	12	0

180

11th Match
INDIA v ENGLAND Fourth Test Match at Bangalore, January 28, 29, 30, February 1, 2
India won by 140 runs

India *First Innings*

S. M. Gavaskar c Underwood b Lever		4
A. D. Gaekwad c Tolchard b Greig		39
S. Amarnath b Greig		63
G. R. Viswanath c Brearley b Underwood		13
B. P. Patel c Randall b Willis		23
Yajuvendra Singh c Knott b Willis		8
†S. M. H. Kirmani b Willis		52
K. Ghavri c Knott b Willis		16
E. A. S. Prasanna c Greig b Willis		6
*B. S. Bedi not out		8
B. S. Chandrasekhar c Knott b Willis		1
Extras (b8, lb6, nb6)		20
	Total....	253

Second Innings

c Brearley b Underwood		50
b Old		9
c Tolchard b Willis		14
(7) not out		79
(4) c Knott b Underwood		17
(5) c Fletcher b Underwood		15
(8) c Randall b Underwood		21
(9) c Amiss b Lever		12
(6) c Old b Willis		12
run out		15
not out		0
(b1, lb6, nb8)		15
Total (9 wkts. dec.)....		259

Fall of Wickets
1 – 9   2 – 102 3 – 124 4 – 134 5 – 153 6 – 170 7 – 236 8 – 240 9 – 249 10 – 253
1 – 31 2 – 80   3 – 92   4 – 104 5 – 124 6 – 154 7 – 189 8 – 223 9 – 257

Bowling	First Innings				Second Innings			
Willis	17	2	53	6	18	2	47	2
Lever	17	2	48	1	9	1	28	1
Old	12	0	43	0	10	4	19	1
Underwood	21	7	45	1	31	8	76	4
Greig	18	5	44	2	23	2	74	0

England *First Innings*

D. L. Amiss c Yajuvendra b Chandra		82
J. M. Brearley c Viswanath b Chandra		4
K. W. R. Fletcher c Yajuvendra b Prasanna		10
D. W. Randall c Yajuvendra b Prasanna		10
R. W. Tolchard b Chandra		0
*A. W. Greig c Yajuvendra b Chandra		2
†A. P. E. Knott b Bedi		29
C. M. Old lbw b Prasanna		9
J. K. Lever not out		20
D. L. Underwood c Yajuvendra b Chandra		12
R. G. D. Willis lbw b Chandra		7
Extras (b3, lb5, nb2)		10
	Total....	195

Second Innings

c Yajuvendra b Ghavri		0
c Gaekwad b Bedi		4
c Yajuvendra b Chandra		1
c Gaekwad b Bedi		0
lbw b Chandra		14
st Kirmani b Bedi		31
not out		81
lbw b Chandra		13
c Ghavri b Bedi		11
c Patel b Bedi		10
st Kirmani b Bedi		0
(b5, lb6, nb1)		12
Total....		177

Fall of Wickets
1 – 13 2 – 34 3 – 64 4 – 65 5 – 67 6 – 137 7 – 146 8 – 154 9 – 175 10 – 195
1 – 0   2 – 7   3 – 7   4 – 8   5 – 35 6 – 61   7 – 105 8 – 148 9 – 166 10 – 177

Bowling	First Innings				Second Innings			
Ghavri	13	3	31	0	4	1	4	1
Yajuvendra	1	0	2	0				
Bedi	23	11	29	1	21.3	4	71	6
Chandrasekhar	31.2	7	76	6	15	3	55	3
Prasanna	28	10	47	3	15	5	35	0
Gavaskar					2	2	0	0

Umpires: M. V. Nagendra and Mohamed Ghouse. Toss won by India

12th Match
MCC v Bombay *Indore, February 5, 6, 7*

Match drawn

MCC   *First Innings*
			Second Innings	
R. A. Woolmer c Mohanraj b Shivalkar	60		c sub b Solkar	16
*J. M. Brearley c Mankad b Shivalkar............	79			
G. Miller lbw b Zarapkar................................	16		(2) c sub b Shivalkar....................	52
K. W. R. Fletcher not out	65		(4) not out	19
G. D. Barlow lbw b Zarapkar	26			
D. W. Randall not out	61			
†R. W. Tolchard			(3) not out	20
C. M. Old				
G. A. Cope } Did not bat				
D. L. Underwood				
M. W. W. Selvey				
Extras (nb1)...	1		(b1, lb4).......................................	5
Total (4 wkts dec.)....308			(2 wkts dec.)....112	

Fall of Wickets
1 – 115 2 – 139 3 – 161 4 – 215
1 – 47 2 – 84

Bowling	*First Innings*					*Second Innings*			
Ismail	16	2	47	0		10	0	32	0
Nayak	19	3	94	0		4	1	24	0
Solkar	3	1	8	0		9	1	25	1
Shivalkar	34	10	74	2		5	0	15	1
Zarapkar	28	3	84	2		1	0	11	0

Bombay   *First Innings*
			Second Innings	
*S. M. Gavaskar c Woolmer b Selvey.............	14		(1) b Selvey..................................	19
S. S. Naik c Barlow b Selvey	2		(2) c Underwood b Old..............	5
†V. Mohanraj not out.....................................	76		(4) b Cope	2
S. Jaywant c Brearley b Old	30		(3) not out	34
E. D. Solkar c Miller b Cope...........................	6		(5) b Cope	13
S. Nayak lbw b Underwood.............................	15		(6) lbw b Woolmer	6
A. Zarapkar c Barlow b Underwood	0		(7) not out	1
S. Bandiwadekar lbw b Miller........................	9			
A. Ismail not out..	19			
R. V. Mankad } Did not bat				
P. K. Shivalkar				
Extras (b10, lb6, nb14)..............................	30		(b9, nb3, lb5)..............................	17
Total (7 wkts dec.)....201			Total (5 wkts).... 97	

Fall of Wickets
1 – 19 2 – 45 3 – 98 4 – 116 5 – 148 6 – 148 7 – 161
1 – 8 2 – 42 3 – 49 4 – 76 5 – 95

Bowling	*First Innings*					*Second Innings*			
Old	18	6	32	1		6	2	10	1
Selvey	20	4	47	2		16	7	27	1
Cope	18	6	36	1		20	9	30	2
Miller	16	5	41	1					
Underwood	7	3	14	2		6	4	2	0
Woolmer	4	3	1	0		5	1	9	1
Barlow						1	0	2	0

13th Match
INDIA v ENGLAND *Fifth Test Match at Bombay, February 11, 12, 14, 15, 16*

Match drawn

India   *First Innings*

			Second Innings	
S. M. Gavaskar c & b Underwood	108		c Willis b Underwood	42
A. D. Gaekwad c Tolchard b Lever	21		st Knott b Underwood	25
S. Amarnath b Underwood	40		run out	63
G. R. Viswanath c & b Lever	4		(5) c Lever b Greig	5
B. P. Patel st Knott b Greig	83		(4) c Fletcher b Underwood	3
Yajuvendra Singh b Greig	6		run out	21
†S. M. H. Kirmani c Knott b Underwood	8		c Greig b Underwood	10
K. Ghavri lbw b Greig	25		c Fletcher b Underwood	8
E. A. S. Prasanna b Underwood	9		not out	0
*B. S. Bedi not out	20		lbw b Lever	3
B. S. Chandrasekhar b Lever	3		b Lever	4
Extras (lb9, nb2)	11		(b4, lb1, nb3)	8
	Total....338			Total....192

Fall of Wickets
1 – 52 2 – 115 3 – 122 4 – 261 5 – 267 6 – 273 7 – 289 8 – 303 9 – 321 10 – 338
1 – 68 2 – 72 3 – 80 4 – 92 5 – 136 6 – 156 7 – 182 8 – 185 9 – 188 10 – 192

Bowling	*First Innings*				*Second Innings*			
Willis	13	1	52	0	6	1	15	0
Lever	17.4	4	42	3	17.4	6	46	2
Selvey	15	1	80	0				
Underwood	38	13	89	4	33	10	84	5
Greig	22	6	64	3	14	3	39	1

England   *First Innings*

			Second Innings	
D. L. Amiss c Viswanath b Bedi	50		c Viswanath b Bedi	14
J. M. Brearley st Kirmani b Prasanna	91		c Yajuvendra b Prasanna	18
D. W. Randall c Gaekwad b Prasanna	22		c Kirmani b Ghavri	15
K. W. R. Fletcher c Viswanath b Chandrasekhar	14			
*A. W. Greig b Prasanna	76		not out	58
†A. P. E. Knott b Chandrasekhar	24		c Bedi b Ghavri	10
R. W. Tolchard st Kirmani b Prasanna	4		b Ghavri	1
J. K. Lever c Gavaskar b Bedi	7		c Gavaskar b Ghavri	26
D. L. Underwood b Bedi	7		c Patel b Ghavri	4
M. W. W. Selvey not out	5			
R. G. D. Willis c Gavaskar b Bedi	0			
Extras (lb13, nb3, b1)	17		(b2, lb3, nb1)	6
	Total....317		Total (7 wkts)....152	

Fall of Wickets
1 – 146 2 – 175 3 – 180 4 – 206 5 – 247 6 – 256 7 – 290 8 – 300 9 – 312 10 – 317
1 – 34 2 – 38 3 – 86 4 – 112 5 – 113 6 – 148 7 – 152

Bowling	*First Innings*				*Second Innings*			
Ghavri	12	2	31	0	15	6	33	5
Gavaskar	2	0	2	0	1	1	0	0
Bedi	56	20	109	4	21	5	52	1
Chandrasekhar	32	7	85	2	4	0	25	0
Prasanna	52	20	73	4	30	12	36	1

Umpires: H. Sharma and B. Rao. India won the toss.

14th Match
MCC v Sri Lanka (not first-class)
Colombo, February 20 (one-day match)
MCC 201–6 (40 overs)
(R. A. Woolmer 63, D. L. Amiss 44, D. W. Randall 40)
Sri Lanka 178–7 (40 overs) (B. Warnapura 58, D. Mendis 34)
MCC won by 23 runs

15th Match
MCC v Sri Lanka Cricket Control Board President's XI Galle, February 22 and 23 (two-day match) (not first-class)
President's xi 238 (G. Houtersz 53*, S. Fernando 31, G. A. Cope 5–64, M. W. W. Selvey 3–48)
MCC 154–3 (J. M. Brearley 81*, G. D. Barlow 46*)
Rain stopped play
Match drawn

16th Match
MCC v Sri Lanka *(see opposite)*

17th Match
MCC v Sri Lanka (not first-class)
Colombo, March 2 (one-day match)
MCC 123 (27.2 overs) (D. L. Amiss 32, T. Opatha 3–20, B. Warnapura 3–24, L. Kaluperuma 3–36)
Sri Lanka 124–7 (26.2 overs) (D. Mendis 41)
Sri Lanka won by 3 wickets

16th Match
MCC v Sri Lanka *(Unofficial Test Match)* Colombo, February 25, 26, 27, 28

Match drawn

MCC   *First Innings*
R. A. Woolmer c & b D. S. De Silva................ 26
G. Miller st Fernando b Kaluperuma 56
G. D. Barlow st Fernando b D. S. De Silva 118
D. W. Randall c Fernando b Opatha 45
D. L. Underwood b Paranathala 9
K. W. R. Fletcher lbw b D. S. De Silva 18
*A. W. Greig not out 59
†A. P. E. Knott not out................................. 4
J. K. Lever ⎫
G. A. Cope ⎬   Did not bat
R. G. D. Willis ⎭
Extras (b16, lb9) 25
Total (6 wkts dec)....360

Second Innings
c Fernando b Paranathala 14
lbw b Opatha.............................. 21
not out 22
c Opatha b D. S. De Silva 37

(b1, lb4).................................... 5
(3 wkts dec.).... 99

Fall of Wickets
1 – 61 2 – 124 3 – 205 4 – 224 5 – 272 6 – 321
1 – 35 2 – 39   3 – 99

Bowling	First Innings				Second Innings			
Opatha	13	0	60	1	11	2	56	1
Paranathala	9	2	17	1	7	0	16	1
D. S. De Silva	36	11	118	3	3.6	1	22	1
A. De Silva	26	7	68	0				
Kaluperuma	22	7	51	1				
Abeynaike	10	4	21	0				

Sri Lanka   *First Innings*
R. Fernando lbw b Lever 5
B. Warnapura c Knott b Lever 34
A. Tennekoon b Woolmer 10
A. Dias c Fletcher b Willis 14
D. Mendis b Underwood 3
T. Opatha hit wkt b Lever............................. 9
L. Kaluperuma c Barlow b Underwood 19
J. Paranathala b Lever.................................. 9
D. S. De Silva c Woolmer b Cope 23
R. Abeynaike c Greig b Willis........................ 15
A. De Silva not out 5
Extras (nb9, lb1) 10
Total....151

Second Innings
c Woolmer b Lever 10
c & b Cope.................................. 69
c & b Underwood 97
c Cope b Underwood 0
c sub b Cope............................... 2
b Willis....................................... 6
not out 1
not out 4

(b8, lb8, nb5)............................. 21
Total (6 wkts)....210

Fall of Wickets
1 – 16 2 – 33 3 – 68 4 – 71 5 – 80 6 – 82 7 – 113 8 – 127 9 – 133 10 – 151
1 – 22 2 – 185 3 – 186 4 – 191 5 – 191 6 – 205

Bowling	First Innings				Second Innings			
Lever	16	2	50	4	14	2	45	1
Willis	10.5	3	25	2	7	0	27	1
Woolmer	8	1	15	1	9	0	37	0
Cope	9	0	19	1	17	5	39	2
Underwood	14	7	21	2	11	4	26	2
Miller					5	2	15	0
Greig	1	0	11	0				

185

MCC v Western Australia *Perth, March 5, 6, 7*

Match drawn

Western Australia *First Innings*

		Second Innings	
R. I. Charlesworth c Knott b Selvey	18	c Knott b Selvey	69
G. Wood c Miller b Greig	37	c Amiss b Selvey	1
R. S. Langer b Selvey	3	run out	83
K. Hughes c Brearley b Old	39	c Knott b Selvey	19
C. Serjeant not out	101	not out	32
I. J. Brayshaw c Knott b Old	0	not out	3
*†R. W. Marsh c Old b Selvey	59		
A. Mann run out	17		
M. Malone c Randall b Woolmer	38		
D. K. Lillee not out	1		
Extras (lb10, nb3)	13	(lb10, nb1)	11
Total (8 wkts dec.)	326	(4 wkts dec.)	218

W. M. Clark did not bat.

Fall of Wickets
1 – 47 2 – 57 3 – 59 4 – 159 5 – 159 6 – 229 7 – 260 8 – 317
1 – 2 2 – 158 3 – 172 4 – 189

Bowling	*First Innings*				*Second Innings*			
Willis	10	1	60	0	6	1	21	0
Greig	12	0	47	1	3	0	11	0
Selvey	16.2	1	102	3	12	1	81	3
Woolmer	10	3	51	1	10	0	70	0
Miller	5	0	29	0				
Old	5	0	24	2	6	0	24	0

MCC *First Innings*

		Second Innings	
D. L. Amiss c Brayshaw b Lillee	9	c Marsh b Lillee	29
J. M. Brearley c Langer b Clark	61	(8) not out	58
G. Miller c Marsh b Malone	56	(2) c Serjeant b Malone	22
R. A. Woolmer c Brayshaw b Malone	6	c Brayshaw b Malone	51
G. D. Barlow lbw b Lillee	60	c Lillee b Mann	10
D. W. Randall c Lillee b Mann	16	(3) c Clark b Malone	31
*A. W. Greig c Marsh b Malone	7	c Marsh b Mann	6
†A. P. E. Knott c Marsh b Clark	11	run out	0
C. M. Old not out	12	c Marsh b Lillee	8
M. W. W. Selvey	did not bat	not out	23
R. G. D. Willis			
Extras (lb5, nb1)	6	(lb1)	1
Total (8 wkts dec.)	244	Total (8 wkts)	239

Fall of Wickets
1 – 10 2 – 119 3 – 130 4 – 154 5 – 180 6 – 197 7 – 215 8 – 244
1 – 50 2 – 60 3 – 100 4 – 115 5 – 127 6 – 140 7 – 153 8 – 182

Bowling	*First Innings*				*Second Innings*			
Lillee	10.5	2	44	2	9	4	25	2
Malone	22	6	56	2	19	2	83	3
Clark	19	3	63	3	11	1	59	0
Mann	14	1	75	1	13	0	71	2

ENGLAND v AUSTRALIA (Centenary Test)

Melbourne, March 12, 13, 14, 16, 17

Australia won by 45 runs

Australia *First Innings*		*Second Innings*	
I. C. Davis lbw b Lever	5	c Knott b Greig	68
R. B. McCosker b Willis	4	(10) c Greig b Old	25
G. J. Cosier c Fletcher b Lever	10	(4) c Knott b Lever	4
*G. S. Chappell b Underwood	40	(3) b Old	2
D. Hookes c Greig b Old	17	(6) c Fletcher b Underwood	56
K. D. Walters c Greig b Willis	4	(5) c Knott b Greig	66
†R. W. Marsh c Knott b Old	28	not out	110
G. J. Gilmour c Greig b Old	4	b Lever	16
K. J. O'Keeffe c Brearley b Underwood	0	(2) c Willis b Old	14
D. K. Lillee not out	10	(9) c Amiss b Old	25
M. H. N. Walker b Underwood	2	not out	8
Extras (b4, lb2, nb8)	14	(lb10, nb15)	25
Total	138	(9 wkts dec.)	419

Fall of Wickets

1 – 11   2 – 13   3 – 23   4 – 45   5 – 51   6 – 102   7 – 114   8 – 117   9 – 136   10 – 138
1 – 33   2 – 40   3 – 53   4 – 132   5 – 187   6 – 244   7 – 277   8 – 353   9 – 407

Bowling	*First Innings*				*Second Innings*			
Lever	12	1	36	2	21	1	95	2
Willis	8	0	33	2	22	0	91	0
Old	12	4	39	3	27.6	2	104	4
Underwood	11.6	2	16	3	12	2	38	1
Greig					14	3	66	2

England *First Innings*		*Second Innings*	
R. A. Woolmer c Chappell b Lillee	9	lbw b Walker	12
J. M. Brearley c Hookes b Lillee	12	lbw b Lillee	43
D. L. Underwood c Chappell b Walker	7	(10) b Lillee	7
D. W. Randall c Marsh b Lillee	4	(3) c Cosier b O'Keeffe	174
D. L. Amiss c O'Keeffe b Walker	4	(4) b Chappell	64
K. W. R. Fletcher c Marsh b Walker	4	(5) c Marsh b Lillee	1
*A. W. Greig b Walker	18	(6) c Cosier b O'Keeffe	41
†A. P. E. Knott lbw b Lillee	15	(7) lbw b Lillee	42
C. M. Old c Marsh b Lillee	3	(8) c Chappell b Lillee	2
J. K. Lever c Marsh b Lillee	11	(9) lbw b O'Keeffe	4
R. G. D. Willis not out	1	not out	5
Extras (b2, lb2, nb2, w1)	7	(b8, lb4, w3, nb7)	22
Total	95	Total	417

Fall of Wickets

1 – 19   2 – 30   3 – 34   4 – 40   5 – 40   6 – 61   7 – 65   8 – 78   9 – 86   10 – 95
1 – 28   2 – 113   3 – 279   4 – 290   5 – 346   6 – 369   7 – 380   8 – 385   9 – 410   10 – 417

Bowling	*First Innings*				*Second Innings*			
Lillee	13.3	2	26	6	34.4	7	139	5
Walker	15	3	54	4	22	4	83	1
O'Keeffe	1	0	4	0	33	6	108	3
Gilmour	5	3	4	0	4	0	29	0
Chappell					16	7	29	1
Walters					3	2	7	0

Umpires: M. O'Connell and T. Brooks.   Toss won by England.

5 STATISTICAL NOTES

MCC v West Zone at Poona

J. M. Brearley (202) scored the first double-century ever for an official MCC touring team in India. The previous highest score was 183 by J. D. Robertson v East Zone at Jamshedpur in 1951. Previous Englishmen to score a double-hundred in India were D. C. S. Compton, 249* for Holkar v Bombay at Bombay (Ranji Trophy) 1944/45, and J. Hardstaff Jnr., 213 for Lord Tennyson's XI v Madras at Madras 1937/38.

J. M. Brearley and K. W. R. Fletcher (118) put on 292 for the second wicket, a record partnership for any wicket for MCC in India.

MCC's first innings of 585–5 declared has only once been exceeded by MCC in India; in 1933/34 MCC made 603 v Madras (A. Mitchell 161, A. H. Bakewell 158).

During the partnership of 215 for the fifth wicket between A. W. Greig (162*) and R. W. Tolchard (67), A. W. Greig went from 94 to 162 in 28 minutes off 23 balls, including seven 6's and four 4's. He scored 28 in an over off his former Sussex colleague, off-spinner U. C. Joshi.

R. G. D. Willis took 4–2 in 17 balls and finished with figures of 5–24.

MCC v Central Zone at Jaipur

C. M. Old dismissed M. I. Ansari with the first ball of the Central Zone first innings and fell whilst delivering his 15th ball. He did not bowl again during the match. Central Zone included in their team Gulrez Ali, son of Mushtaq Ali, and Vijay Nayudu, a grandson of C. K. Nayudu.

First Test Match—Delhi

D. L. Amiss (179) reached his century with a 6 off K. Ghavri and in making his eleventh Test hundred passed 150 for the eighth time in Tests. His score was the highest by an Englishman in a Test in India, beating T. W. Graveney's 175 at Bombay in 1951–52.

S. M. Gavaskar (71) became the first Indian batsman to score 1000 runs in Test matches in a calendar year when he reached 47 in India's second innings. This figure he took to 1024 made in 20 innings in 11 Test matches between January 24 and December 21. In so doing he became the tenth batsman to achieve this feat, K. F. Barrington having achieved it twice in 1961 and 1963.

J. K. Lever had a match analysis of 36.4-12-70-10 and became the sixth Englishman to take ten wickets in his first Test. The previous ones were:

12–102 F. Martin v Australia, The Oval 1890
10–156 T. Richardson v Australia, Manchester 1893
11–96 C. S. Marriott v West Indies, The Oval 1933
10–179 K. Farnes v Australia, Trent Bridge 1934
11–145 A. V. Bedser v India, Lord's 1946

The last bowler to take ten wickets in his first Test was R. A. L. Massie at Lord's for Australia v England in 1972. His match figures were 16–137. Other than Massie, the only bowlers to have exceeded Lever's first- innings figures of 23–6–46–7 and to have taken 8 wickets in their first Test innings are A. E. Trott for Australia v England at Adelaide 1894–95 and A. L. Valentine for West Indies v England, Old Trafford 1950. His 7–46 was the best Test analysis by any England bowler in India, beating Headley Verity's 7–49 at Madras in 1933–34.

B. S. Bedi and B. S. Chandrasekhar both registered 'pairs'. They had thus been dismissed for a 'duck' more often than any other Test cricketers: B. S. Bedi, 19 'ducks' in 78 Test innings, and B. S. Chandrasekhar, 18 'ducks' in 60 Test innings. B. S. Bedi became the third player to have completed three 'pairs' in Test cricket, joining J. Briggs and D. L. Underwood—all of them, incidentally, left-arm spinners.

England's victory was their first since 25 February 1975, when they beat New Zealand in Auckland.

Second Test Match—Calcutta

A. W. Greig (103) reached his eighth Test century for England in 6 hours 55 mins., the third slowest ever for England—P. E. Richardson took 8 hours 8 mins. v South Africa at Johannesburg in 1956/57 and K. W. R. Fletcher 7 hours 37 mins. v Pakistan at the Oval in 1974.

A. W. Greig's century was only the second ever scored for England at Calcutta, the other one being by M. C. Cowdrey in 1964.

A. W. Greig, when he had made 3, reached 3000 runs in Test cricket in his 49th Test.

In his first innings in Test cricket R. W. Tolchard scored 67 in 5 hours 20 mins. with two fours.

England's victory was their first in a Calcutta Test match in six attempts.

MCC v Combined Indian Universities and 'Under 22' XI—Nagpur
This was MCC's first victory outside a Test match in India since M. J. K. Smith's tour in 1964.

Third Test Match—Madras
England, by winning this Test, had beaten India in six consecutive Test matches, three in England in 1974 and three in India, giving them victory in a series in India for the first time since D. R. Jardine's team won the 1933/34 series two matches to nil with one drawn.
    This was the first time India had lost the first three Tests of a home series.
    India's second-innings total of 83 was the lowest total ever made in a Test match in India, the previous record being 88 by India v New Zealand, Bombay 1964/65.
    B. S. Bedi in his 51st Test took his 200th Test wicket when he dismissed A. W. Greig in the first innings. He was the first Indian bowler to reach this figure and the 12th in all Test cricket.

Fourth Test Match—Bangalore
Yajuvendra Singh in his first Test match equalled two world records for fieldsmen other than wicket-keepers by taking five catches in an innings (so joining V. Y. Richardson, Australia v South Africa at Durban 1935/36) and seven in a match (G. S. Chappell, Australia v England, Perth 1974/75).
    R. G. D. Willis produced his best figures in Test cricket by taking 6–53 in the Indian first innings.
    In the history of Test cricket England's fourth wicket has only fallen once previously for eight runs or less. This was v Australia at Melbourne in 1903/04 (5 runs for 4 wickets).

Fifth Test Match—Bombay
J. M. Brearley in his 7th Test played his highest Test innings (91) and with D. L. Amiss put up England's first century opening partnership (146) for 12 Test matches (since J. H. Edrich and B. Wood put on 111 v Australia at Lord's in 1975) and the highest since D. L. Amiss and D. Lloyd made 157 together v India in July 1974 25 Test matches before.
    S. M. Gavaskar, in scoring his tenth Test century, scored his second against England and his second in India. He had previously scored a century against New Zealand at Bombay in November 1976.
    K. Ghavri in his eighth Test produced his best bowling figures of 5–33, bowling slow left-arm rather than his normal left-arm medium.
    D. L. Underwood in India's second innings took 5–84, the first time he had taken five wickets in a Test match v India. He has now taken five wickets or more in a single innings against all Test-playing countries. It was the 100th time Underwood had taken five wickets or more in an innings in a first-class match.
    D. L. Underwood, in taking his 29th wicket of the series when dismissing K. Ghavri in the second innings, equalled F. S. Trueman's record of 1952, the best by an England bowler v India. In addition, he beat F. J. Titmus's record of 27 wickets by an England bowler in India, achieved in 1964.
    At the end of this Test D. L. Underwood had taken 248 Test wickets, thus equalling R. Benaud and leaving only J. B. Statham (252), Trueman (307) and L. R. Gibbs (309) ahead of him. B. S. Bedi had taken a total of 215 Test wickets by the end of the series.

MCC v Sri Lanka—Colombo (Unofficial Test Match)
In Sri Lanka's second innings A. Tennekoon and B. Warnapura put on 163 for the second wicket, a record for Sri Lanka v MCC for any wicket, beating the 119 put on by Ranjit Kernando and Buddy Reid in 1969.

189

England's first-innings total of 95 was the lowest score by England since they were dismissed for 87 by Davidson and Meckiff also at Melbourne in 1958–59.

R. W. Marsh by catching J. K. Lever off the bowling of D. K. Lillee in the first innings surpassed the late A. T. W. Grout's record of Test wicket-keeping dismissals by an Australian of 187.

D. K. Lillee's first-innings bowling performance of 13.3-2-26-6 was the best of his Test match career, although he did take 8–29 for Australia v Rest of the World at Perth in 1971–72.

A. P. E. Knott in dismissing G. J. Cosier in the second innings took his 85th Australian victim in Test matches, beating the record of A. A. Lilley established in 1909.

R. W. Marsh (110*) in scoring his third Test century became the first Australian wicket-keeper to score a century against England.

D. L. Underwood in dismissing D. Hookes equalled J. B. Statham's total of 252 Test wickets.

D. W. Randall in making 174 became the fourteenth batsman to score a hundred in his first Test match v Australia, the last batsman to do so being J. H. Edrich who made 120 v Australia at Lord's in 1964. It was the first century by an English batsman on his debut in Australia for England since the Nawab of Pataudi scored 102 at Sydney in 1932–33. He is also only the second batsman to have achieved this feat at Melbourne, having been preceded by Maurice Leyland who scored 137 in 1928–29.

When he had made 161 Randall was given out by umpire Tom Brookes to a catch by Marsh off Chappell but was recalled after Marsh indicated to umpire Brookes and Chappell that the catch had not been taken cleanly.

D. W. Randall's 174 was made in 448 minutes off 354 balls with 21 fours; he was awarded A$1600 as 'Man of the Match'.

D. K. Lillee in taking 5–139 took his match aggregate to 11–165 and brought his haul to 47 wickets in his previous six Test matches.

England's total of 417 was 11 runs higher than the highest winning fourth innings in any Test match.

The final margin of defeat was 45 runs—exactly the same as in the first-ever Test between the two countries.